THE YOUNG AUGUSTINE

The Young Augustine

The Growth of St. Augustine's Mind
Up to His Conversion

JOHN J. O'MEARA

<small>SECOND REVISED EDITION</small>

ALBA·HOUSE   NEW·YORK

SOCIETY OF ST. PAUL, 2187 VICTORY BLVD., STATEN ISLAND, NEW YORK 10314

ST PAULS

BR
1720
.A9
O5
2001

Library of Congress Cataloging-in-Publication Data

O'Meara, John Joseph.
    The young Augustine : the growth of St. Augustine's mind up to his
conversion / John J. O'Meara. — 2nd rev. ed.
       p. cm.
    Includes bibliographical references and index.
    ISBN 0-8189-0833-5
    1. Augustine, Saint, Bishop of Hippo.   I. Title.

BR1720.A9 O5 2000
270.2'092—dc21
[B]
                                 99-049350

Produced and designed in the United States of America by the
Fathers and Brothers of the Society of St. Paul,
2187 Victory Boulevard, Staten Island, New York 10314-6603,
as part of their communications apostolate.

ISBN: 0-8189-0833-5

Printing Information:

Current Printing - first digit   1 2 3 4 5 6 7 8 9 10

Year of Current Printing - first year shown

2001 2002 2003 2004 2005 2006 2007 2008 2009 2010

Too late have I loved You, O Beauty ever ancient, ever new, too late have I loved You! You were within me, but I was outside, and it was there that I searched for You. In my unloveliness I plunged into the lovely things which You have made. You were with me, but I was not with You. Created things kept me from You; yet if they had not been in You they would not have been at all. You called, shouted and broke through my deafness. You flashed, shone and dispelled my blindness. You breathed Your fragrance on me; I drew in breath and now I pant for You. I tasted You, now I hunger and thirst for more. You touched me, and I burned for Your peace.

(Confessions 10:38)

Biblical Abbreviations

OLD TESTAMENT

Genesis	Gn	Nehemiah	Ne	Baruch	Ba
Exodus	Ex	Tobit	Tb	Ezekiel	Ezk
Leviticus	Lv	Judith	Jdt	Daniel	Dn
Numbers	Nb	Esther	Est	Hosea	Ho
Deuteronomy	Dt	1 Maccabees	1 M	Joel	Jl
Joshua	Jos	2 Maccabees	2 M	Amos	Am
Judges	Jg	Job	Jb	Obadiah	Ob
Ruth	Rt	Psalms	Ps	Jonah	Jon
1 Samuel	1 S	Proverbs	Pr	Micah	Mi
2 Samuel	2 S	Ecclesiastes	Ec	Nahum	Na
1 Kings	1 K	Song of Songs	Sg	Habakkuk	Hab
2 Kings	2 K	Wisdom	Ws	Zephaniah	Zp
1 Chronicles	1 Ch	Sirach	Si	Haggai	Hg
2 Chronicles	2 Ch	Isaiah	Is	Malachi	Ml
Ezra	Ezr	Jeremiah	Jr	Zechariah	Zc
		Lamentations	Lm		

NEW TESTAMENT

Matthew	Mt	Ephesians	Eph	Hebrews	Heb
Mark	Mk	Philippians	Ph	James	Jm
Luke	Lk	Colossians	Col	1 Peter	1 P
John	Jn	1 Thessalonians	1 Th	2 Peter	2 P
Acts	Ac	2 Thessalonians	2 Th	1 John	1 Jn
Romans	Rm	1 Timothy	1 Tm	2 John	2 Jn
1 Corinthians	1 Cor	2 Timothy	2 Tm	3 John	3 Jn
2 Corinthians	2 Cor	Titus	Tt	Jude	Jude
Galatians	Gal	Philemon	Phm	Revelation	Rv

NOTE TO THE SECOND REVISED EDITION

THE FIRST EDITION of this book (1954) presented some of the material of my Oxford thesis (1945) and my edition of Augustine's *Against the Academics* (1950), but also anticipated some of the conclusions of my *Porphyry's "Philosophy from Oracles" in Augustine* (1959, 1969). Its argument is that the Neo-Platonist that played the most significant role in Augustine's conversion was Porphyry: he who felt that the mass of mankind could not be brought to salvation except through a Mediator between the Father and man. Porphyry's rejection of Christ as that Mediator, because of his birth of a woman and death on a cross, was absolute. Augustine, however, in turn totally rejected Porphyry's rejection: he "put on Christ" and accepted the Incarnation and Redemption. Thus his conversion was not to Neo-Platonism, but to Christianity. The work of Porphyry involved in this development is referred to in this book as the *Return of the Soul*. My work of 1959 and 1969, however, argued that this title was merely *descriptive*, and that the book's formal (and authenticated) title was the *Philosophy from Oracles*, a book much controverted by Christian writers. Over the years my argument has gained in acceptance:[1] Beatrice (1988, 1996), in particular, has used it as "the starting point of a series of essays" which culminate in the conclusion that Porphyry's notorious "Against the Christians" is in fact his notorious *Philosophy from Oracles*. This was, one should note, the initial published opinion of Harnack, later editor of the supposed fragments of an "Against the Christians," the existence of which is now questioned by scholars.

---

[1] Cf. E. DePalma Digeser, *Journal of Roman Studies*, lxxxviii, 1998, p. 136: "It is, I think, a compelling thesis."

FOREWORD

THE FIRST STATEMENT made in almost every book on Augustine is that, although the bibliography on the subject is immense, the author feels that there is still room for his book. In point of fact, however, instead of there being too many books — in English, at any rate — on Augustine, there are too few (cf. the Select Bibliography, p. 217ff.). If the reader were invited to suggest the titles of serious studies in English of either Augustine's life or thought, embarrassment for him would arise not from a wealth but from a dearth of such books.

It is far otherwise abroad. In France alone, for example, there has been a succession of remarkable works describing various aspects of Augustine's career and writings, those of Portalié, Alfaric, Boyer, Gilson, Marrou, and Courcelle — to mention but a few. One may disagree with the conclusions of some of these scholars, but one must allow that their work is of great importance. The present writer cannot accept, for instance, the main theses of Courcelle's *Recherches sur les Confessions de saint Augustin* (Paris, 1950), but he is very willing to hail it as a book of the greatest value for the understanding of the *Confessions* and Augustine's earlier life.

Of the books that are available in English, some are frankly unsympathetic. One author has written: "Augustine's influence extended for evil over practically the whole field of human activity, social and political no less than religious." This is at best an unhelpful exaggeration. At the other extreme we have books of simple piety. In between there are a number of studies where psychology, at various levels of crudity, is applied to Augustine's life and his account of it in the *Confessions*. It may be said that few of the authors of these books show undue scrupulosity in controlling their speculations by the evidence at hand. Indeed the great weakness in the literature about Augustine in English is that the writers have been too keen to present him from some particular angle and have tended to neglect the facts.

The present book makes some attempt to remedy part of that weakness. It does not, therefore, seek to interpret Augustine in terms of any psychological theory. It aims merely at presenting in English as much of the information about Augustine's ideas up to the time of his conversion as is now available and can be transmitted to a wider public without all the panoply of *Wissenschaft*.

Nevertheless we can hardly avoid giving some opinion of the kind of man Augustine was: how sensual and at the same time spiritual; how attracted by the things of this world and how devoted to the life of intelligence; how yielding in friendship on the one hand and how firm to shake it off on the other — in brief, how compounded of excess and restraint, imagination and reason, mysticism and dialectic. There is no simple formula that will explain him. To say that he was sensual, for example, is true but misleading. When one has attempted to distinguish between his sense of sin in youth and the sin itself and between both and his polemical purpose in the *Confessions* — and then measured all against his lifelong yearning for Truth, one will not be satisfied that one has done him justice in presenting him, however sympathetically, mainly as a sensualist. But to ignore his sensuality would also be a mistake.

The time is opportune for a serious study of the development of Augustine's mind. Recent evidence has changed our notions, for example, of the distance traveled, so to speak, by Augustine away from Christianity when he became a Manichee, and traveled by him back again when he was converted. Moreover, the century-old controversy on the sincerity of Augustine's conversion to Christianity and his alleged preference for Neo-Platonism, has left us with knowledge at once abundant and fairly precise on a most interesting and vital phase of his development. Scholars too have gleaned some additional pieces of information from sources hitherto neglected.

The story of Augustine's conversion is of extraordinary interest and appeal. A Manichean opponent of the saint once expressed doubt as to its sincerity on the grounds that it was too sudden and too radical. People do commonly believe that it was radical and sudden. But Providence does not normally work in that way, and it is our duty to explain what we can of the change that came upon Augustine in terms of human reasoning alone. If the conversion as described in the following pages seems too gradual, too closely knit from one phase to another, too inevitable in the long run, and too little invested with wonder and the miraculous, our account may for all that still be true. When one speaks of ideas and the intellect one speaks of a faculty which, paradoxically enough, is "blind," and must yield automatically to truth on its presentation. But what miracle may lurk in a change of will can easily escape the coarse mesh of understanding. This miracle we cannot explain.

Newman has likened Augustine's conversion to that of St. Paul. Here for the purpose of illustration, and because readers may be interested in the comparison, we have compared it to that of Newman himself. Newman in fact invites the comparison, and it is sufficiently close to justify extensive quotation from the *Apologia*. In this connection it is well to say that the author has given the words of Augustine also at considerable length from time to time, in the belief that these words cannot fail to be of interest, and so that the reader may have some direct acquaintance with the evidence. On one point especially, that of Augustine's discovery of the importance of the Incarnation both in his own life and in the lives of all men, it seemed essential to give a very liberal measure of quotation, because, although the theme in question is central to the study of Augustine's conversion, it has not been presented in this way before.

The *Confessions*, together with Possidius' *Life of Augustine* and some of Augustine's other works, are the principal sources of our information. No careful reader of the *Confessions* will be unaware of the many and complicated difficulties to be encountered in that famous book. Of these difficulties something is said in an Introductory Note, which some readers may prefer to skip. The translation of the *Confessions* used throughout is an updated version of Pusey's adaptation of Watts' which goes back to 1631. This translation is not always satisfactory and is frequently inaccurate; it is corrected here only where it seemed essential that this should be done. Readers may find a modern translation easier to follow, but for many this translation has the charm of an Authorized Version. Similarly the author has elected for the traditional English spelling of the name of Augustine's mother, although some recent writers have used the manuscript spelling "Monnica."

It remains for me to express my thanks to the many friends and scholars who have helped me in one way or another with this book.

CONTENTS

xiii

INTRODUCTORY NOTE
The *Confessions*

W HEN WE OPEN the pages of a book that bears the title *Confessions*, we normally expect to read of the past aberrations, frequently moral, of its author. We may, perhaps, believe that the writer has reformed and has been induced to set down the sorry record of earlier days, partly to humble himself before men, and partly to show to others that no matter to what depths one has descended one can rise again. Some such notion as the author's admission of guilt, for whatever purpose, comes to our minds.

But as we read on through the book — be it the *Confessions* of Rousseau, *La Confession d'un enfant du siècle* of Musset, *A la recherche du temps perdu* of Proust, *Si le grain ne meurt* of Gide, De Quincey's *Confessions of an English Opium-Eater*, or Joyce's *Portrait of the Artist as a Young Man* — whatever else it be, we are likely to find that it does not quite correspond to that first notion.

Thus De Quincey, for example, says in the preface to the original edition of 1822:

> My self-accusation does not amount to a confession of guilt. Infirmity and misery do not, of necessity, imply guilt. If opium-eating be a sensual pleasure, and if I am bound to confess that I have indulged in it to an excess not yet recorded of any other man, it is no less true that I have struggled against this fascinating enthralment with a religious zeal, and have at length accomplished what I never yet heard attributed to any other man — have untwisted, almost to its final links, the accursed chain which fettered me.

Rousseau's words are not greatly different:

> Let the last trump sound when it will, I shall come forward
> with this work in my hand, to present myself before my Sov-
> ereign Judge, and proclaim aloud: Here is what I have done,
> and if by chance I have used some immaterial embellishment
> it has been only to fill a void due to a defect of memory. I
> may have taken for fact what was no more than probability,
> but I have never put down as true what I knew to be false. I
> have displayed myself as I was, as vile and despicable when
> my behavior was such, as good, generous, and noble when I
> was so. I have bared my secret soul as Thou thyself hast seen
> it, Eternal Being! So let the numberless legion of my fellow
> men gather round me, and hear my confessions. Let them
> groan at my depravities, and blush for my misdeeds. But let
> each one of them reveal his heart at the foot of Thy throne
> with equal sincerity, and may any man who dares, say I was
> a better man than he. (Book One, 1712-19, translated by J.M.
> Cohen, Penguin Classics, 1953.)

We see at once that the author expects to be as much admired
for his virtues as forgiven for his faults, and the recital is often as much
concerned with the one as with the other. Sometimes the author
glories in his shame, and this either because he has been delivered
from his iniquity or because he feels no need of such deliverance.

These confessions are rarely full autobiographies. Frequently
they present only a selection of incidents or a period from the author's
life, and the selection or period is determined by the author's purpose or the theme which he wishes to illustrate.

These thoughts come naturally to our minds when we open the
most famous of all Confessions, the *Confessions* of St. Augustine. Here
we have the story of one who fell and, by the grace of God, rose again.
From the most cursory examination one sees that it is obviously no
mere autobiography and no mere admission of guilt. Since we have
to rely upon these glowing pages penned by Augustine for nearly all
of our information about his early life and conversion, we must at
the outset decide how we can use this document. How far is it historical in the facts it relates? What special significance is there in

the actual selection of the facts? We must, in short, describe the kind of book it is, and then we shall be better able to interpret it.

Scholars with one or two exceptions have agreed that the word "confession" has all three of its contemporary significations when it is applied to the book of Augustine. It is a confession of sin; it is a confession of faith; and it is a confession of praise. It is a mistake, however, to seek to separate these three elements, for though the emphasis varies from place to place the confession of sin nearly always implies faith and praise, and likewise each of the other two implies the others.

> Let the arrogant mock me, and those who have not been, to their soul's health, stricken and cast down by You, O my God; but *I would still confess to You my own shame for Your praise.* Allow me, I beseech You, and give me grace to go over in my present remembrance the wanderings of my past time, and to offer to You the sacrifice of thanksgiving. (4:1)

There we have the confession of sin and praise, and the confession of faith is everywhere implied.

Some authors, when they recite the history of their past, do so in the presence not of God, but of men only whom they address. They invite the sympathy, if not the admiration of the reader. But Augustine's *Confessions* are made to God, to confess belief in Him, to render Him a sacrifice of praise, and to acknowledge His grace in the healing of his sins. Nevertheless, if the *Confessions* were meant for the ears of God alone, they would never have been written; for God needs no reminder of our deeds nor of the operation of His grace, and He knows the mind of every man. Augustine admits this:

> Lord, […] are You ignorant of what I say to You? […] Why then do I lay in order before You so many things? Not, in truth, that You might learn them through me, but to stir up my own and my readers' devotions towards You. (11:1)

Others are allowed to listen in, so to speak, to this confession made to God. Indeed, God is magnified in their knowledge of Augustine's life. This is tantamount to saying that he did have some readers in mind when he embarked upon his *Confessions*. It is not likely, however, that he foresaw the countless men and women who would read his words. He wrote this book as he wrote most of his other books — for a particular occasion, with the thought, naturally, that the appeal of his work might prove to be general.

In the year A.D. 395 Alypius, then Bishop of Thagaste, Augustine's birthplace, wrote to Paulinus of Nola to pay certain polite compliments and make a certain definite request: he wanted a copy of Eusebius' famous *Ecclesiastical History*. He himself sent five works of his lifelong friend, Augustine, in advance — to encourage, we must suppose, Paulinus to comply with his request. Paulinus sent the book and asked in his turn that Alypius should send him "the whole story of his holiness's life." He wants to know Alypius' birthplace and parentage and the details of his vocation to the priesthood. He wonders especially if Alypius had come under the influence of Ambrose of Milan as had Paulinus himself. In short, he wants to know everything about Alypius.

We do not know Alypius' reply to this flattering request. Feeling, doubtless, that he could not comply with it himself, he asked Augustine to do so, who in a letter to Paulinus informed him that Alypius was on the one hand too modest to recount his life and on the other under too great an obligation to Paulinus' benevolence to refuse to do so. Accordingly Augustine undertook to do it for him. Augustine and Paulinus exchanged compliments and each expressed a great desire to know the other. Unfortunately their office prevented them from meeting face to face. Some scholars suggest that at this point Paulinus requested Augustine to send him an account of his own life, similar to that which he had written of Alypius, and that the *Confessions* is that account. The suggestion is not improbable, for Augustine did compose the *Confessions* in the few years preceding A.D. 400 and Paulinus must have been among those spiritual persons who, Augustine says, would be amused in a friendly way in learning what kind of man Augustine had been.

There is a certain tension, then, in the *Confessions*. Augustine addresses his thoughts and words to God, who, however, knows all in advance. The thoughts and words which are directed towards God find the occasion of their formulation in an audience of men, Augustine's friends. In a sense Augustine is attempting to address God and his friends at the same time; and through his words, whether they recount facts or fancies, he informs men while praising God.

This aspect of the *Confessions* deserves very careful attention, for it is intimately connected with what is called the *historicity* of the document — its reliability as evidence for the facts of Augustine's life. It has to be remembered that Augustine, although employing a literary form where some conscious adjustments, if not unconscious modifications, may be found, is writing for an audience which in the main knew him well. They knew more than he puts in writing — which accounts for the many omissions of important details which we would wish to know. They could not easily be misled. Above all, his words were written, as it were, before the face of God who saw clearly into his heart and knew what truth was in his words. But much depended on his memory and his use of it and so we must say something of this.

Augustine was very interested in the question of what memory was and how it worked, as can be seen from his lengthy discussion of it in book ten of the *Confessions*. These few lines, for instance, are particularly illuminating for our present purpose:

> And I come to the fields and spacious palaces of my memory, where are the treasures of innumerable images. [...] When I enter there, I require what I will to be brought forth, and something instantly comes. Others must be longer sought after, which are fetched, as it were, out of some inner receptacle. Others rush out in troops, and while one thing is desired and required, they start forth, as if to say: "Is it perhaps I?" These I drive away with the hand of my heart from the face of my remembrance; until what I wished for is unveiled, and appears in sight, out of its secret place. Other things come up readily, in unbroken order, as they are called

for; those in front making way for those following; and as
they make way, they are hidden from sight, ready to come
when I will. (10:12)

The passage is strictly applicable to what Augustine did in the
first nine books of the *Confessions*. The dominant point is that he
selects among all the memories which present themselves to him
those which can be used for his purpose. "These I drive away with
the hand of my heart, from the face of my remembrance; until *what
I wished for* is unveiled, and appears in sight, out of its secret place."
We shall see presently what pattern he wished to paint. Memories
which help to make or make clear that pattern are readily accepted
and even, when they do not easily come to his mind, sought after.
Others which do not fulfill this purpose are driven away with the
hand of his heart from the face of his remembrance. And sometimes
a whole series of relevant memories comes together when they are
called for, and these are gladly accepted.

One can hardly exaggerate the importance of this point in as-
sessing the biographical value of the *Confessions*, which, accordingly,
must not be regarded as being fully autobiographical even for any
period or section of his life. Augustine, that is, does not pretend to
tell the whole truth about even part of his life. He picks and chooses
exactly as he wishes. He has a perfect right to do so, and he does not
expose himself to any charge of playing false. He wishes to illustrate
a theory, which he believed to have been verified in his own life.
He chooses from the memories of his life only those that illustrate
that theory. He is not bound to choose any others. It is indeed remarkable how few, relatively, are the precise facts recounted in the
Confessions.

One can see very clearly the mind of the Bishop of Hippo at
work upon its memories. When one offers itself to him, his present
mind judges its relevance to his purpose and then very properly asks
if when the event happened, it wore for him then the guise that it
now wears. A very good instance of this scrupulous honesty is found
in the third book, where we are told of Monica's attempt to get a
bishop to bring Augustine out of Manicheism into the true Church.
"This woman entreated him to consent to talk with me, refute my

errors, unteach me ill things, and teach me good things (for this he was accustomed to do when he found persons fitted to receive it). He refused, *wisely, as I afterwards perceived*" (3:21). At the time, of course, Augustine was convinced that the bishop was afraid to argue with him; for Augustine felt certain of winning.

He presents, therefore, his memories of events as they seem to him in retrospect *at the time of writing*, while being fully aware that the events themselves may have seemed otherwise to him at the time of their occurrence. He does not conceal this. He draws attention to it. But the fact recounted is still the same. The bishop refused to see him. He looked on the refusal in one way then and looks on it in another way now. Which is the correct way? In a sense both, but with reference to him at different times. The one thing absolutely constant and which links his two attitudes, is the fact of the refusal. Another instance, perhaps, is his reading of Cicero's *Hortensius*. We shall see that he invested that reading with extraordinary significance which it probably did not have at the time. Out of thousands of other incidents it beckoned to him in retrospect as being one to suit his purpose. But that he did read it is certain.

He tells us that sometimes he has great difficulty in recalling a single memory, and sometimes, on the contrary, a whole interconnected series presents itself to him. We can be sure that he experienced difficulty in trying to piece together relevant memories from his earlier life; some of the details which he considers relevant to his theory, such as his behavior as a baby, he does not remember at all. He knows of these things through information, observation, or by conjecture:

> Afterwards I began to smile; first in sleep, then waking. So it was told me of myself and I believed it; for we see the like in other infants, though of myself I remember it not. (1:8)

It was not so, however, for the series of events which culminated in his conversion. They offered themselves to him *en bloc* and as such they are presented to the reader, for they played a part more than anything else in revealing to him God's Providence over him and all mankind.

Augustine, therefore, scrutinizes his facts with quite extraordinary care. He distinguishes clearly between those which he does not personally remember and those which he does, and these in turn are examined for what they were and what they are.

Although his handling of his material is rigorously honest, as indeed befitted a bishop addressing his God in words which would be read by men, he quite openly adds moral disquisitions — sometimes to our notions, perhaps, in a rather forced way — by way of comment on some fact or conjecture. Thus we are given at various points the bishop's views on the errors of the Manichees, on Neo-Platonism, original sin, the conversion of the sinner, baptism, marriage, love, friendship and a great variety of topics which occupied his mind at the time of writing the *Confessions*, and which are treated in his other works of that period. These moralizations can prove fatal to the unsympathetic reader. If the doctrine taught is not to his taste, he will be at best offended by what may seem to him irrelevant, if not false; and at worst he will so violently disagree with the doctrine which is added to the fact for good measure that he will begin, perhaps, to distrust the fact as well.

What is the modern reader to make of the following passage?

> In Your sight none is pure from sin, not even the infant whose life is but a day upon the earth. [...] Was it then good, even for a while, to cry for what, if given, would hurt me? Bitterly to resent, that free persons, and my own elders, yes, the very authors of my birth, served me not? That many besides, wiser than me, obeyed not the nod of my good pleasure? To do my best to strike and hurt, because commands were not obeyed, which if obeyed would have been to my hurt? The weakness then of the infant's limbs, not its will, is its innocence. I myself have seen and known even a baby to be envious; it could not speak, yet it turned pale and looked bitterly on its foster-brother. (1:11)

Even if he subscribe to the doctrine of original sin, the modern reader may feel that Augustine has forced the issue somewhat. It is desirable, therefore, to spare the reader the effects of some of these moralizations — partly in order to sustain his confidence in the truth of the *Confessions*, and partly to help him to retain or not be prevented from acquiring true sympathy for one whose friendship was much sought after.

It is often suggested that religion made Augustine ruthless and inhuman, all the more so because he was by birth an African and therefore had no sense of moderation. Yet a religious man is not necessarily inhuman, and an African not necessarily immoderate. Even if Augustine were ruthless and inhuman and immoderate, religion and place of birth had no necessary connection with his being so. For the moment we are concerned merely with a certain inhumanity, we might say, or immoderation in passages such as that just quoted, and we are confident that this can be explained quite simply without ever raising the question of Augustine's race or religion.

For Augustine was a rhetorician. His whole training and profession until the time of his conversion centered on making his point, whatever it was, clear by every means within the resource of rhetoric. And forced, unfeeling exaggeration was a means only too frequently employed. Augustine's relatively mild return here to what he himself called "windy rhetoric" will not distress anyone who has made the acquaintance, for example, of the excruciatingly frigid infelicities of Lucan. He will know what allowances he must make if he is to be just. But the man who knows nothing of the extravagances, both in matter and form, perpetrated by Latin rhetoricians must understand that in the passage quoted and elsewhere in the *Confessions*, immoderation in sentiment and expression are often merely a rhetor's tricks of style. They are not in fashion with us, it is true. We will do well if we reduce to the dimensions of our own experience the picture painted. We will not do well if we reject the whole thing as thoroughly insincere, much less as revealing an immoderate and inhuman mind.

So much, then, for the moralizing passages. To some they seem full of charm, eloquence and truth. To others they may seem tasteless, artificial and irrelevant. The point for our present purpose is to remember that Augustine does not conceal that they are moralizations on the facts of his life, and not the facts themselves, and that we should rather admire the restraint exercised by this rhetorician-become-bishop when provided with the whole of Christian doctrine as his theme, than think hardly of one who did as most men are constrained to do — conform to the fashion of the day.

There is one feature of Augustine's rhetoric which, however much it conform to established practice, needs a little more explanation. When he speaks of "a certain Aeneas" and of "a certain Cicero," he presents the reader with a problem. For it is obvious not only from the most elementary acquaintance with the African school curriculum of his day, but even from the *Confessions* itself, that Augustine knew of both Aeneas and Cicero not merely as an English-speaking schoolboy knows of Hamlet and Macaulay, but indeed with a warm intimacy cultivated over many years of careful and detailed study. How then can he talk of "a certain Cicero," or "a certain Aeneas"?

We must not lightly suppose that Augustine was accommodating himself to the possible ignorance of his hearers — in the same way as Cicero himself assumed ignorance of well-known Greek artists and their work when he was addressing Romans who were presumed to have neither knowledge of these artists nor respect for those who knew about them. Augustine could hardly assume such an attitude concerning Aeneas and Cicero before the audience of his friends in Africa or in Nola.

The explanation, perhaps, is somewhat different. Augustine had a great fondness for indefinite expressions, especially at crucial points in his story. He does not tell us, for example, the name of his mistress or of the friend whose death affected him so profoundly. And there are many more instances, particularly in his references to the Neo-Platonists. Most puzzling of all is his professed — or genuine — ignorance as to whether his first work *On the Beautiful and Fitting* was made up of two or three books. There is reason to believe that this fondness for an indefinite formula reflects his belief in Providence which disposes all things, however unrelated, disparate and haphazard they might seem to be, in a pattern which is later to emerge. Augustine had such confidence in this unerring Providence that he is content sometimes to indicate a detail in the pattern in the most general way only — as if to be too precise and explicit about petty facts were to distract one's attention from the really important thing

— the working of Providence. Hence, even when he knows a thing precisely, he sometimes forbears to give a precise indication, as if impatient with the triviality of mundane things; or as if wishing, through having a certain want of order in his expression, to show forth the greatness of the highest order, that of Divine Providence. Whether this be an explanation or not, his fondness for indefinite expressions can be of crucial importance. At the very climax of the *Confessions* we read:

> Thus was it then with me, and he [Alypius] perceived something of it; for *something* I suppose I had spoken, in which the tones of my voice appeared choked with weeping, and so had risen up. […] I cast myself down, *I know not how*, under a *certain* fig tree, giving full vent to my tears. […] And, *not indeed in these words, yet to this purpose*, I spoke much to You. […] I heard from a neighboring house a voice, *as of a boy or girl, I know not*, chanting, and repeating: "Take up and read; take up and read." (8:28-29)

Augustine had the most vivid recollection of this scene; but whether because of his extreme agitation at the time of its happening, or his desire at the time of writing to bring out the central point of the episode by relegating to the background the details which he judged unimportant, there is no other part of the *Confessions* where so much indefinite phrasing abounds. It would be quite erroneous, however, to conclude that the episode is therefore unhistorical. Here more than anywhere Augustine employs indefiniteness, real or rhetorical, to heighten the dramatic quality of the episode and to mark the intervention of Providence.

But rhetoric did not stop at expressions of indefiniteness. It employed dreams, visions, voices, and supernatural terrors, admonitions and interventions of all sorts. Of these the *Confessions* has its share. Contemporary readers would have little difficulty in deciding what was merely rhetorical, but for us it will be necessary to examine these matters where they are important and especially the case of the "voice, as of a boy or girl, I know not, chanting: 'Take up and read.'"

It is hardly necessary to remark that the account of his life as set out by Augustine in the *Confessions* is not strictly chronological. For the most part it does observe the order of events; but sometimes the reverse order is employed, the order of Augustine's memory working its way backwards from the present to the past. From time to time this may puzzle the reader, and may argue some carelessness in the composition; but it does not at all affect the historical value of the facts recounted.

The chief theme of the *Confessions* — now to be mentioned briefly — reveals not only one of the most important senses in which he uses the word *Confessions*, but also determines his selection of episodes, his choice of moralizations, and matter to which rhetorical device is applied. Furthermore, it guarantees the historicity of the *Confessions* as a whole inasmuch as it is found with the same articulation in the early *Dialogues* of Augustine composed within a few months of his conversion — and it is eminently edifying and likely to have pleased Paulinus of Nola and the other spiritual persons who seem in the first instance to have prompted Augustine to write.

The central point in the *Confessions* is the conversion. The conversion itself falls into two parts or moments: the conversion of the intelligence and the conversion of the will. Augustine represents the first as achieved through Platonist learning and the reading of the Scripture, which for some Platonists issued in presumption, and the second through Christian submission, which for him issued in confession:

> I might discern and distinguish between *presumption* and *confession*; between those who saw where they were to go [the Neo-Platonists], yet did not see the way, and the way [Christ] that leads not to behold only but to dwell in the beatific country. (7:26)

The story of mankind was the story of Augustine. Of himself he was weak and earthy; but through a series of aberrations, accidents, admonitions, and adversities Providence had brought him to the Incarnate Word, who both elevated and supported him by His

grace and was for him the Way of authority to the Father. Augustine was convinced of the truth of this theory of life through its operation in his own. The *Confessions*, therefore, centers around this
theme, and its composition is guided by the various elements in it.
Greed for worldly things expressed by a consuming passion for success in his profession is given great prominence. Augustine's life of
fleshly sin is brought out in the highest relief. His acquaintance with
a high and pure philosophy receives an emphasis which to some may
seem remarkable, not to say puzzling. The wandering from one quack
to another, from astrologer to demonologist, is brought strongly to
the reader's attention. But Augustine represents himself as never
giving up in his search for truth. Eventually, under the tender guidance of a kindly Providence, he comes face to face with the challenge to accept or reject Christ and this challenge is the *dénoûment*
of the story. What follows afterwards can be of little significance
beside the great thing that has happened to him in his life.

It is easy to see, then, why he omits much, while at the same
time lingering on certain vital episodes. There is little about his childhood which could easily be exploited for his purpose, and much of
the little there is in the *Confessions* lacks the simplicity of a straight
account. On the other hand the preoccupation with Neo-Platonist
pride and Christian humility in submission to the Word made flesh
is naturally very evident. Moreover, the story as applied to his life is
greatly foreshortened: the suddenness of his conversion is brought out
in great relief — so much so that it has left readers breathless and
uncomprehending. How could the change be so sudden, radical and
permanent? The submission of the will did, of course, happen quickly
— but it had long been prepared for, and when the change came it
was gradual and leaves us with less difficulty in understanding how it
was enduring. Finally, Augustine has included in his *Confessions* not
only the account of his own life, but part also of the lives of Monica,
Alypius and Victorinus. All three had their excesses and all three were
led through adversity by a tender Providence to a sudden conversion.
The story of Augustine's own conversion, therefore, is to some extent the story of a typical conversion: it is the story of Everyman.

One of the strongest reasons for believing in the historicity of
the *Confessions* is precisely the fact that it is dominated by this theme;

for the very first extant work of Augustine, written within a few months of his conversion, is likewise dominated by it. This is only natural for the theme *is* the story of his conversion.

A cursory examination of the *Confessions* will reveal that, of its thirteen books, the first nine deal mainly with Augustine's conversion and what preceded it, and the last four with Augustine's life at the time of writing. There is no account given of the twelve important years which intervened between the death of his mother soon after his baptism and his present life as Bishop of Hippo. But even in the last four books Augustine was trying to do two things: on the one hand, tell those who had requested the information from him how he was now faring in the conflict with the world, the flesh, and the devil; and on the other, expound the beginning of Genesis. He combines all these various parts rather awkwardly, merely placing them in succession one after the other. The result is a badly composed book.

Scholars have been unwilling to believe that Augustine could be content with this. They admit that, for all his training in rhetoric, he was not very good at planning a book: we have only too many instances of his failures in this matter. But they will not believe that that could be true of the most famous and lauded of all his works, the *Confessions*. In not believing they at once deny the evidence of their senses and forget that Augustine had no expectation of producing what has come to be regarded as a masterpiece. He meant it as a work of edification, and he had no scruple in including at the end of the main work his efforts to comply with some requests.

All kinds of theories have been advanced to discover an alleged latent unity and design in the work.[1] Stiglmayr believes that unity is achieved in taking the word *Confession* in the sense of a sacrifice of praise to God as applied to the three topics of the work; namely, the first nine books leading up to his conversion, his present

---

[1] A convenient summary is given by P. Courcelle, *Recherches sur les Confessions de saint Augustin*, Paris, 1950, pp. 21ff.

state, and the commentary on Genesis. Landsberg and Le Blond say that these three topics achieve unity for the work inasmuch as they correspond to Augustine's past, present and future. Courcelle aptly remarks that he has difficulty in seeing how the commentary on Genesis corresponds with Augustine's future. Others suggest that, as edification is to be found everywhere in the work, edification confers the desired unity. Still others suggest that this unity is contrived by the whole book being a confession of faith.

Courcelle adopts and develops a suggestion made by Wundt some years ago, according to which the *Confessions* is the application to Augustine's own life of a technique in catechetical instruction which he was probably evolving at the time of the writing of the book and which is fully displayed in the work *On Catechizing the Uninstructed* (cf. 5:9). According to this book the catechist's work is easiest if the uninstructed has been brought to Christianity through a series of admonitions, terrors of divine origin, miracles or dreams. The catechist's first duty is to show the subject how God has taken care of him in all this. His second duty is to show him that the best of all ways to God and the surest oracle is Holy Scripture. The catechist is to begin his instructions with the explanation of Genesis.

Courcelle agrees that the first nine books of the *Confessions* are a history of the exhortations, terrors, consolations, directions, dreams, oracles, miracles, and admonitions that had led Augustine to Christianity. But he goes on to say that all this is, in Augustine's eyes, of secondary importance. The point of the *Confessions*, Courcelle argues, is precisely the commentary on Genesis. Augustine, on several occasions throughout the first nine books, says that he is in a hurry and cannot delay on the matter he has raised and is omitting very much that might be included, because he wants to get on to the important thing:

> for much I pass by, hurrying to those things which more press me to confess to You. (3:21)
> And when shall I have time to rehearse all Your great benefits towards us at that time, especially when hurrying on to yet greater mercies? (9:7)

Eventually, in the beginning of the eleventh book we come upon the words:

> But how shall I be able with the tongue of my pen to utter all Your exhortations and all Your terrors, and comforts, and guidances, by which You brought me to preach Your Word, and dispense Your Sacrament to Your people? And if I am able to utter them in order, the drops of time[2] are precious with me. I have long burned to meditate on Your law, and to confess to You my skill and unskillfulness, the daybreak of Your enlightening me, and the remnants of my darkness, until infirmity is swallowed up by strength. And I would not have anything else steal away those hours which I find free from the necessities of refreshing my body and the powers of my mind, and of the service which we owe to men, or which though we owe not, we yet pay. (11:2)

Courcelle supposes that Augustine's original intention was to describe as quickly as possible the various steps which led him to Christianity and then to set forth a detailed exposition of Christian doctrine, based on all the Scripture, beginning with the early part of Genesis. As from the third book on he was trying to bring the biographical section to a close; but in this he was not successful. When he had reached the ninth book he began to get into a panic. But on the other hand in the eleventh book he is content to expatiate at great length on the first verse of Genesis. His exposition of Genesis is so slow indeed that in the twelfth book he begins to worry again, not on his own account, but lest none of his readers should be able to stick it out: *quis legentium capere durabit?* His worry abides and, in the end, the work (although his exposition has not got beyond the first thirty verses of Genesis) is published — unfinished.

But the first readers of the *Confessions*, Courcelle goes on to suppose, being more attracted by the biographical part than by the exposition of Genesis, asked Augustine to tell them of his present life. He obliged them and inserted after the ninth book, and before

---

[2] The image is taken from a water-clock, which operated like an hour-glass.

the exposition of Genesis, the account which is set forth in the tenth book. Williger had already shown good reason to believe that this book had been inserted with some inevitable derangement of the material.

While one may be only too ready to agree that Augustine was not at his best in planning his books, one may not be convinced of the correctness of a supposition so paradoxical as to represent Augustine setting out to write a short account of his life up to his conversion, followed by a *detailed* exposition of Christian doctrine based on the whole of Sacred Scripture,[3] and actually succeeding in writing a relatively long account of his life, followed by a commentary on a mere thirty verses of Scripture. One cannot easily believe that he ever intended at any stage to give in the *Confessions* a detailed exposition of Christian doctrine based upon Scripture.

The haste shown throughout the first nine books and at the beginning of the eleventh (which on Courcelle's own admission followed at first immediately after the end of the ninth) is indeed due to his burning desire to get on to the exposition of Scripture; but Augustine nowhere says that he wished in the *Confessions* to embark upon the task of expounding Christian doctrine based on the whole of Scripture: a task which would take even Augustine a lifetime and very many books. Courcelle's supposition is, in short, without foundation and in the highest degree incredible.

What Augustine does say in the beginning of the eleventh book is: "long have I burned to meditate on Your law. [...] And I would not have anything else steal away those hours which I find free." This means quite simply that he has been impatient (or represents himself as being impatient) to come to a task more congenial, he asserts, at the time — namely the exposition of Scripture. Courcelle has been misled by some words which follow shortly upon these just quoted: "Let me confess to You whatever I shall find in Your books, and hear

---

[3] "Augustine, without a doubt, had in mind a great overall plan: in the guise of an exhortation, he related all that had taken place 'in [chronological] order', up to the present moment in order to reveal through his own personal experiences some admonitions of God; then he would expose the Christian doctrine in detail, basing it on the whole of Scripture beginning with the opening words of Genesis." — Courcelle, *Recherches*, p. 23f.

the voice of praise, and drink You in, and meditate on the wonderful things out of Your law; even from the beginning, when You made the heaven and the earth, to the everlasting reigning of Your holy city with You." (11:3) Augustine intends to meditate on the whole of Scripture indeed, but he neither says nor implies that that extended meditation is to complete the present *Confessions*: it was to be the occupation of every hour he could find free for the rest of his life and was to result in his many expositions on Sacred Scripture.

No one of his contemporaries and no one in modern times has shared the view, attributed to Augustine by Courcelle, that the biographical part of the *Confessions* is of secondary importance. We feel certain that Augustine, in fact, held no such view. When we come to the story of his conversion, we shall find that he was profoundly moved by the consideration of how Providence had prepared him for his conversion and discovery of all truth in the Scripture. The story of that preparation seemed to him not of small, but — within the context of the *Confessions* — of the greatest importance.

Wundt was to this extent correct, that he saw the correspondence between the text from the work *On Catechizing the Uninstructed* and the composition of the *Confessions*, which composition becomes all the more clear if the tenth book is left out of consideration. He might have gone further and shown that there was here not so much question of a technique in instruction and explanation as a theory about life in general and Augustine's life in particular.

❦

To sum up: the book is a confession by Augustine to God of sin, praise, and especially of faith — of faith in the Incarnate Word as against the proud rejection of Christ by the Neo-Platonists. The confession is made to God, but before men and for their edification. It contains in its first nine books the history of Augustine's life up to and including his conversion; in the tenth — a book apparently intercalated after the first publication of the whole work — a history of his present conflicts with the world, the flesh and the Devil; and in the last three books a commentary on the first chapter and the first two verses of the second chapter of Genesis. If there is unity in the *Confessions* it lies, to the exclusion of book ten, in the contrast between the search for Truth under the guidance of Providence in the first part of the work, and the enjoyment of Truth in the Scriptures in the third part. This contrast is the theme of the *Confessions*, the first part of which — seeking for Truth under the guidance of Providence — is of primary importance within the *Confessions* itself and essential for the proper understanding of the second.

Augustine believes that all men have similar experiences in the search under Providence for Truth — up to a certain point. Then they are challenged to accept the authority of Christ: some confess to Christ; others in their presumption reject him. Victorinus, his friend and fellow-countryman, submitted to Christ. So did Augustine, and instantaneously with that submission all his former difficulties were overcome.

The *Confessions* therefore is no autobiography, and not even a partial autobiography. It is the use of Augustine's life and confession of faith in God as an illustration of his theory of man.

The facts of his life are discovered by him in memory and the road of memory he traverses, back and forth, visiting only such places as can be of use in the present purpose. If he has no memory of a particular point which is useful for his theory, he conjectures with easy probability what must have happened. Hence the *Confessions* is not wholly a purely personal history; it is in part typical.

Certain consequences for its historicity can be seen to arise from a book of this nature. To begin with, not all of the facts, not necessarily all the important facts even, of Augustine's life are here related: many are forgotten and many would not fit into the pattern of his theory. The events even as given are presented as seen by the writer at the time of composition and not always as they seemed when they occurred. There is appended, moreover, to the relation of facts many moral disquisitions which again are aimed at interpreting the facts in the light of later beliefs rather than in the light of Augustine's views at the time. Added to all this are a rhetorician's fondness for overstatement on the one hand and understatement (manifesting itself in deliberate vagueness both in recollection and language) on the other, and the employment of extraordinary means such as dreams, visions and voices for the furtherance of his arguments especially at a crucial juncture.[4]

What is rhetorical, however, is not necessarily false. Where we have a control for certain sections of the *Confessions*, we find that the facts as given there are correct. Where Augustine has recourse to conjecture, he conjectures with reserve. If he does examine events in the light of recent beliefs and add a moral lesson, he is both conscious of what he is doing and occasionally reminds the reader of it. His audience expected him to use the various techniques of rhetoric, and we have only ourselves to blame if we are misled by them; and God, whom Augustine solemnly addressed, is not mocked. It would have been dangerous for him, to put things at their lowest, to attempt to deceive his many friends and enemies.

The *Confessions*, in short, gives a true account of Augustine's life up to the time of his conversion. But since this account is presented in the pattern of a theory and with the methods of a technique, it needs careful elucidation. Neither the theory nor the technique must be considered as unhelpful, much less harmful. They not only reveal to us the facts of Augustine's earlier life, but also give us the clue to their interpretation and to the mind and heart of that towering figure who built upon a city of philosophers and rhetoricians a city of Christian thought.

---

[4] For an examination of the "elements of fiction" in the *Confessions*, see my *Studies in Augustine and Eriugena*, ed. Thomas Halton, The Catholic University of America Press, 1992, pp. 39-56. For the serious implications of the *Confessions*, see my *Understanding Augustine*, Dublin, 1997, pp. 31-42.

1

BIRTH-PLACE

THERE WAS A TIME, we are told, when Europe was joined to Africa, and a man could walk over dry land from Gibraltar to Tangier. If he made his way eastwards along what is now the coastline of Algeria and Tunisia, he would have found little change from what he had seen in Southern Europe. The flora and fauna were much the same, and the physical appearance of the fertile belt that runs the whole length of the littoral between the mountains and the sea did not greatly differ. The climate there was humid in those days, and what is now the waterless waste of the Sahara was steppe country on which men and beasts could live.

There came a time, however, when the sea swirled past Gibraltar, when the humidity left the air, and when the sun blazed down mercilessly on a trackless desert within the hinterland. But always the belt of land along the coast was fertile. And for the last three thousand years and more a people has lived here that in the main has blue eyes, fair or brown hair and fair skin. No one knows whence they came. It is possible that they came from Europe by Gibraltar, or across the narrow waters from Sicily, or in some other way. Here they have remained, living their own peculiar life, speaking their own languages, and phlegmatically enduring the domination of one culture after another. In Mommsen's words: "The civilized foreign dominions changed; the Berbers remained like the palm of the oasis and the sand of the desert."

For these people are now called Berbers, a name inherited

from the Romans, by whom some of them at least were described as *barbari* — almost barbarians. But the Romans knew them generally as Afri, and their land as a whole as Africa. They were also called Libyans and their language Libyan.

Although it is thought that they all belong to the same racial stock, they have had some internal variations and much intermingling with their successive conquerors and other peoples who settled on their shores. Thus in historical times the Libyans who lived east of a point opposite to Sicily, were considered to have very fair complexions and are represented in this way on monuments of the nineteenth Egyptian Dynasty. On the other hand the Numidians (formerly, simple "nomads") and the Mauri (Moors) were regarded as rather sallow and darkish in appearance. These internal variations can, however, be greatly exaggerated. An authority on this question, Albertini, holds that the names of Libyan, Numidian, Moor, Gaetulian and so on correspond to no intrinsic differences of race, but only of geographical position.[1] Here and there one would find the characteristic physical traits of Phoenicians, Greeks, Romans, Jews and other nations by whom the Berbers were conquered or with whom they had come into contact. All these, however, they easily absorbed or ignored and the racial stock has remained substantially the same down to our own days.

The language of this people has not been widely studied although it is spoken in many parts by Berbers even still. Philologists, however, appear to be certain that it is a native African language belonging to the same family as that spoken by the Ancient Egyptians.

Scholars tell us a good deal more of their religious beliefs. In certain places and occasions and when confronted by natural phenomena such as thunder and lightning, they felt themselves in the presence of a power or powers infinitely stronger than they, and of whom they walked in fear. Religious cult took the form of placat-

---

[1] *Cambridge Ancient History*, XI, p. 481. Cf. the same author's *L'Afrique Romaine*, Algiers, 1950.

ing innumerable "spirits" or gods by means of magical practices and the wearing of amulets and various apotropaic emblems. Among these spirits to be placated were especially the spirits of the dead, for whom Africans, and among them the Christians, always had an extraordinary respect and reverence. Later under the influence of the Phoenicians they worshipped personal deities who typified certain physical forces and events, such as the rebirth of vegetation in the spring, the dry weather which saves the harvest, and the terrible destruction which lay harnessed in the sea. They multiplied sacrifices to appease the powers, now become deities, which were hostile, and retain the favor of those which were well disposed. In due course two deities became of supreme importance and the principal objects of cult, especially at Carthage, Baal Hammon and his consort Tanit. In this the influence of the native religion upon the foreign cult introduced by the Phoenicians becomes very plain, for all the details of the cult were magical. The efficacy of the sacrifice to the deity was considered to depend upon the magical power of the victim. In normal times an animal might be considered to have the necessary magical force; but in times of crisis only a human victim would do, and sometimes in the greatest crises that victim was the head of the community who voluntarily sacrificed himself or herself to avert doom. The self-immolation of Dido and Hamilcar are but two stories known to us. We have the more horrific tale from Diodorus of how the Carthaginians sacrificed three hundred of their members in the fourth century B.C. to prevent Agathocles from taking their walls. These and other instances indicate how the magical character of the native religion persisted in the assimilation of imported cults. Even if we now know that there was no god called Moloch, we are still not relieved of the knowledge that human sacrifice was practiced in Africa; for the word Molk itself means human sacrifice. Recent discoveries to the south of Carthage prove only too clearly that these magical offerings were made.

Into this land and among this people Augustine was born on 13 November A.D. 354. His mother was a young woman, twenty-three years of age, who already had, or was soon to have, at least two other children. Of her children Augustine was destined to be by far the greatest.

His birthplace is now called Souk-Ahras, which is situated in Algeria on the confines of Tunisia. Then it was called Thagaste, situated in Numidia on the confines of Africa Proconsularis. The names have changed and so has the state of cultivation of the soil. In Roman times Numidia and the whole of what is now North Africa generally enjoyed a degree of agricultural wealth and prosperity which seems scarcely credible to one who looks upon the relative barrenness of that land today. Thagaste, when Augustine was born there, was still a fine example of the prosperity brought by the Romans.

The Phoenicians, who had come to Africa before the Romans, had built most of their cities on the coastline. The Romans took over those cities, but also opened up the inland districts. There they had built towns connected with one another and the ports by the all-conquering Roman roads. Roman roads, however, would never in themselves have made Africa wealthy. The Romans did much more to Africa than conquer it. They built bridges across rivers, dammed the smallest as well as the largest torrents, built up reservoirs and dug cisterns big and small. These same cisterns, unused today, bear silent witness to the prosperity which was brought here through the effort of man, and which through his negligence, has largely passed away. The Romans did not try to irrigate the country as a whole. Instead they used the natural advantages of the terrain as best they could. Where there were river-basins of any size they grew grain. Where the land was parched for want of water, they planted immense groves of olive-trees, whose roots reach well below the surface to that earth which even in Africa still retains some moisture. Sheep and horses were put to pasture in odd patches here and there. They did, however, irrigate market-gardens and orchards, and Africa was famous for its artichokes and beans.

So rich did Africa become in corn and olive oil that Rome
at first depended on her for two-thirds of her corn and later for
nearly all her oil. In the beginning the oil sent over was coarse and
was used for lamps only. But the Africans refined their produce until
eventually their oil was also used in the kitchen and even in the
toilette. Cultivation of the soil was constantly being extended or
intensified, and all kinds of inducements were given to entice the
industrious husbandman to produce more. Among these inducements was that known as *emphyteusis*: a contract between the land-
lord and a tenant for the latter to cultivate an unproductive part
of the estate on the condition that he enjoyed all the fruits of that
land for a certain number of years and after that paid an agreed
rent. Africa was mainly held by big landlords, of whom the largest
was the Emperor himself. These landlords were not much concerned how their money came to them, provided that it came. They
encouraged the farmers to take any step which would increase the
overall production and consequent financial return. If the tenants
preferred to pay them indirectly through a local municipal tax, or
directly in rent, they did not seem to mind: they were presumably
interested only in the returns.

It is no wonder then that at the height of its prosperity in
Roman times the country carried a population as large, according
to one calculation, as any that ever lived on the banks of the Nile,
and that it was dotted with towns and cities enjoying all the advantages of urban life of the day. Public buildings adorned the
towns and villages, the smallest of which could boast of its baths
and temples, if not also of theaters and triumphal arches.

The valley of the Medjerda in which Thagaste stood, was particularly fruitful. In Augustine's day the river was known as the
Bagradas. Then, as now, it was the only river worthy of the name
in all that area; and then, as now, it carried enormous alluvial de-
posits to the sea between Tunis and Bizerta. The annual rainfall
here is about seventeen inches — much the same as Madrid, which
has a similar altitude. This rain is distributed over the autumn,
winter, and spring, when the weather can be very capricious and

rainy. The summer is dry and hot, varied only by the coming of the *sirocco* with all its attendant discomforts.

We can picture the town where Augustine was born and its surroundings. Perched high on the uplands of northeast Numidia it had a vista of mountains rising to a height of 3,000 feet further to the East. The river brought fertility to the soil and a wealth of corn, pasture and market-gardens. There were olive groves on the drier ground, and up the hills in the scrub and the forests of oak and pine were to be found wild beasts, lions, bears and panthers which were trapped in large numbers and sent to Rome for the Games in the Amphitheater.

The population must have been mostly Berber with a fair sprinkling of Roman officials and traders. There would have been no recent Roman settlers, for the settling of war veterans in Africa had ceased in the second century; and previous settlers would long ago have been absorbed. There may have been a few Greeks and Jews and individuals or families from neighboring peoples. But in the absence of positive information we must suppose that the permanent population of the town was nearly all of Berber stock.

What language was spoken in the streets and homes of Thagaste? Latin was certainly used on public occasions and in official documents and by officials in the discharge of their duties. The educated classes, too, mostly used Latin both at home and abroad. Some families probably spoke Punic; but in the main the language of the ordinary people must have been Berber. Augustine's family belonged to the better class, and the ordinary language in the house would have been Latin.

Patricius, the father of Augustine held an office which was given the title of *decurio*. It meant, in effect, that he was a member of the town council. From this it seems clear that he was not a Roman official residing in the town as his place of work. He was, in fact, a small landowner and this alone would make it fairly certain that if he had Roman blood in his veins it must have come down from the second century when the settling of Roman veterans stopped. It is safest then to presume that he was a native Numidian. He was a man of some standing, however, as the honor conferred upon him shows.

We can take it that the family into which Augustine was born was not a lowly one. We can also take it that it was not a wealthy one. There may have been other reasons for this, but one evident reason is nearly enough to account for it. The office of *decurio*, once it was inflicted on a man, passed by inheritance to his children, unless they escaped from it by joining one of the reserved occupations, such as the very profession later adopted by Augustine, that of teaching rhetoric. The *decuriones* had to make up for deficiencies in the revenue and at the same time spend large sums of their own money to finance public services and entertainments. At the time when Augustine was born, the *decuriones* had been drained of every penny they inherited or earned in the effort to maintain the excessively high standard of public service and entertainment already mentioned. Many of them sought to evade their onerous obligations by fleeing to monasteries and overflowing into the reserved professions. But a series of edicts against such subterfuges and pursuing soldiers held them to their task until they broke under it.

Whether Patricius was building up family wealth and had just been the recipient of this uncomfortable honor, or had inherited the honor and was quickly losing his wealth, we do not know. We do know, however, that his property did not extend beyond a few poor fields, although when Augustine talks about it in this way he may be exaggerating. In addition, we know that his parents had great difficulty in finding the money to send Augustine to, what we would call, the University of Carthage. Augustine expressly tells us that his father was much commended by his friends for the efforts he had made in pinching and scraping in order to provide his son with this superior education.

We are fortunate in being able to indicate the limits between which Patricius' estate must have fallen. On the one hand we have a famous inscription, called the *Inscription of the Harvester of Maktar*, which tells eloquently the story of a poor man who has struggled and made good:

> I was born of a poor family. My father had no income or house of his own. Since the day of my birth, I have always tilled the land; my land and I have not rested. When the season of the year came round when the harvest was ripe, I was the first to cut my stalks. When the bodies of harvesters who hire themselves out round Cirta, the capital of the Numidians, or in the plains overlooked by the Mountain Jupiter, appeared in the country, I harvested for other men for twelve years under a burning sun. For eleven years, I commanded a gang of harvesters and reaped corn in the fields of the Numidians. By my work, having been able to do with little, I at last became owner of a house and an estate. Today I am comfortably off. I have even risen to honors; I have been inscribed among the Decurions of my city, and my colleagues have elected me Censor, me who at the beginning of my life was only a small peasant. I have seen my children and grandchildren come into the world and grow up round me, and my life has gone by, peaceful and honored by all.[2]

Was Patricius such a person? It seems possible indeed; for there is no doubt that his spirit is not broken. Rather his ambition is whetted with the prospect of giving a higher education to his son. There is a feeling of optimism and success conveyed in those passages of the *Confessions* where Patricius' efforts on behalf of his son are described. There is, moreover, a tone of respect and deference in Augustine's own later attitude to a local magnate named Romanianus that suggests that Augustine's family was happy to be noticed by him. One cannot argue very much on this kind of evidence, however.

But if Patricius had inherited a large estate which was dwin-

---

[2] *Corpus Inscriptionum Latinarum*, Berlin, 1863, VIII, 11824, as translated in J. Toutain, *The Economic Life of the Ancient World*, London, 1930, pp. 279 ff. (Routledge and Kegan Paul).

dling under the expenses of the honor conferred on his family, we can see from many splendid mosaics found in Africa the kind of house which would have been his. One mosaic from Tabarka,[3] about sixty miles from Thagaste, for example, shows the master's house with its square forecourt and tall, square flanking towers connected by a *loggia*. One can see the coach-houses and the offices, and all the varied life of the small community: the ducks, geese and pheasants in the yard; the orchard and the vineyard; the sheep watched over by a spinning shepherdess. From another mosaic, this time from Oudna south of Carthage, we are given a number of scenes from daily life on a medium-sized property: men hunting with spear and net; a ploughman following his two oxen; sheep attended by their shepherd; a horse drinking at a trough; one slave driving an ass, another picking olives, another milking a goat, and still another playing a flute while watching his beasts.[4]

Somehow one has the feeling that if Patricius owned such an estate he would have been anxious to hand it on to Augustine, even if it were encumbered by the office of *decurio*. He would hardly have encouraged him in a profession which held great rewards, it is true, but only for those who were eminently successful, and which in the meantime would take him away from the estate. And what confidence could Patricius have, for all his early brightness, in Augustine's ultimate success? Augustine was not the only son in the family; but that he might expect to inherit the estate is not unlikely since in the end he did inherit it.

One may be inclined, then, to place Patricius nearer to the level of the Harvester of Maktar than to that of Romanianus, the friend and patron of Augustine. Augustine may not have been too modest when he spoke of the few poor fields.

It is sometimes suggested that Augustine's mother, Monica, was of lowly extraction. The only reason given is that, according to Augustine, when she was a young girl, she used to be sent to

---

[3] Cf. P. Gauckler, *Inventaire des mosaïques de la Gaule et de l'Afrique*, II, no. 940.
[4] *Ibid.*, no. 362.

the cellar to draw wine. But to have a cellar at all is something, and whether we are dealing with high or low, it is difficult to take too seriously an argument relying on the allocation to a child of a household chore. The words of St. Paul are apposite: "As long as the heir is a child, he differs in nothing from the servant, though he be lord of all" (Gal 4:1). Moreover the context supposes that there were domestics in her parents' house. It is also suggested that she was of a lower race. She was certainly Berber and her name may be derived from the Libyan deity Mon, worshipped in the neighboring town of Thibilis. But there is no good reason for believing that her husband was not a Berber also.

There is some evidence, in fact, for a Berber background to the upbringing of Augustine. Thagaste was a center of Berber culture; in no other area are early Berber remains so numerous. Augustine himself followed certain Berber traditions in his life, as for example in choosing a name for his son: Iatanbaal (*given of Baal*, translated into Latin as Adeodatus), which preserves the Berber custom of having Baal in some part of a child's name — and in certain other matters. Frend[5] supposes that Augustine's later attitude to the cult of martyrs reveals a reversion to Berberism.

If Augustine's parents were Berbers, their aspirations, nevertheless, were in the main towards what was Roman. They belonged to the upper classes and were probably somewhat out of sympathy with the mass of their fellow-Numidians. Frend puts forward the theory that the ultimate failure of Catholicism and Augustine *within* Africa was due to the fact that both identified themselves too closely with the Roman power and were at variance with the native agrarian, Numidian, and (in religion) Donatist movement. Frend, perhaps, simplifies things too much. The indications, however, in the case of Augustine's own family are that although they were Berber and Numidian (and there were some Donatists even on Monica's side) they and their better-class friends had thrown in their lot with the Roman rulers, if not also with Catholicism, that is, as opposed to the Donatist Church.

---

[5] Cf. W.H.C. Frend, *The Donatist Church*, Oxford, 1952.

One other point which seems of peculiar interest to those who are curious about Augustine: what color was his skin? If, as Albertini says, the difference between the Libyans and Numidians is mainly topographical, and if the Libyans — and Berbers — are mainly fair, then, in spite of the recurring belief that Numidians were dark, Augustine on general grounds is more likely to have been fair than dark! Certainly the Romans in Italy had no prejudice against his color when they honored him with high office in Milan. He felt even that he could easily become the governor of a province. On the whole his color can hardly have been much darker than that of the average Roman.

Augustine came into life in a family where the mother was a devout Christian, and the father a pagan. There were very many such families in Africa, although not all perhaps were as harmonious. Not all Christians were as pious or as restrained as Monica, and not all pagans as indifferent as Patricius. Taking a broad view of the situation, we can say that in the fourth century A.D. Christianity in Africa, as elsewhere, was gaining and Paganism as an organized religious system, was losing perceptibly.

Apart from other considerations, a faith which placed the native Africans on the same level before God as the Romans was welcomed by those who were interested in improving their condition. In addition there had been a succession of imperial edicts against Paganism from the time of Constantine onwards. It was only during the short reign of Julian the Apostate (361-363) that any respite was given. In the very year in which Augustine was born there was one such edict promulgated, and it was followed by twenty more in the last twenty years of the fourth century. Four edicts in all were passed in the year A.D. 399, as though a serious attempt was being made to wipe out Paganism forever before the dawn of a new period. Idols were to be thrown down; temples were to be converted to public use; bishops were to report laxity in the administration of the law in this matter; and judges were to be fined for not enforcing it.

There were, however, no such edicts after the first year of Augustine's life until he was twenty-seven. Indeed the tide seemed to run in favor of Paganism for a short period when Julian supported it against Christianity. He could observe that there remained many among the lower elements of the population, and quite a number among the more cultured and influential, who sincerely professed Paganism and led lives as good as any Christians — to outward appearances, at any rate. They continued to worship as their Berber, Punic or Roman ancestors had worshipped before them either through conviction or for want of something they judged better.

Nevertheless the cult of Saturn and Coelestis and all the magical rites and practices of the local pagans seem to have had little appeal for Augustine at the time. And he was to see his father yield to Christianity shortly before he died, when Augustine was in his seventeenth year.

Christianity had more obstacles to deal with than Paganism. There was Manicheism and above all there was schism: there was the Church of the Donatists. As it happened, Thagaste was peculiarly free from this schism, which must have made it easier for Monica to teach Catholicism to the boy Augustine. But the scandal was too great, too obvious, and too widespread to have escaped the attention of the growing lad.

The schism arose, at least partly, and was maintained, again at least partly, because of certain characteristics of the Church in Africa. Christianity in Africa was remarkable for — among other things — the number of its bishops, and the extraordinary enthusiasm of its veneration for martyrs.

Bishops were very numerous indeed. Nearly six hundred of them turned up at the famous Conference at Carthage in A.D. 411, and although that figure included the Donatist bishops, it does not allow for the number of absentees and the sees that were vacant. They enjoyed a good deal of power and privilege, but very often their ecclesiastical jurisdiction did not extend beyond what would nowadays be a parish.

The African Church, however, was distinguished above all in its veneration for the martyrs of the Faith. The first we hear of Christianity in Africa is, in fact, in connection with the martyrs of Scillium and Madauros. On August 1, we are told, of the year 180 they were summoned to sacrifice and deny Christ. They refused. They were asked to think better about their refusal. They refused to open the matter again. They were then sentenced, and all said: "Thanks be to God." Immediately they were beheaded for the name of Christ. Doubtless many had died for the Faith before the martyrs of Scilli and Madauros, as many certainly did after them.

To such an extent did the thought of the martyrs color the attitude of African Christians that shrines of martyrs began to spring up everywhere and relics multiplied in a surprising way. The ecclesiastical authorities had to intervene and take action against certain misguided cults, and this was one of the principal causes of the Donatist schism. An archdeacon, named Caecilian, reproved a woman, called Lucilla, for her excesses in this matter and immediately provoked her powerful and lasting hostility. Subsequently he was elected to the bishopric of Carthage, but his fellow-bishops had not waited for the Numidian representatives to arrive for the election. When they did arrive, Lucilla bribed them to elect a bishop of their own on the ostensible ground that one of the bishops who had consecrated Caecilian had betrayed the Church in handing over the Scriptures to the civil authorities in order to escape persecution. They did so, and thus schism was established. It was not long until there were two bishops in nearly every petty see, with disastrous consequences, of course, for the peace of the Church.

Apart, however, from the short reign of Julian, who as he favored Paganism, so also favored the Donatists, the Donatist Church was always on the losing side until it was finally broken at the Conference at Carthage in A.D. 411. But from the time of Julian, when Augustine was just emerging from childhood, until the end, when largely through the work of Augustine and his friends they were rendered powerless, the Donatists kept up a constant attack upon

Catholics, even going so far as to use roving bands of brigands, *circumcelliones* as they were called, to do physical violence on those who dared to differ from them.

It is not necessary to say here that many of the Donatists led bad lives, and that many of those who opposed them were no better. Some bishops were unworthy and full of worldly ambition. There were scenes of debauchery during the banquets that took place on feast days in the basilicas. There were, in short, the thousand and one imperfections, great and small, which are incidental to institutions that use the services of man. To wonder greatly at these things or to dilate at length upon them would reveal little knowledge and little understanding. But can we be surprised if many pagans and Manichees were slow to yield to the Church? Can we be surprised to learn that many Christians were Christians only in name? And can we be surprised if a clever and impetuous young lad, such as Augustine, should grow up with strange notions about Christianity and a certain disdain for what he believed it taught?

2

EARLY TRAINING

W HEN WE BEGIN to assess the influences that played upon the growing Augustine we find ourselves immediately confronted with the name of Monica. Psychologists interpret the relations of this mother and son in a variety of ways according to the theories of their schools. Writers in a more romantic vein trace the history of the love of these two, the one for the other, from the beginning, through many disappointments, to the final ecstasy of a more than human delight. And they who seek to edify give in some ways the major role to Monica; for was it not through her tears that such a son was not allowed to perish? Here, although our aim is not to edify, nor to excite romantic *frisson*, nor to illustrate a psychological theory, we must attempt to give due importance to the influence of his mother upon Augustine. He considered that his conversion was in some ways her achievement; and, once he was baptized, she regarded her mission in life as over. Hence, after the climax of the *Confessions*, we have the remarkable description in the ninth book of Monica's life, character and final union with Augustine in mind and spirit, in the sublime contemplation of God, before she died.[1]

Monica did more for Augustine than could be expected of an ordinary mother. But Monica was no ordinary mother. We shall see her planning everything for him. We shall see how she over-

---

[1] See further my *Understanding Augustine*, Dublin, 1997, pp. 34f.

came every obstacle that stood in the way first of Augustine's worldly career and later, insofar as it was in her power, of his spiritual salvation. If she was not physically present wherever he was, she was there in spirit, absorbed in everything he said and did. If, when he came back to Thagaste a Manichee, she refused to have him in her house, on another occasion she insisted upon following him to Rome and Milan in order to be near him. She remained with him to the end of her life, keeping house for him and his friends, devoting herself entirely to them. Monica was not merely a good and pious woman given to prayers, dreams and tears. To begin with, she had faults — although those mentioned by Augustine are slight indeed. She managed, or attempted to manage him, even if she did not always succeed. It is true that one whole side of his life, the intellectual, must have been almost closed to her; and much of his life was led independently of her when it was not in opposition to the principles she held most dear. Nevertheless, for one reason or another, she had sufficient influence with him shortly before his conversion to prevail upon him to send away his mistress, who had been faithful to him for fifteen years, and to consider marrying a girl not yet of marriageable age but, apparently, of Monica's choosing. Truly she was in some respects a *mulier fortis*.

It will be best, perhaps, first to take account of what her son says of her, before we attempt to describe her character and see to what extent it is reflected in that of her favorite son.

In the *Confessions* Augustine gives us a short "life" of his mother in the understanding of which we shall have to recall our observations for the interpretation of the *Confessions* as a whole. In particular, one might notice how, we might almost say, he invents a fault for her so that Providence might, through adversity, suddenly convert her.

Monica owed much of her good habits of life to an old nurse who had served her father when he was a child and who consequently had a position of peculiar authority in the house. This old woman insisted that Monica and her sisters should not drink between meals — not even water: "'You drink water now, because you do not have wine in your power; but when you come to be married, and be made mistresses of cellars and cupboards, you will scorn water, but the custom of drinking will abide.' By this method of instruction, and the authority she had, she restrained the greediness of childhood, and moulded their very thirst to such an excellent moderation, that what they should not, that they would not."

> And yet (as Your handmaid told me, her son) there had crept upon her a love of wine. For when (as the custom was) she, as though a sober maiden, was bidden by her parents to draw wine out of the hogshead, holding the vessel under the opening, before she poured the wine into the flagon, she sipped a little with the tip of her lips [...] by adding to that little, daily littles [...] she had fallen into such a habit, as greedily to drink off her little cup brimful almost of wine. [...] Would anything avail against a secret disease, if Your healing hand, O Lord, watched not over us? [...] How did You cure her? How heal her? Did You not out of another soul bring forth a hard and sharp taunt, like a lancet out of Your secret store, and with one touch remove all that foul stuff? For a maidservant with whom she used to go to the cellar, falling to words (as it happens) with her little mistress, when alone with her, taunted her with this fault, with most bitter insult, calling her a wine-bibber. With this taunt she, stung to the quick, saw the foulness of her fault, and instantly condemned and forsook it. (9:17-18)

The young Monica, as soon as she was of marriageable age, was bestowed upon Patricius who took her into his own house, where his own mother still ruled. At first, the old lady listened to the gossip of the servants against their new mistress and became incensed against her daughter-in-law. But Monica's respectful attitude, her patience and her meekness won the day and soon his mother invited Patricius to whip the mischief-making servants. From then on all went well — as between her mother-in-law and herself.

Patricius was more difficult to win over, and it took her until the end of his life. He was frequently unfaithful to her until, shortly before he died, he became a Christian; but she bore the injury without complaint. His choleric temper must have been a very great trial; still, while other women bore on their faces for all to see the marks of the punishment generously meted out to them by their spouses, Monica went unscathed by her tempestuous lord to the wonder of all. For she humored Patricius and forbore to answer back when he spoke hot words to her. Only later when he had calmed down did she attempt to justify herself; and even then showed him that she loved and respected him. She advised her women friends to maintain the same respectful attitude towards their husbands and, as Augustine says: "Those wives who observed it found the good, and returned thanks; those who did not observe it found no relief, and suffered." In all matters inside the house or without she behaved with discretion, and thought only of spreading peace in every way she could.

Thus far the life of Monica up to the time that Augustine came upon the scene. After that her life becomes part of his. The qualities in Monica which Augustine calls upon us to admire in what has been recounted are briefly: perseverance, discretion, respect for authority and a love of peace. These same qualities are to be seen on a greater scale in the course of her life as mother of Augustine; and as she was loved and admired by her husband, so was she admired and loved by her son. The characteristics which seem most dominant are: her perseverance, her power to endure; her discretion, and her ability to bide her time. Indeed both are connected, and her life is the story of a controlled ambition, a constant striving upwards towards temporal and, especially, spiritual goals, which no present disappointment and no lapse of time could lessen or suppress. Her deliberate campaign for Augustine's conversion took nearly twenty years, but in the end she won. She was affectionate and attracted affection, and had a certain simplicity, sincerity and goodness. But it would be a mistake to think of her as merely a tearful visionary, for she was strong, practical, ambitious and determined. As Augustine grew up in childhood within the household, which he himself depicted for us, he cannot have failed to be drawn into sympathy with his mother. Children are not slow to feel disturbances in the atmosphere of a home, and the young Augustine would, when his father was in a temper, have instinctively gone for shelter to his mother's bosom. Whether Patricius was or was not as bad-tempered as Augustine says is of no great consequence now. The important thing is that that was the impression that Augustine got of his father in his childhood. One natural result would be that the boy began to share the feelings of his mother and the other "little women," as he calls them, who lived in the house. This does not, however, mean that he never had sympathy for his impulsive and frequently discomfited father.

The day came when Augustine was sent to school, to learn to read and write, to add, subtract, multiply and divide:

> Next I was put to school to get learning, in which I (poor wretch) knew not what use there was; and yet, if idle in learning, I was beaten. For this was judged right by our forefathers; and many, passing the same course before us, constructed for us weary paths, through which we had to pass; multiplying toil and grief upon the sons of Adam. But, Lord, we found that men called upon You, and we learned from them to think of You (according to our powers) as of some great One, Who, though hidden from our senses, could hear and help us. For so I began, as a boy, to pray to You, my aid and refuge; and broke the fetters of my tongue to call on You, praying to You, though small, yet with no small earnestness, that I might not be beaten at school. And when You heard me not (not thereby giving me over to folly), my elders, yes my very parents who yet wished me no ill, mocked my stripes, my then great and grievous ill. (1:14)

It does not, one may hope, detract from the charm of the passage quoted to realize that while Augustine was doubtless consulting his own unhappy experience in all of this, he has his eye very much on a commonplace of Stoic literature. Labriolle pointed out long ago that Augustine is here following a passage from Seneca,[2] who maintains that there is no essential difference between the "business" of grown-ups and the games of children. To Seneca they are both equally unimportant. To Augustine they are both equally bad. Even the comparison, which he was to make on more than one occasion again, of punishments inflicted on schoolboys to the racks and hooks and other torments inflicted on the martyrs is inspired by his later reading in Stoic literature.

It would not, however, have been surprising if the thought of a Christian martyr's experience had come to him as he submitted to the master's ferule. His mother had taken great care to indoctrinate him with as much of Christianity and, we can suppose, the local veneration for martyrs, as he could take at this early stage. Even from the womb of his mother he was, he tells us, sealed with the mark of Christ's cross. Naturally, then, when in a sudden violent sickness it was thought that he was about to die, he asked to be baptized. Since he as quickly recovered, his mother did not proceed with the baptism, for she felt, as did many other Christians of the day, that the grace of baptism which left the soul spotless before God, no matter how it had been defiled, could more advantageously be used when adolescence would have passed with all its perils, if not calamities. He saw nothing wrong in this at the time; but later he was to blame his mother for her decision. In the meantime, however, he was a catechumen, an aspirant to baptism and, as he says himself, a believer.

> I then already believed; as did my mother and the whole household, except my father. Yet he did not prevail over the power of my mother's piety in me, that as he did not yet believe, so neither should I. For it was her earnest care, that You my God, rather than he, should be my father; and in this You helped her to prevail over her husband. (1:17)

Men have too often forgotten these first years of Christian

---

[2] *De const. sap.* 12:1. Augustine returns to the theme in 1:30.

belief and piety when Augustine was the willing pupil at his mother's knee. How long that period lasted we do not know. He can hardly have been sent away from home to another town to school much before ten years of age — and perhaps he was somewhat older. But it lasted long enough to leave an indelible impression on his mind. Some writers suppose that because of the *disciplina arcani* — the keeping secret of Christian doctrine from those who were not full Christians — Monica taught little, if anything, of Christian doctrine to Augustine. But this is taking the *disciplina arcani* far too seriously. From these early years with Monica he got, possibly, certain childish notions of God's nature and a child's approach to Scripture, which, because their development was interrupted, may have hindered him at a later stage. But it would be wrong to underrate the effect of these years upon his attitude towards Christianity. Augustine was first, though not formally, and last a Christian: the years between were an important interlude, it is true, but still an interlude. In adolescence and early manhood he always preserved a great reverence for the name of Christ, and a strong link between him and Christ was always in the background in the person of his mother. It is significant that when he is converted his mind goes back to these early days and he feels that he is but taking up again the threads which he had let drop as a boy.

He had hated his years of schooling in reading, writing and arithmetic at Thagaste; but for all that he had shown enough promise to encourage his parents in the belief that he would profit by being sent to school to Madauros, a good-sized town about fifteen miles to the south of Thagaste.

Here he was away from the influence of his mother, unless we suppose that she accompanied him thither. But it does not follow that because there were pagans in Madauros that he boarded with them. Surely it is more reasonable to suppose that Monica took what care she could to see that he was well looked after, if possible by Christians whom she might trust. It is idle to conjure up a picture, as some writers do, of the young impressionable boy, coming from the simplicity of a Christian home in a small town, brought suddenly and unprotected face to face with an overpowering flood of paganism, pagan life, and pagan rites. He could see paganism even in his own home in Thagaste. One can concede, of course, that there was less supervision, that there was a richer pagan life to see, and that he himself was becoming more and more curious.

It will not be necessary, then, to dwell on the evidences of pagan life which met his enquiring gaze as he walked to school in the streets of Madauros. They were much greater in themselves, and had a far greater influence on him, as we shall see, when he found himself later on in Carthage. He always remembered the statue of a naked Mars in the Forum, and the eccentric behavior of the respectable people of Madauros on the feast of the Bacchanals. But the town remained in his memory for other reasons besides its paganism. It was the place of origin of at least one of Africa's greatest writers in Latin, Apuleius, and it was there that he began in a serious and systematic way to experience the educational training of the day.

This was essentially a training in language, literature and oratory. The product arrived at was the eloquent man who could apply himself successfully either to the public service or elsewhere to public affairs and the management of men. There were three stages in the training; the first, that of reading, writing and arithmetic, which Augustine had already passed through in Thagaste; the second, that of Grammar, which he was now to encounter at Madauros; and the third, that of Rhetoric, which he would meet with partly at Madauros but mostly at Carthage. Grammar and Rhetoric were not very sharply divided and there was a good deal of overlapping both in matter and technique between the two. It will be convenient, therefore, at this stage to take the two together.

Grammar consisted in the understanding of the poets and in the right method of writing and speaking. It was therefore much more than mere grammar in our sense of the word: it was, in fact, both a training in grammar and, according to the capacity of the pupil, a study of literature.

The latter half of the fourth and the whole of the fifth century was the Golden Age of grammarians. Some of their work has come down to us, and there we can see their fondness for definition and precise classification. Augustine, although he does not discuss this part of his training in the *Confessions*, does tell us in his *On the Usefulness of Believing*[3] of the best known grammatical authors of his day, Asper, Cornutus, Donatus, and for meter (which was added to grammar) Terentianus Maurus. Some, at least, of their works he used, and we can see from them the quality of the training which he received. The language discussed was not the Latin of his day: it was the Latin of Cicero, which was, even to Augustine, a classical language. Hence there was much emphasis on fixed rules and authority. This thorough training in a very precise, reasoned and positive science, left a mark on Augustine for the rest of his life. According to Alfaric[4] he remained for the whole of his life a grammarian, and Marrou[5] sees in the author of *On the Trinity* or the *City of God* the grammarian of Madauros. He always had a fondness for grammatical illustrations, for subdivisions and definitions; but perhaps the effect of this strict and searching discipline on his mind itself and general mental outlook was more fundamental and of greater consequence. It gave him a canon by which to judge all things, the canon of logical sequence: this led him later to embrace Manicheism and later still to forsake it. If he had come to this discipline with the persevering diligence of his mother, then he must have found it peculiarly satisfying and in it he must have been unusually successful.

The second part of the Grammar course dealt with literature and it was here that it tended to overlap with Rhetoric which in its turn began with literature and went on to eloquence. It was here also that an exact and reasoned discipline became less exact and less reasoned; for the appeal was no longer to reason but to emotion and imagination. This left an even greater mark on Augustine.

The principal authors studied were Virgil and Cicero, with

---

[3] P. 17.
[4] P. Alfaric, *L'évolution intellectuelle de Saint Augustin*, I, Paris, 1918, p. 13 ff.
[5] H. Marrou, *Saint Augustin et la fin de la culture antique*, Paris, 1938, p. 3 ff.

Terence next perhaps, and then Horace, Lucan, Persius, Ovid, Catullus, Juvenal, Seneca, Sallust and possibly Apuleius. Many if not all of these were studied in excerpts and in Madauros there would have been special emphasis, perhaps, put on those authors and passages which were African or dealt with African topics. The study of authors was conducted in a long-established procedure. The passage was first read aloud or recited from memory, due attention being given to diction and punctuation. Punctuation was often uncertain and the master's help was needed here. He gave direction, often according to his fancy, on variations in the readings of the texts — and these were many in those days when every book had to be copied by hand. He then made comments on the style of the passage. The next item was the one which took up most of the time: it consisted in giving a literal explanation of everything in the passage and a literary comment. The literal explanation frequently involved a good deal of etymology, and the explanation and comment was so exhaustive that the general sense of the passage — to say nothing of the book or work as a whole — was often lost. Servius' commentary on the *Aeneid* is a good example of this kind of thing; and the last three books of the *Confessions* where Augustine comments on the first chapter of Genesis enable us to see how Augustine put something like this process to work for himself.

Marrou attributes to the authors of detailed commentaries a "psychological atomism" and a myopia which prevents them from seeing the whole. The criticism is not perhaps relevant to this kind of work when practiced as a discipline in a class and for a limited time. That Augustine, however, retained a taste for the method is abundantly clear from his many detailed expositions of Holy Scripture; and he sometimes tended to be carried away with present interest and forget the proportion needful in the whole. But for all that he has at least as much taste for synthesis as analysis — and perhaps more.

The fourth and final stage in the treatment of the author was a short review of the three previous ones and a final summary judgment. This in itself obviated somewhat the dangers of psychological atomism and myopia.

When the student proceeded to Rhetoric, he brought with him some of the same authors, but his use of them was different. Here Cicero reigned, and his oratorical works — especially his earliest such as the *On Invention* — were treated with the greatest reverence. The training in rhetoric was partly in theory and partly in practice. The *aim* was eloquence, which could be used to demonstrate a point, to prove one's case before a court, or to offer advice to one in doubt — three situations which were supposed to embrace generically the occasions when success in the art of exposition meant success in one's career. The *theory* went back to the time of Cicero and before him to the Sophistic movement in Athens at the end of the fifth century B.C. It had changed hardly at all with the passage of years. It gave the student various main headings under which to consider any topic proposed: they helped him to discover what he should say and the proper order of his discourse.

The *practice*, however, was the important thing and took up most of the time of pupil and master. As already in Grammar, the pupil here too engaged himself in preparatory exercises of about a dozen different kinds arranged in a scale of increasing difficulty. Augustine seems to have a keen recollection of one of these in which he himself met with success amongst his schoolmates at Madauros. It was the preparatory exercise called "delineation of character," the ninth in the scale:

> Bear with me, my God, while I say something about my intelligence, Your gift, and on what trifles I wasted it. For a task was set me, troublesome enough to my soul, upon terms of praise or shame, and fear of stripes, to speak the words of Juno, as she raged and mourned that she could not "This Trojan prince from Latium turn," [*Aeneid* 1:36 ff.] which words I had heard that Juno never uttered; but we were forced to go astray in the footsteps of these poetic fictions, and to say in prose what he expressed in verse. And his

speaking was most applauded, in whom the passions of rage
and grief were most preeminent, and clothed in the most
fitting language, maintaining the dignity of the character.
What is it to me, O my true life, my God, that my declamation was applauded above so many of my own age and class?
Is not all this smoke and wind? And was there nothing else
upon which to exercise my mind and tongue? (1:27)

The main practical exercise of Rhetoric proper, however, was
the preparation and delivery of an actual speech. There were two
kinds of such declamations, one in which the speaker gave advice
(the *suasoria*) which he conceived would have been useful to some
great man at some famous crisis in his career. The elder Seneca
gives us some favorite instances of this, such as the occasion of
Cicero's doubt as to whether he should or should not ask Mark
Antony to spare his life. For success in this exercise one obviously
needed a great deal of historical information, much psychological
insight, and of course a certain dramatic power to make the situation real for one's audience. The second kind of declamation was
somewhat more difficult: it argued for the proper course of action
in a debatable matter (*controversia*) often arising from a point of
law and that law purely fictitious! The more fictitious the law and
fanciful the situation, the more scope the student had for showing
his ingenuity in disentangling the knot, the pithy wisdom of his
advice, and the richness of his eloquence. The topics which have
come down to us are sufficiently improbable, and often almost gro-
tesque, to show us how far removed from actual life were the exercises in which the students of rhetoric were engaged. We should
not, however, conclude that the rhetoricians were unaware of this.
They must have been aware, and they must have seen some profit
in this manner of training.

When one examines carefully the two overlapping disciplines, that of Grammar, which Augustine completed while he was
at Madauros, and that of Rhetoric, the preparatory exercises of
which — and little more — were encountered by him before he
went to Carthage, one will perhaps come to the conclusion that

the whole training was aiming at two very different things; for both Grammar and Rhetoric while putting emphasis on dry and formal analysis, on precise definition, division and subdivision, at certain points encouraged deliberate digression, the scarcely-controlled exploitation of imagination and emotion and above all a certain largeness and overflowing abundance in theme and language. The question may be asked: which of the two aspects of this training appealed the more to Augustine? The answer is, the second. Although during the rest of his long life he was to employ, with apparent relish, the various technical aids which Grammar and Rhetoric gave him — recourse to definition, division, classification, etymology, and the method of the detailed commentary, to say nothing of the various figures of speech and rhythmical patterns in language — he showed from the beginning until the end a great fondness for following his fancy wherever it led. His works are incontestable evidence of the little success he had in careful methodical planning and the requirements of form. Something has already been said of the weakness in the *Confessions* from this point of view. But the same weakness is to be seen in greater or less degree in many of his other works, in his *Against the Academics*, *On the Agreement of the Evangelists*, *On the Trinity* and the *City of God*. It is a commonplace of Augustinian scholarship to say that Augustine was not able to plan a book. There is, however, a little justice in Marrou's contention that Augustine was not interested in doing so: his spirit was impatient of the restraints. Marrou compares Augustine's notions of order in a book to that of other people's notions of order in a room: it is purely superficial; the room looks neat but the drawers are crammed with tossed and ill-assorted objects. Whatever truth there be in that view, we can be sure that Augustine's genius was too great, too independent, too tumultuous to find easy expression in a neatly articulated plan. He loved to think rather in terms of one large, all-embracing idea.

Nevertheless he consciously aimed at what was more formal, methodical and controlled; and it is one of the great interests of his story and one of the clues to his character to know of this oscillation between restraint and excess. When in the first book of the *Confessions* he came to consider the defects of the life he led at school, he seized immediately on what he felt was a weakness. He tells us how he deeply disliked what was useful to him, namely, reading, writing, arithmetic and the Greek language, and became overenthusiastic about what he later, with too much harshness, judged useless, if not altogether irrational, namely, entering into the emotions of some literary personage, such as Dido in the *Aeneid:*

> But why did I so much hate the Greek, which I studied as a boy? I do not yet fully know. For the Latin I loved; not what my first masters, but what the so-called grammarians taught me. For those first lessons, reading, writing and arithmetic, I thought as great a burden and penalty as any Greek. And yet whence was this too, but from the sin and vanity of this life, because I was flesh, and a breath that passes away and comes not again? For those first lessons were better certainly, because more certain; by them I obtained, and still retain, the power of reading what I find written, and myself writing what I will. Whereas in the others, I was forced to learn the wanderings of one Aeneas, forgetful of my own, and to weep for dead Dido, because she killed herself for love. (1:20)

The passage quoted above raises one point on which something must be said: how much Greek did Augustine know? Some scholars believe that in the last fifteen years or so of his life he knew considerably more than he did when he was converted. That just may be. But the real question of interest is how much he knew immediately before his conversion. It is evident that he began to learn it at school and that his plain statement that not one word of it did he understand cannot be taken literally. It is equally evident that he always found great difficulty with it — how great, is the problem. Could he sit back and read, for example, a Greek author of average difficulty with ease; or did he make out the Greek only with great difficulty and constant recourse to various aids? It seems almost certain that his performance for most, if not all of his life, was nearer the second. The knowledge he shows of Greek in his books is confined to elementary words, etymologies common to discussions of a special nature, technical and some Christian terms. The conclusion must be that until late in life at least he could use a Greek text only as a control against which to check a doubtful word or passage in the Latin.[6]

As for the rest, his life in Madauros cannot have been very different from that of an ordinary boy. He speaks of his enormities: "So small a boy and so great a sinner," and again:

> For I saw not the abyss of vileness, into which I was cast away from Your eyes. Before them what was more foul than I was already, displeasing even those as myself? With innumerable lies I deceived my tutor, my masters, my parents, from love of play, eagerness to see vain shows, and restlessness to imitate them! Thefts also I committed, from my parents' cellar and table, enslaved by greediness, or that I might have something to give to boys, who sold me their things, which game all the while they liked no less than I. In this play too, I often sought unfair conquests, conquered myself meanwhile by vain desire of preeminence. And what could I so ill endure, or, when I detected it, upbraided I so fiercely, as that which I was doing to others? And for which if detected, I was upbraided, I chose rather to quarrel than to yield. And is this the innocence of boyhood? [...] These very sins are transferred from tutors and masters, from nuts and balls and sparrows, to magistrates and kings, to gold and manors and slaves, just as severer punishments displace the cane. (1:30)

He also tells us of his good points and successes: "I learned to delight in truth, I hated to be deceived, had a vigorous memory, was gifted with speech, was soothed by friendship, avoided pain, baseness, ignorance." (1:31) And again: "I learned willingly with great delight, and for this was pronounced a boy of promise." (1:26)

---

[6] For some discussion of this point see B. Altaner, "Die Benützung von original griechischen Vätertexten durch Augustinus," *Zeitschr. f. Rel.-u.Geistegesch.* (1948), 77.

It is difficult to believe that a boy who had come so much under the influence of a woman such as Monica was not at least a little more sensitive, a little more aloof, a little more ambitious and independent than the ordinary boy. His success in his studies confirms this. As for his enormities, we must not take too seriously the words in this connection of a bishop and rhetorician. In any case we shall immediately look more closely at greater disorders, for Augustine has reached his sixteenth year.

3

ADOLESCENCE

But while in that my sixteenth year I lived with my parents, leaving all school for a while (a season of idleness being interposed through the narrowness of my parents' fortunes), the thorns of unclean desires grew over my head, and there was no hand to root them out. When my father saw me at the baths, now growing to manhood, and endued with a restless youthfulness, he, as already anticipating grandchildren, gladly told it to my mother, rejoicing in that tumult of the senses. [...] But in my mother's breast You had already begun Your temple, and the foundation of Your holy habitation, whereas my father was as yet but a catechumen, and that only recently. (2:6)

Readers of the *Confessions* will readily recall the emphasis which Augustine places upon his moral transgressions at the time of his adolescence and, indeed, up to the year of his conversion. From this emphasis on, if not preoccupation with, moral issues people generally have formed the impression that Augustine was in these matters a great sinner, and that the power of the grace of God is best shown in the sudden transformation of this ardent sensualist into a man of well-nigh perfect chastity. In fact, however, the greater emphasis in the *Confessions* is not placed upon these matters in themselves, but only in so far as they form part of his theory of man and every man. In any case a careful reading of the text may induce us to ask if, judged by the standards of his time and place, he was a great sinner at all.

If one were to take everything he says quite literally, one might get the contrary impression. He speaks, as we have seen, of the year interposed between his schooling in Madauros and his higher training in Carthage in such terms as might, at first, lead one to believe that his conduct was unusually bad. He talks of the madness of lust, of the muddy concupiscence of the flesh, and the bubbling over of adolescence. His language is strong:

> I was deafened by the clanking of the chain of my mortality, the punishment of the pride of my soul. I strayed further from You, and You let me alone, and I was tossed about, and wasted, and dissipated, and I boiled over in my fornications. (2:2)

He tells us of his mother's advice to him: "not to commit fornication; but especially never to defile another's wife" (2:7), which advice, he immediately adds, he would have blushed to obey. We can hardly go far wrong in taking it that he both disobeyed Monica's injunctions about his relations with women, and also allowed himself such other practices, including, possibly, relations with those of his own sex, as were freely condoned by pagans in antiquity. But in none of these things was his conduct unusually bad.

There is, in fact, abundant evidence that, although he gave himself without too many qualms of conscience to the practices we have mentioned, he had to make an effort to keep up with his companions:

> Among my equals I was ashamed of being less shameless, when I heard them boast of their exploits. Yes, and they boasted more, the more they were degraded. I took pleasure, not only in the pleasure of the deed, but in the praise. What is worthy of dispraise but vice? But I made myself worse than I was, that I might not be dispraised. When in anything I had not sinned as the abandoned ones, I would say that I

had done what I had not done, that I might not seem contemptible in proportion as I was innocent; or of less account, the more chaste. (2:7)

Even here, however, we have to be on our guard against his words. He is so anxious to demonstrate his major error in those days, that is to say his utter perversion of will, that while he wishes to paint his sexual misdeeds in as black a color as possible, he may yet feel constrained to exaggerate his relative chastity so that if he is behindhand in physical sin, he more than compensates in sheer perversity.

The situation is somewhat paradoxical, but it may have been so. Nonetheless, Augustine, bad and all as he was in sexual matters, was probably not as bad as some of his companions. Therefore when in 400 he came to pass judgment on the adolescent that he had been, he blamed himself more for his evil motives than for what he had actually done.

This accounts, perhaps, for what may seem to us the quite undue emphasis laid by him at this stage in the *Confessions* upon the episode of the pear tree; for more than half of the second book, some two thousand words, is taken up with it.

The story is simply this. There was a pear tree next door to his father's vineyard. Its fruit was tempting neither in color nor taste. There were more and better pears at home. Nevertheless, late one night, with some lewd companions, he robbed the tree, taking away, as he says, huge loads of the pears — not to eat them, but to fling to the hogs, having only tasted them. They did this because they liked to do what was wrong. It was gratuitous evil springing, he tells us, from a cloyedness of well-doing and a pamperedness of iniquity.

This is the example Augustine gives from this period of his life of what he calls "fornication of soul," which, of course, he must consider as of greater consequence than fornication of body. The perversity lay in his wishing to do what he might not, only because he might not. This adolescent defiance, this perverse wantonness, this fornication of the spirit, is the primary fault, according to Augustine himself, during this time, and its manifestation in sensuality seems to him of less consequence than its expression in an act without apparent motive. He goes on to observe, however, that he never would have done this act of theft by himself:

> Alone, I would never have committed that theft, in which what I stole did not please me, but that I stole; nor alone would I have wanted to do it, nor would I have done it. O friendship too unfriendly! […] When it is said, "Let's go, let's do it," we are ashamed not to be shameless. (2:17)

The truth probably is that because of a greater sensitivity, connected possibly with his greater interest in more intellectual pursuits, Augustine had a greater consciousness of the evil of his life. That evil both seemed, and in a sense was, therefore, greater. In this way, the more intellectual and the more apart he was, the greater sinner he felt himself to be.

It is difficult, all the same, to take too serious a view of his misdemeanors during this sixteenth year. He was adolescent. He was idle. He frequented the baths and the streets at night with bad companions. If he had not already embarked upon a carnal way of living, he was very soon to do so. But in all these things he was not as wicked as his companions — and not to be as wicked as one's companions in a situation such as his, is already some indication of greater worth and nobler aspirations. Vincent the Rogatist[1] says that Augustine was known among the students as a quiet and respectable young man. We believe that that judgment is more likely to convey the correct impression of the kind of youth Augustine was, than such pronouncements — founded by popular writers on too literal an understanding of Augustine's rhetoric — that he was a rebellious scholar, a zealous comedian, a cheat, a liar: in a word, a thorough good-for-nothing.

---

[1] Cf. *Ep.* 93:51.

Patricius and Monica in the meantime were using every en-
deavour to gather together the money necessary to send their promising boy to Carthage. This was the first thought in their minds.
Even Monica was prepared, for the moment at any rate, to put his
moral welfare in the second place:

> Neither did the mother of my flesh, as she advised me to
> chastity, so heed what she had heard of me from her hus-
> band, as to restrain within the bounds of marriage what she
> felt to be pestilent at present, and for the future dangerous.
> She did not heed this, for she feared that a wife should prove
> a clog and hindrance to my hopes. Not those hopes of the
> world to come, which my mother reposed in You; but the
> hopes of learning, which both my parents were too desirous
> I should attain; my father, because he had next to no thought
> of You, and of me but vain conceits; my mother, because
> she considered that the usual courses of learning would not
> only be no hindrance, but even some furtherance towards
> attaining You. For thus I conjecture, recalling as well as I
> may, the disposition of my parents. The reins, meantime,
> were slackened to me, [...] and my iniquity burst out from
> me. (2:8)

Some writers have been less than fair to Patricius and more
than fair to Monica. They represent Augustine as never saying
anything but evil of his father, and tell us even that that father
was the sole author of Augustine's lust. Contrariwise, they commend Augustine's praise for his mother and make her the human
author of what was good in him. They speak of Augustine's dual
heredity, of his nature harboring both the unbridled sensuality of
his father and the gentle mysticism of his mother, and of his having within him a tangle of seething, overflowing passion, yet as
being also possessed of the power to raise himself to the *templa
serena* of metaphysics. They see a radical division of Augustine's
ego, due to his parents, a dualism within him which kept him
stranded for nine years in the dualistic heresy of Manicheism.

This picture is crudely drawn. It is true that Augustine speaks better of Monica than of Patricius. But Augustine does praise his father and does find fault with his mother. He speaks with some little pride of how Patricius, although poor, did more for his son in sending him to Carthage to be educated, than did many wealthier citizens of Thagaste for their children. And he dwells on the greater fault of Monica in not seeking to control his sensuality, for, as his Christian mother, she had greater consciousness of his sin and a greater responsibility to prevent it. Both husband and wife, in fact, were consumed with worldly ambition for their son, and both were determined not to let anything stand in the way of that ambition. It was not the first time that Monica had postponed the taking of a step towards Augustine's spiritual good: for had she not also postponed his baptism?

One feels, however, that the good Bishop's censure of his mother is not without sympathy for, and understanding of her position in those far-off years. If she had behaved no better than her husband, she had along with him sacrificed her own convenience for his advancement. It is not only a mistake to take his censure too seriously; it is also unjust, because it represents Augustine as an ecclesiastic too ready to condemn smugly a well-intentioned imperfection in his mother. The truth is that Augustine is justly proud of his parents at this juncture and grateful to them. "Who did not praise my father, because going beyond the ability of his means, he furnished his son with all necessities for a far journey for his studies' sake?" (2:5) And he conjectures that his mother's motive for not wishing to see him married at that time was that marriage would hinder his intellectual advancement, which in due course would help his spiritual welfare. Her mistake was a mistake in judgment — but she meant well and deserved credit.

It is difficult to believe that the son for whom they scraped together their pennies was a thorough good-for-nothing. A good-for-nothing does not usually inspire such confidence in his ability on the one hand and stability on the other as to lead his parents to make great sacrifices to send him "on a far journey for his studies' sake."

To Carthage I came, where there hissed all around me in my ears a cauldron of unholy loves. I did not love yet, but I wished to love, and out of a deep-seated desire, I reproached myself for not desiring more. I sought what I might love, in love with loving, and I hated both safety, and a path without snares. [...] To love, then, and to be loved, was sweet to me; but even more, when I obtained to enjoy the body of the one I loved. I defiled, therefore, the spring of friendship with the filth of concupiscence, and I beclouded its brightness with the hell of lustfulness. [...] I fell headlong then into love, in which I longed to be ensnared. I was both beloved, and secretly won the chains of enjoyment. (3:1)

When his parents sent Augustine to Carthage alone in his sixteenth or seventeenth year they were certainly exposing him to moral risk. Precautions, doubtless, were taken, but the risk must have remained great. For by all accounts Africa led Italy and every other country in lust, and Carthage led the rest of Africa. Salvian tells us in his rhetorical way that an African, whether he was a Christian or not, who was not impure was as hard to meet as an African who was not an African. He speaks particularly of Carthage: it overflows with vice and boils over with iniquity; it teems with people and teems even more with turpitude; riches are heaped up within her, and so too is vice. Men are there each more criminal than the other, fighting now from greed and now from impurity. Here they are drunk with wine, and there they are bloated from overeating. Sometimes their heads are crowned with flowers, and sometimes they reek of perfumes, but always they are plunged in the rottenness of debauchery. Salvian's picture continues in this exaggerated strain; and if one is not on one's guard against his pious rhetoric, one may believe that there was in Carthage a concentration of all the possible moral filth and vice that ever was. But Salvian is not our only source of information, and the moral laxity of the city was indeed considerable.

In two passages from the *City of God* Augustine tells us of the public manifestations of paganism which met his eyes from time to time:

I myself, when I was a young man, used sometimes to go to
the sacrilegious entertainments and spectacles; I saw the
priests raving in religious excitement and heard the choris-
ters; I took pleasure in the shameful games which were cel-
ebrated in honor of gods and goddesses, of the virgin
Coelestis, and Berecynthia, the mother of all the gods. And
on the holy day consecrated to her purification, there were
sung before her couch productions so obscene and filthy for
the ear — I do not say of the mother of the gods, but of the
mother of any senator or honest man — nay, so impure, that
not even the mother of the foulmouthed players themselves
could have formed one of the audience. For natural reverence for parents is a bond which the most abandoned cannot ignore. And, accordingly, the lewd actions and filthy
words with which these players honored the mother of the
gods, in presence of a vast assemblage and audience of both
sexes, they could not for very shame have rehearsed at home
in presence of their own mothers. And the crowds that were
gathered from all quarters by curiosity, offended modesty
must, I should suppose, have scattered in the confusion of
shame. If these are sacred rites, what is sacrilege? If this is
purification, what is pollution? (2:4, translated by Marcus
Dods, Nicene and Post-Nicene Fathers series)

Where and when those initiated in the mysteries of
Coelestis received any good instructions, we know not. What
we do know is, that before her shrine, in which her image is
set, and amidst a vast crowd gathering from all quarters and
standing closely packed together, we were intensely interested spectators of the games which were going on, and saw,
as we pleased to turn the eye, on this side a grand display of
harlots, on the other the virgin goddess; we saw this virgin
worshipped with prayer and with obscene rites. There we saw
no shame-faced mimes, no actress overburdened with modesty; all that the obscene rites demanded was fully complied
with. We were plainly shown what was pleasing to the virgin deity, and the matron who witnessed the spectacle returned home from the temple a wiser woman. Some, indeed,
of the more prudent women turned their faces from the im-

modest movements of the players, and learned the art of wickedness by a furtive regard. For they were restrained, by the modest demeanor due to men, from looking boldly at the immodest gestures; but much more were they restrained from condemning with chaste heart the sacred rites of her whom they adored. And yet this licentiousness — which, if practiced in one's home could only be done there in secret — was practiced as a public lesson in the temple. (2:26)

These festivities in honor of the Great Mother, with whom the Africans identified Coelestis, Augustine witnessed for himself. He saw too the procession of her emasculated priests with their dank hair, painted cheeks, and feminine gait: and looked with his own irreverent eyes upon the realistic representation of the love of Cybele for the shepherd Attis.

These pagan rites were not the only public representations that could be interpreted in a scabrous way by a restless adolescent and his friends. There were also the public festivities in the great open-air theater, or in the closed-in Odeon. At various times, we gather from other writings of his, Augustine saw represented in the theater the loves of Jupiter, the labors of Hercules, the stories of Agamemnon, Achilles, Priam and Hecuba, Hector and Andromache, and of Aeneas' descent into Hades, and of course a number of comedies, in which the African Terence was acknowledged master. In the theater he saw various acrobatic turns and decent and indecent pantomimes. And there too he was present at great oratorical exhibitions and contests in which he himself was later successfully to take part.

He visited the colossal Amphitheater, too, and the Circus. In one, where martyrs had one time suffered, he saw gladiators contend with one another and with wild animals; and in the other he may have caught something of the ardent passion for chariot-racing which swept the Roman Empire.

Augustine speaks, then, with some justice of "the whirlpool of the lives of the Carthaginians, who get very excited about these spectacles." Nor was this colorful life to be seen only in certain places and at certain times. It met him, in less ceremonial form it is true, in the straight and regularly-placed streets around the Byrsa, the old and natural center of the city; it met him in the immense baths in the Forum, the favorite lounging-place for students, and on the esplanade with its famous series of bizarre mosaics; it met him in the mean little streets beside the harbors, where lived a riff-raff of sailors and petty traders; and it met him in the spacious suburbs to the West where the princes of government, commerce, and the land, had their splendid dwellings.

Merely to describe how pagan, and even dangerous, his general environment was, is not to prove, however, as some authors seem to think, that Augustine ran wild and welcomed every opportunity to sin. The truth is surely that he was more exposed to sin than he was at Thagaste; that he yielded more, perhaps; but that he still remained a catechumen. We know that he even went to church from time to time, not with the best of intentions always and not always to his apparent spiritual gain. But the important thing is that he still regarded himself at seventeen years of age as an aspirant to Christianity.

It was in church, in fact, one day that, as he tells us, he dared to conceive of a desire for a certain sinful action, and dared also while there to arrange for it. Some writers think that these words refer to his first meeting with his faithful mistress and the mother of his son. Of these writers some suggest that the encounter was quite accidental; others think that Augustine went to the church deliberately to plan the deed: that he was not just overcome by a temptation but rather was behaving with cynicism. But whether or not his mistress is in question and whether the meeting was accidental or contrived, one may feel inclined to believe that Augustine's relations with women were, after all, relatively moderate — for having made a *liaison* he kept to it for upwards of fifteen years, supporting mother and child, loving him and, it must be, her during all his early manhood until his conversion. His contemporaries would not have regarded him as acting the libertine in this — far from it. Even his Christian mother seems to have been happy enough for many years with the situation. One does not get the impression that Augustine succumbed completely to his passions at this time.

Indeed, apart altogether from the responsibility in which his mistress and his son involved him, he was more absorbed in two pursuits than a libertine in the late teens would naturally be. One, the lesser, was demonology, and the other was his studies, which began to develop into a search for truth.

Carthage was full of magicians, haruspices, astrologers and demonologists. They had various names and various techniques in their divination — but most of them worked for money, although a few were more serious and dangerous. The magicians would sell you a charm which would ensure the defeat of the rival to the chariot on which you had put your money. Their ceremonies, incantations, and imprecations could be employed in almost every contingency in life. The haruspices, who plied a more respectable trade, read the future in the flight of birds or the entrails of animals. The astrologers, also called *genethliacoi* or mathematicians, catered for a less uneducated clientele: they dealt in horoscopes and presented their findings with an impressive show of mathematical calculation and complexity. Then there were those who paid cult to demons, powers, usually evil, who were intermediate to God and men — who could, through their union with these demons, do uncanny things.

These various purveyors of good fortune and foreknowledge exercised a peculiar attraction over Augustine for many years, even up to his conversion. He speaks of his service of demons and his sacrificing of his evil actions to them. One should not treat this matter too lightly. Augustine was later to consider the cult of demons as one of the chief reasons why Porphyry, among others of the Neo-Platonists, did not accept Christ. That he was fascinated by this mysterious and somewhat eerie cult there can be no doubt; it was yet another of the many terrible dangers through which Providence led him. "And Your faithful mercy hovered over me from afar." (3:5) At this stage, however, he was but approaching the abyss.

His progress in studies was at the same time highly satisfactory, and was due, doubtless, to hard work as well as to natural capacity; for he had no part in the doings of the rowdier students, whose conduct in fact he abhorred. It is noticeable that he was more independent of bad companions and cared less for their esteem than when he was younger. "And now," he says with some pride, "I was chief in the rhetoric school."

There is, however, the crowning evidence of the seriousness of this young man, which must be given in his own words:

> In the ordinary course of study, I fell upon a certain book of Cicero, whose speech almost all admire, but not his heart. This book of his contains an exhortation to philosophy, and is called *Hortensius*. But this book altered my affections, and turned my prayers to Yourself, O Lord; and made me have other purposes and desires. Every vain hope at once became worthless to me; and I longed with an incredibly burning desire for an immortality of wisdom. I began now to arise, that I might return to You. For not to sharpen my tongue (which is what I was purchasing with my mother's allowances, in that my nineteenth year, my father being dead two years before), not to sharpen my tongue did I employ that book; nor did it infuse into me its style, but its matter.
>
> How I burned then, my God, how I burned to rise from earthly things to You, nor did I know what You would do with me. [...] And since at that time the Apostle's writings were not known to me, I was delighted with Cicero's exhortation. Thus I was strongly roused, and kindled, and inflamed to love, and seek, and obtain, and hold, and embrace not this or that sect, but wisdom itself whatever it were. This alone checked me thus enkindled, that the name of Christ was not in it. For this name, according to Your mercy, O Lord, this name of my Savior Your Son, had my tender heart, even with my mother's milk, devoutly drunk in, and deeply treasured. And whatever was without that name, though never so learned, polished, or true, did not entirely take hold of me.
>
> I resolved then to bend my mind to the Holy Scriptures, that I might see what they were. But behold, I saw a thing

not understood by the proud, nor laid open to children, lowly
when entering, in its recesses lofty, and veiled with mysteries. I was not such as could enter into it, or stoop my neck
to follow its steps. For not as I now speak, did I feel when I
turned to those Scriptures. They seemed to me unworthy
to be compared to the stateliness of Cicero: for my swelling
pride shrunk from their lowliness, nor could my sharp wits
pierce their interior. Yet their meaning was such as would
grow within a little one as he matured. But I disdained to
be a little one; and, swollen with pride, took myself to be a
great one. (3:7-9)

There are several remarkable things about this passage. One
is that the *Hortensius*, from anything we know directly of it, was
not the inspiring book which Augustine's words here and elsewhere
would lead us to believe it to have been. We have some fragments
of it, culled chiefly from Augustine's own works, and these fragments do not rise above Cicero at his best — as for example his
Dream of Scipio at the end of his *Republic*, where the heavenly re-
ward of the good Roman is described — and Cicero's best in philosophy is not very inspiring; for Cicero was partly an eclectic and
partly a sceptic, and neither an eclectic nor a sceptic is likely to
set the world on fire. The *Hortensius*, which, as Augustine says, was
an exhortation to philosophy, was at least in part based on
Aristotle's dialogue *On Philosophy*, the fragments of which in turn
are not likely to effect any very profound change in one. Augustine later tried the *Hortensius* on two young pupils of his; but, if we
are to judge by the *Against the Academics*, where the trial is described, it had little result, and no passages from it of any power or
inspiration have been recovered from that work of Augustine's.
Nevertheless, because of the importance attributed to it by Augustine, the *Hortensius* enjoyed an extraordinary fame for many
centuries and to this day arouses our avid curiosity. If it was a great
book, how explain its comparative obscurity until Augustine read
it, and its eventual disappearance? And if it was a great book, what
positive teaching did it contain? Or was it after all just an ordi-

nary book that happened to set off a flame in Augustine's mind when that mind was prepared to be inflamed? Or is it another case of the pear-tree, a thing of no great significance in itself, but used as a symbol of something very much more important and of greater consequence?

It seems likely that the book was at least as inspiring as Cicero could make it; that it did come into Augustine's hands when it could have most effect on him; but especially that he uses it as a symbol.

The story of his reading of the *Hortensius* is the story of what some people choose to call his first conversion. It was a conversion to philosophy in effect, although it might have resulted in Christianity, and it was a conversion which did not last. It came when Augustine's intellectual life was burgeoning, and its actual result was that Augustine gave up what allegiance he paid to Christianity and became a Manichee. Between this time and the time when he met St. Ambrose he was definitely not a Christian — unless one regards the Manichees as Christian — and his final conversion was a conversion from those years between.

The episode is most skilfully placed. It is a minor climax in the *Confessions*. It shows how near Augustine came to baptism in the Christian Church, and when he fell away he was farther away than ever. Providence watched over all this: it was but one of the crises through which Augustine was led to God. "Nor knew I what You would do with me."

The full significance of the text referring to the *Hortensius* episode will emerge only when Augustine's final conversion is discussed.[2] There it will be brought into relation with other texts and especially one from the *Against the Academics* (2:5). For the moment, however, one may remark that in both instances the episode is introduced in a dramatic way: in both cases the books were a revelation. In both the books are described in an indefinite way — "a certain book," and "certain books," although he knew quite

---

[2] See pp. 189 ff.

well their titles. He describes the effect on him in both cases as "incredible" and he compares that effect to fire. The result is likewise the same: all worldly hopes became of no account. That result was in both effected suddenly. He began, without knowing it, to return to God, to the religion he had drunk in with his mother's milk. He opened the Scriptures to see how their message fitted in with what he read in the *Hortensius* and the Platonist books. Here the great difference is found. In the one case he learns in his pride only to despise Scripture and turns away from Christianity. In the other he learns in humility to wonder at it and is converted.

The conclusion is evident. Augustine in describing the effect the *Hortensius* had upon him has imported back into the earlier period his recollection of the later effect of the Platonist books. The tone in the *Against the Academics* is higher and more intense. And when, at a later stage in the *Confessions*, he comes to describe his conversion yet again, and goes through exactly the same details in the same way, the tone is higher still and the whole is more developed and sustained. But here in the episode of the *Hortensius* we have described for us an abortive conversion, at a crucial point, and for a significant purpose.

The prominence given to the reading of the *Hortensius* is meant to stress Augustine's awakening to a real interest in truth. The book did not, in fact, directly work any greater change in him: he still pursued his worldly career with restless energy and determined ambition. But its reading in part provoked, and in part coincided with, the true beginning of philosophy in his mind.

4

MANICHEISM

WHEN AUGUSTINE, under the influence of Cicero's *Hortensius*, examined the Scriptures and found them wanting, one may be allowed to suspect that the *Hortensius* was not alone responsible for this result. He mentions that his mind was occupied with three considerations: the desire for truth, the love of the name of Christ, and dissatisfaction with the Scriptures. It is not without significance that the Manichees professed to offer him satisfaction on just these three points precisely. Augustine in other words had fallen for their propaganda. It was no accident that within a few days of his reading of the *Hortensius* he joined the Manichees: "Therefore I fell among proud, glib men exceedingly carnal and prating, whose mouths were the snares of the Devil, limed with the mixture of the syllables of Your name, and of our Lord Jesus Christ, and of the Holy Spirit, the Paraclete, our Comforter. [...] They cried out 'Truth, Truth,' and spoke much of it to me, yet it was not in them." (3:10)

The Manichean system was partly negative and partly positive. It was much engaged in showing up the defects, for example, of Scripture; but it had also a positive teaching of its own. It is evident, however, that Augustine was at first much more influenced by its polemic against Christianity than by anything else; while in the end he was greatly dissatisfied with its positive teaching. We must, therefore, say something about their system in general. But first a word about Mani and the Manichees themselves.

Our information on both has been enormously increased during the whole of a century, and although some of the material discovered is only recently published or only partly studied, it is possible to be more confident about one's assertions than it would have been some time ago.

Mani was born in the year A.D. 216 in Babylonia, where his name is one commonly found at the time. He was lame, and spent part of his early years in some kind of gnostic settlement and for these reasons, perhaps, grew up to have a horror of the body and a love of a rather morbid asceticism. He would appear to have been of aristocratic lineage, and it is even possible that part of the religious movement which centered about him had in the beginning the political purpose of restoring his family to power. Be that as it may, he was the recipient of two great heavenly visitations in one of which he "discovered" that he was the Paraclete. His relations with the reigning Shahpuhr I, while friendly, were unsatisfactory; but it was not until the reign of Bahrâm that, after having travelled widely in the cause of his religion, he was arraigned by the established clergy and having endured a month's Passion was crucified on 26 February, 277.

The religion which he founded had its origin in many sources but may also have derived partly from the Marcionites and partly from Christianity. In any case, it was gnostic: it was the revelation of a knowledge that brought salvation. Puech[1] discovers in it three main points: it was *universal*, inasmuch as it quite literally covered the known world in the West and the East, and was at the same time a full and complete revelation as opposed to local and partial revelations such as, in the opinion of the Manichees, was Christianity; it was a *missionary* religion, pledged to redeem the whole human race; and it was a *book* religion, inasmuch as, making little use of ritual and none of sacraments, it concentrated on preaching the word contained in its seven holy books — *Shabuhragân, Living Gospel, Treasure of Life, Pragmateia, Book of Mysteries, Book of Giants,* and the *Letters of Mani.* This last point explains why there

---

[1] H.-C. Puech, *Le Manichéisme,* Paris, 1949.

was such little schism within Manicheism — although there was much local variation — and why the feast of the Bema, the principal feast, took precedence of all others: for the chair (Bema) from which the word was taught was the greatest symbol of all.

This gnostic religion spread very rapidly and endured until very recently — indeed some scholars hold that it still survives in the East. It had reached Africa within twenty years of Mani's death and was well established there when Augustine came under its spell. In this connection it is most important to stress the fact that Manicheism in general claimed to complete the revelation of Christ, and while it criticized Christianity, also allowed that Christianity was partially true. African Manicheism in particular, while maintaining a stand against Christianity, had surprisingly close affiliations with the Catholic Church. Indeed, it had friendlier relations with it than had the schismatic Christian Church of the Donatists. Men could change their allegiance from Catholicism to Manicheism — and vice versa — without attracting as much attention as they would if they changed to Donatism. It even happened that Christian ministers were, after many years' performance of their functions, discovered to have been Manichees all the time. The Donatists, in fact, accused Augustine, bishop and all as he was, of never having ceased to be a Manichee. Part of the reason, perhaps, for this close link between Christianity and gnostic Manicheism was the traditional gnosticism of the Christian Church of Africa, the Church of Arnobius and Lactantius. Much of that original Christian gnostic element seems to have been eventually absorbed into Manicheism.

Another point which must be strongly emphasized here is the reverence in which St. Paul was held by the African Manichees. Frend[2] goes so far as to say that African Manicheism was a Paulinist heresy and rightly wonders how far Augustine had studied St. Paul's Epistles during his ten years as a Manichee. It is quite impossible to believe that Augustine had not read St. Paul fairly thoroughly

---

[2] W.H.C. Frend, "The Gnostic-Manichaean Tradition in Roman North Africa," *Journal of Ecclesiastical History*, April, 1953, p. 21.

— with Manichean eyes, of course. Hence, when his conversion to Christianity does take place, he is naturally very curious to read St. Paul with Christian eyes — which partly accounts for the great prominence of St. Paul in Augustine's conversion.

One must also stress the fact that Manicheism attracted men who were of an enquiring turn of mind and more educated and sophisticated than the average: its gnosticism made a strong appeal to them and it was certainly for this reason above others that Augustine embraced Manicheism when he did. It promised to teach a saving doctrine and give a reason for what it taught.

Finally, Manicheism was, from a practical point of view, very much occupied with evil — demoniac evil in particular. The reason for this will be seen presently. But in the meantime it may be remarked that the Manichees regarded life as governed by the conjunction of planets and stars at the time of one's birth and that, since the demons manipulated the planets, one's only recourse was to avail oneself of religion and astrology to outwit them. Astrology, in short, was essential to Manicheism, and demonology — for those who felt it safer to placate than to outwit the spirits of the air (usually evil) — was clearly a temptation. It will be easy, therefore, to understand Augustine's long interest in both astrology and demonology and his subsequent hostility to them — to say nothing of his continued preoccupation with the problem of evil.

It is evident that one cannot hope to understand Augustine's mind or conversion without being well acquainted with the teaching of the Manichees. If, as Frend says, it is true that in becoming a Manichee Augustine had no thought of renouncing Christianity, and if it is true, as was said of him in the fifth century, that Augustine could not free himself from Manicheism no more than an Ethiopian could change his skin or a leopard his spots, then it is important to know something about that African sect which approximated so closely to Christianity in its theory of the Paraclete, the eminent role it accorded to Christ, and its reverence for St. Paul, but which, for all that, was as different from true Christianity as the night is from the day.

Augustine sometimes implies that there were many Manichees

in Carthage, and at other times that there were few. To judge from the number of books he wrote against them when he had gone over to Christianity, they cannot have been an inconsiderable force in that great city with its many religions and many cults. Even though they had been outlawed by the civil authorities on a number of separate occasions before and during Augustine's association with them which began about 373, he nevertheless met many of them as his companions in the baths and in the classrooms. They were prominent in intellectual circles, for their appeal was primarily, not to faith and authority, but to reason and finding out for oneself. They were, moreover, very active in proselytizing, and seized every opportunity, a chance conversation or public debates (in which they frequently took part despite the decrees against them), to disabuse Christians and others of their errors.

The sources which are used here for both the negative and positive teaching of the Manichees are principally the many works written by Augustine at a later stage against them. For the present purpose there could be no better source. Prominent among these are his works against Faustus, Fortunatus, Felix, and Secundinus; but there are very many more in which the Manichees are directly attacked or incidentally referred to. These include *On Genesis Against the Manichees*, *On the Morality of the Manichees*, *On the Usefulness of Believing*, *On the Two Souls*, *Against the "Foundation Letter" of the Manichees* and *On the Nature of the Good Against the Manichees*.

It goes without saying that no matter how scrupulous the controversialist may be, one has to interpret very carefully his account of the doctrine which he attacks. Augustine does some injustice to his former friends and exaggerates the ridiculousness of some of their teachings so that one naturally wonders, if what he says of them is true, that he ever could have become a Manichee. But he was young when he joined them and never proceeded beyond the first stage in their organization. One must, moreover, always allow for the rhetoric of an enemy.

In the following remarks on the *negative* teaching of the
Manichees, mention is made only of their polemic against the Old
and New Testaments, and particularly to that part of it which is
echoed in the *Confessions*.

The Manichean attack on the Old Testament was serious and
detailed.

To begin with, the God of the Old Testament, according to
the Manichees, is an irresponsible, immoral and irascible person.
His favorites are utterly worthless and the Law handed down by
them is ridiculous and unworthy of a God.

The Manichee sees all kinds of flaws in the story of the Creation as given in Genesis: no reason is given why God chose to
create at the moment at which he did create — why did he not
create before then — or wait even longer? How could he have created the heavens and the earth, when it is also said that the earth
was already there, invisible and without shape? God himself must
have dwelt in the darkness which covered the abyss. Where did
the darkness come from? And whence the abyss? When he had
made the light to appear — whence, it is not said — he was overcome with pleasure, as one who had not the remotest idea of what
he was doing. He then made day, but with usual caprice it began
by the evening and not, as one would expect, by the morning. He
waited until the fourth day to create the sun, but how were the
days marked off before then? He made man in his own image:
therefore he must have a nose and mouth, and beard, and entrails!
He made man from the slime of the earth: couldn't he have chosen something more decent for one who was to be like himself?
And why did he create a sinner — and noxious animals? And if
the first sin was committed by a woman, why did he place her by
the side of Adam? To the Manichees it seems evident that the
God of the Old Testament could not foresee the consequences of
his actions.

Moreover, the God of the Old Testament manifests various
unworthy feelings. He shows fear, envy, gluttony and anger. He is
biased: he robs the Egyptians to enrich the Israelites. He chooses
only as his own those whose reproductive organs have undergone

a shameful mutilation. His ideals are low; for his precept to the first man and woman was: increase and multiply.

It is unnecessary for us to detail the various criticisms of the patriarchs and prophets made by the Manichees. Abraham, Lot, Isaac, Jacob, Judah, David, Solomon, Hosea, Moses — all come under the lash for their carnal acts and other alleged misdemeanors as outlined in the Old Testament; and the Law delivered by Moses, in particular, is held up to ridicule, and the only good in it was alleged to be what it had got from the influence of the Gentiles.

Against the common contention that the Old Testament has at least the merit of both prophesying the coming of Christ and preparing for that coming, the Manichees were strongly opposed.

They professed to be willing to believe that this was so: they were only too happy to find a rose in the midst of thorns or gold in the earth — but they denied that any of the texts which were alleged to foretell Christ's coming could bear such an interpretation. In fact, the Law was the very antithesis of the New Testament. They contradicted one another in a thousand places and the Manichees took great delight in making plain the opposition. According to Genesis, they pointed out, the world was made by God; according to the Gospel of St. John, it was made by Christ. Genesis says that God rested on the seventh day. St. John says that the Father never ceases to act. In Genesis, Cain is told that in spite of his labor, the earth will remain sterile; in St. Matthew God promises to nourish us, as he does the birds of the air, without our taking thought of the morrow. According to Genesis Adam was made in the image of God. In the New Testament Christ calls his questioners "a brood of vipers" and "the children of the Devil." These are but a few of the alleged contradictions between Genesis alone and the New Testament. The Manichees went through every book of the Old Testament and conducted their inquiry in exactly the same way.

In brief, the Old Testament is an old garment on to which one should not sew a new patch; an old bottle into which one should not pour new wine. The Old Testament produced only bitterness: the New some sweetness. One should be abandoned, if not contemned; the other should be embraced with reservations.

Manichean criticism of the New Testament was of almost equal violence. It was contended that the Christians had fabricated a relationship between the New and the Old Testaments; that the New Testament was not to be relied upon as a source of information for the life and teaching of Jesus; and that it was in conflict with the truth, as enshrined in the pure faith of the Manichees.

The New Testament, it was alleged, was not written by faithful and immediate witnesses of the events described — in spite of the claim of some of the books to have been written by the Apostles of the Lord. They were, in fact, written by later disciples who had been so enamored of Judaism that they inserted texts which are quoted as establishing the relationship between the Testaments. Where these texts were not mere fabrications, they could be interpreted best by excluding a Jewish reference. For example, the text: "Do not think that I am come to destroy the Law or the Prophets. I am not come to destroy, but to fulfill" (Mt 5:17). The Law and Prophets referred to were not the Jewish Law and Prophets but rather those of the Gentiles. In any case, Christ may not have used these words at all: they may well have been an interpolation. And so for the other texts.

What little confidence one can have in the New Testament as a source of information for the life and doctrine of Christ, is, the Manichees claim, easily demonstrated.

Take the beginning of the Gospels of Matthew and Luke. Both tell us that Christ was conceived of the Holy Spirit and born of the Virgin Mary. Nevertheless not only is there no mention of this in John and Mark, but John begins his Gospel with: "In the beginning was the Word," and expressly reports the Savior as saying that he was not of this world, that he proceeded from the Father, and he came from heaven. Even Matthew reports him as saying that he has no other parents than those who do the will of his Father who is in heaven. And there are many other such texts directly contradicting the story of Christ's being born of man on earth. Moreover, Matthew and Luke give differing accounts of Christ's generation which cannot be reconciled. Matthew's account goes back through the father of St. Joseph through Solomon to David; while Luke's goes back through Heli through Nathan to David. In any case there is no point in giving Christ's generation through St. Joseph who according to Matthew himself had nothing to do with the generation of Christ. Even in Matthew's Gospel itself there is a serious discrepancy: for the first few chapters tell of the generation and birth of a privileged man — it is another Jewish Genesis — while the rest of the book is the story of the real Christ. Matthew is not even able to add correctly, for while he says that there are three groups of fourteen generations between Christ and Abraham, he gives in fact in his account only forty-one, that is, one less.

In passing we may remark that Augustine was deeply impressed by all these difficulties raised by the Manichees on the question of Our Lord's generation as set out in Matthew and Luke. He was even more deeply impressed as we shall see by the two following points which also formed part of the Manichean objection against the Christians.

The whole account of Christ's birth of a woman and death on a cross was, said the Manichees, utterly repugnant.

It was impossible that God should descend to a woman's womb and deliberately expose himself to the indignities attending upon conception and birth. How much more proper to believe with St. Paul, as interpreted by the Manichees, that Christ humbled himself in assuming, but only apparently, the body of a man to show all men the way to heaven? To do this he did not even have to appear to be born.

It was not impossible, however, that Christ should suffer — but only apparently — death. Because while to be born was a bad thing, since one imprisoned in one's matter some divine spirit which otherwise might have escaped from matter, to die was a good thing, inasmuch as the spirit one had imprisoned was freed forever. Hence Christ could laudably appear to die. It was a follower of the Devil, according to one Manichean account, who was clothed in the purple garment, bore the crown of thorns, and was nailed to the cross. According to another account it was Simon of Cyrene, whom Christ transfigured so as to be like him, while he smiled at all that happened. In short, the Manichees had a special and profound abhorrence for the Christian belief in Christ's birth of a virgin and his death on a cross. We are told that the Manichee Agapius would blaspheme a thousand times the cross of Christ.

The reader of the *Confessions* will immediately perceive how deeply the Manichean polemic against the Scriptures affected Augustine. He had to wait until he heard the sermons of St. Ambrose and read the books of the Neo-Platonists before he could read the Bible with due reverence again.

Although Augustine was turned away from the Church of Christ partly at least by the Manichean criticism of the Christian Scriptures, he could hardly have become a Manichee without being in some way impressed by the *positive* teaching of the followers of Mani. Their claim to use reason only, and not faith, flattered him just when he was beginning to feel the confidence of a very young man in his own intellectual powers.

The Manichean teaching may be presented under the headings of dogma, morals and eschatology. In general their doctrine arises from their radical solution to the problem of evil; that is to say, they posit two independent Principles, the Good and the Evil, existing independently and apart from all eternity. They come into conflict and from that conflict results the world and man as we know them. It can be seen immediately that the system is rigorously dualistic.

The dogmatic teaching of the Manichees revealed the Kingdoms of Good and Evil. The one is all light; the other all darkness. In the Good is harmony; in the Evil chaos and confusion. The Father is enthroned, as a sun, in the Kingdom of the Good. He has all possible perfections; he is eternal, glorious, happy, wise. About his throne stand Dominations, Eons, and an innumerable company of angels who honor and hymn his majesty. In his Kingdom there blows a health-giving breeze over fragrant meadows; and mountains, sea and air delight the senses.

Nothing, however, of all this is grossly material, for all here is Spirit and all is One. With the atmosphere and the earth of the region of the Good the Father of Light forms a Trinity which is yet a Unity — for although three, they form the one spiritual substance. This spiritual substance of the Manichees, it must be emphasized, was not spiritual in the full technical sense. Rather was it material, without appearing to be material. Later on we shall see that one of the great obstacles for Augustine in his acceptance of Christianity was his inability to conceive of a pure spiritual substance; for he had become inured in his Manichean period to thinking of a "spiritual" God who was in fact composed of some tenuous matter, to which were attributed purely immaterial properties. Nevertheless, the Manichees were not accustomed to thinking of the Father as a kind of person — but rather as Light Resplendent.

The Father of Light is, unlike the Christian God, finite and limited. He is limited through the existence of the independent Principle of Evil. Where the Kingdom of the one begins, the other necessarily ends.

The region of Evil has five provinces in which live five different kinds of inhabitants: serpents in the province of darkness; fish in the province of muddy waters; birds in the province of boisterous winds; quadrupeds in the province of devouring fire; and bipeds in the province of thick smoke. These groups of inhabitants are, in spite of their diversity, of one nature and although each of the other four has its own leader, they all obey the leader of the bipeds in the land of smoke. He is called the Prince of Darkness and his followers are called "demons."

The Prince of Darkness is a cruel and unjust tyrant who does nothing but evil and ruthlessly rules subjects as evil as himself, whose sole occupation is doing as much evil to one another as possible. This Prince cannot be called "divine" nor "God," no more than black can be said to be white. On the contrary he is called Matter or, more popularly, the Devil or the Demon.

The conflict between the Good and Evil Principles, between the Father of Light and the Prince of Darkness, between God and the Devil, was caused by the latter.

One day the bipeds noticed the light shining from the region of the Good and were so entranced by it as to wish to have it for themselves. Their chief thereupon invited them to follow him on a raid to conquer it. All the inhabitants of the five provinces assembled, the denizens of darkness, muddy waters, boisterous winds, devouring fire and thick smoke, and all marched against the Good. Suddenly the Father of Light was aware of a great commotion on the confines of his Kingdom and was afraid. He employed none of his followers, whose destiny was peace and tranquillity, against the Prince of Darkness, but drew from the luminous earth, which was identical with himself, a "Virtue" or "Soul" or "Word" which he called the "First Man," his Son, to do battle for the Light.

In engendering this Son, the Father was in no way decreased, no more than is one who speaks when the word is spoken. The Son thus spiritually engendered was, as it were, another Eon to do the will of the Father, who himself must live in untroubled peace. This "First Man" must not be confused with Adam, who was produced by the Devil.

The Word of the Father, then, armed himself with the armor of light, water, wind, fire and air and went forth to do battle with the Prince of Darkness. The Word, not being able to vanquish the Prince of Darkness in a straight fight, resorted to a ruse. He made a bait of the elements with which he was armed and tempted the gluttony of the Devil with it. The bait was, of course, of the same substance as God and when the Devil ate it, he at once imprisoned in the realm of Darkness something of the realm of Light, and at the same time his own rage and fury were calmed. From this circumstance arose the intermingling of the two regions, of the Good and the Evil. The pieces of spiritual substance or soul have been submerged in the matter which engulfs them, and they have lost nearly all intelligence and nearly all memory of their previous state. Their presence in matter is, of course, temporary. They are there to reduce the strength of matter. Eventually they will escape to the region of Light.

The Father next sent a second envoy to rescue the First Man and to help the escape of the elements of Light. This second envoy is called the Spirit of Life. He brought order into the chaos which

confronted him and in this way was the world made — a mixture
of the Good with the Evil in which, however, the Good is destined
to be superior. Above the world he placed the sun, composed of
fire and light, and the moon, composed of wind and water. It is here
that the First Man was placed. He looks in pity on the unhappy
souls below him who as yet have not escaped from matter, and from
time to time veils his face, thus causing what we know as an eclipse.
The Spirit of Life also formed five other planets, and about them,
here and there, placed the stars, those Demons possessed of a notable quantity of soul, which, however, only occasionally shines out;
for it is mostly enshrouded in matter. All the other evil powers
which had been conquered were scattered over the world which
we know: their bones are the rocks we see and their bile is our wine.

The Spirit of Life is assisted in all these operations and in the
continuance of his work by a number of Eons who help him. One
suspends the earth over the abyss and weeps for the unhappy lot
of the souls therein who are involved with matter. Another sup-
ports the earth from below upon his shoulders: he is kneeling on
one knee and when he shifts his burden from shoulder to shoulder, we feel the earth quake beneath our feet. A third takes his place
in the depths of the earth, there to stir up the fires and winds and
waters. A fourth ceaselessly patrols the air emitting rays in all directions to help in delivering soul-particles from their vesture of
matter. The Spirit of Life presides over all their activities, which
are aimed ultimately at the deliverance of souls.

The sun and moon particularly help in this, as it is to them
that the souls make their way when they have escaped. When they
free themselves they are mixed with the pure air of the milky way,
and when they are there purified by angels of light they are brought
to the barque which is the moon. She, during the course of fourteen days, attains her fullness through the constant addition of
these souls, and then transfers her precious cargo to its fatherland,
the realm of the Light. The movements of the sun and moon by
day and night in Solstice and Equinox throughout the four sea-
sons of the year are explained simply in terms of their primary func-
tion — to deliver souls.

But the First Man and the Spirit of Life are especially helped by another Eon who is called the Third Messenger. He dwells in the sun and moon and is both masculine and feminine. He has many assistants who likewise can appear to be either masculine or feminine. At the order of the Third Messenger they present themselves before the Demons. The Demons being consumed with concupiscence emit seed, wherein principally the soul-particles are to be found. If that seed has a large proportion of soul particles, it is brought eventually to the barque of the moon. If, however, it contains but little soul, it falls upon the earth. The appearance of these androgynous helpers — Virtues as they are called — before the Demons causes the lightning; and the angry reaction of the Demons, who are cheated, is manifested to us as thunder. The seed falls upon the earth as rain.

The development of all vegetation depends upon the seed of the Demons. If that seed is rich in soul-particles it finds its way to flowers which are highly colored and fruits which have a melting taste. As a result of this, unfortunately, divinity is always exposed to unworthy uses, being eaten by panthers, lions, elephants, gluttons and dogs: in this sense the Manichees agreed that the Son of God is always nailed to the wood or cross of suffering, for the world is indeed a cross whereon Light is afflicted.

Animals arise in two ways. Some very small animals develop spontaneously from matter. The others are Abortions produced by the Demons and their mates before there was any mixing of the Good and the Evil. They are in themselves, therefore, entirely evil; but as they have eaten vegetation they have become possessed of some good.

Man, too, arose from the Demons and certain Abortions which they produced after the world was made. These latter were gathered together by their leader, Ashaqloun, who promised to make for them a sun in the region of Darkness if they would render to him whatever of soul there was in them. They agreed to this and transferred the soul particles, which they had received from eating vegetation, to him by engendering offspring and offering all the offspring to their leader to be eaten. In eating these Ashaqloun took upon himself all their good and all their evil. He in his turn sought to beget offspring by his mate, who, being fruitful, in due course gave birth to the first man, Adam. Adam inherited the concentrated good of all the Abortions.

Man was destined to symbolize and perpetuate on this earth the mixture of Light and Darkness, Good and Evil. He is a microcosm. His body comes from the Demon; his soul from God. More precisely, he has two warring tendencies, two souls, within him. The good soul, coming from God, can of itself do no evil; but driven by the evil soul, which is identified with carnal concupiscence and comes from the Devil, it does what it would not do. Here the Manichees appealed to St. Paul: "Because the wisdom of the flesh is an enemy of God. For it is not subject to the law of God, neither can it be" (Rm 8:7). "But I see another law in my members, fighting against the law of my mind and captivating me in the law of sin that is in my members" (Rm 7:23). This evil soul is the root of all our badness; it is indeed evil incarnate and ever subsisting. It drives us to reproduce ourselves and in so doing prevent the soul from escaping the bonds of the flesh.

Adam himself had less of this evil in him than any of his descendants. In fact, he in a way abounded with good. Unfortunately his parents begot another child, Eve, who abounded as much in evil as Adam in good. She was the very incarnation of concupiscence. Eve was the ruin of Adam, and all her daughters are the ruin of all his sons. Some Manichean writers go so far as to say that Eve had no soul at all. At any rate woman conspires to keep all soul fettered in the flesh.

Our only hope, then, is to be born again, this time spiritually, in Christ — to put off the old man and put on the new. This new birth can come only when the soul remembers her former estate in God and works hard to recover herself. Salvation is worked by knowledge; and Christ, as Matthew says, is our one master. He chooses us freely. He is the way to God, and truth, and the door which leads to the Kingdom. No one can come to the Father save by him. Whoever sees him, sees the Father. Whoever believes in him, lives and will live forever.

Christ is as old as the world and is identified with the First Man, entrusted with the salvation of men. He is called the Son of God and the "Wisdom and Virtue" of the Father. By his virtue he dwells in the sun; by his wisdom he dwells in the moon.

His mission is to liberate the souls of men. In the Garden of Eden it was he, and not the Devil, who presented himself to Adam and Eve as the serpent to "open their eyes" and make them as gods. On the other hand it was the Demon who tried to prevent them from eating of the tree of knowledge of good and evil. Adam learned of his former state and led a holy life; Eve continued in a perverse way until eventually she led Adam to sin — but his sin was a sin of weakness.

Since the time of Adam and Eve men have been divided into two groups: those who serve God; and those who serve the Devil. Of the latter we are born into the flesh. We can always, however, have a rebirth in the spirit. Towards this end perfect chastity of body is the first essential step. The test is to do what Christ commands us to do; it is not merely to believe, but to act.

One can hardly fail to notice how much of this teaching is concerned with the taming of the flesh and the putting on of Christ. It will be seen that at the moment of Augustine's conversion, although he approaches these ideas with a Christian outlook, they dominate his thoughts. Similarly, although the inspiration for his *City of God* may owe something to Tyconius and other sources, it must surely owe something also to the Manichean teaching on the two Kingdoms. One must remember, however, that even Neo-Platonism may to some extent seem to imply the same dualism and to commend the same *gnosis* for salvation and return to the Father. This kind of teaching, in fact, seems to answer a fundamental demand in the minds of many sensitive and intelligent men.

Manichean morality aimed at the control of three activities, that of the mouth or head, that of the hand or body as a whole, and that relating to reproduction.

The "seal of the mouth" forbade blasphemy, perjury, oaths of any kind, and lies. But more emphasis was placed on what was eaten by the mouth. The strict Manichee did not eat flesh nor even fish. For flesh, even when alive, holds little Light, and when dead is nothing but an unclean mass that can but defile him who eats it. Similarly when an eggshell is broken all the good departs and there is nothing left to eat but dead matter. Even milk loses whatever divinity it holds as it is pressed from the teats by the milker. All animal food is therefore forbidden, and wine, being but the bile of Demons and ruinous to the senses, is particularly to be shunned.

The good Manichee, however, could have a large choice of fruits and vegetables: grapes, apples, pears, figs, lettuce, chicory, mushrooms, and various kinds of cereals. He might use olive oil, pepper and spices. All of these possess a notable quantity of the divine substance, and some of them, as for instance the melon, an extraordinarily high proportion of it — hence the melon's beautiful color and taste. Fruit juice is allowable instead of wine.

In eating these things the Manichees not only do no evil, but perform the worthiest of services — for they free the divine substance from its imprisonment in these material objects: in fact they free Christ born of the Virgin earth and everywhere crucified here below. Nevertheless, they must not only not eat these fruits to excess, but must at regular times practise abstinence so as to bring their own flesh into subjection and allow their own spirit to free itself from the bonds of their flesh.

The "seal of the hand" forbids homicide of any kind and war. To kill another, no matter what the reason, is to violate the divine substance in him, and war is the occupation of the devils. One may not kill an animal, harmful or not harmful, for food or sport. Farmers, therefore, are much exposed to committing these crimes which are tantamount to homicide, and the penalty for homicide, according to one account, is to be reborn an elephant.

A good Manichee will not cut down a tree or root out a weed. To pluck a fig even, as Augustine says in his *Confessions,* is to do violence to Christ who is suffering on the tree.

The divine substance is, moreover, everywhere — in the air,

in the rocks, in the waters. The Manichee will disturb that divinity as little as possible. Hence he will never take a bath, for he would tear the divine substance in the water. He will do as little manual work as possible, for in handling objects he is causing pain to Christ. The Manichee should desire to possess nothing; still less should he covet or steal or engage in usury. He should content himself with food for a day and clothes for a year. He should have no interest in honors of any kind, nor should he take part in public affairs. He should live only for God. He could appeal to the words of Christ who praised poverty and the endurance of persecution for justice' sake.

The "seal of the bosom" seeks to prevent the propagation of evil and therefore the reproduction of the species. All sexual relationship is forbidden. Marriage especially was instituted by the Devil. Our parents have done us the greatest disservice in bringing us into the world: hence we should leave them and follow Christ. We should not even, Christ says, return to bury them when they are dead.

One sins less with a concubine than with a wife — for to intend to propagate men is a greater evil than merely to seek one's pleasure. At all costs, therefore, the Manichee should avoid becoming a father. He should take every step to avoid this; but the best step is total abstinence.

Manichean eschatology centers around the destiny and duties of three classes of men — the Manichean Elect, Manichean Hearers ("Auditors" or Aspirants), and the Wicked.

The Elect who can be men, women, or even children, are few in number, practice all the obligations of Manicheism as perfectly as possible, and are destined at death to enter the Kingdom of God. They are enrolled as Elect when they receive the Manichean "baptism," and live henceforth a life of poverty and asceticism.

A member of the Elect observes with the greatest scrupulosity the three seals. He would die sooner than eat even a fish. He could do no violence to anything, and would rather starve than pluck an apple. He lives a life of the most absolute chastity. The pallor of his face is an indication of the sanctity of his life.

When he eats fruit it must be supplied to him by others, and then he thinks only of releasing from the fruit the divine substance within it. He is bound, in fact, to eat every particle of such food as is brought to him and allow none of it to perish. And while he eats, he prays and hymns the Lord.

Some of the Elect do more than sanctify themselves: they attempt the salvation of their neighbors. Some become deacons, others priests. Over these are seventy-two bishops; and over these again twelve masters. Finally, a representative of Mani presides over all.

It is evident from the mere statement of the requirements for the perfect Manichee that most "Manichees" were never full Manichees and were, in fact, merely aspirants. These were called the "Auditors."

The Auditors were unwilling, as yet at any rate, to follow the life perfectly. Hence their name — "For not the hearers of the law are just before God: but the doers of the law shall be justified" (Rm 2:13).

Nevertheless they do observe certain obligations. They profess the faith and pray to the Father, Son and Holy Spirit. They pay special devotion to the sun and moon. They take part in all the religious exercises of their church and obey the ordinary precepts of the Gospel. As for the rest, they do what little they can to imitate the Elect. They do not observe the seal of the mouth; for they eat meat and drink wine. All the same they do fast severely from time to time. They do not observe the seal of the hand; for they practice as farmers, take part in public life, and aspire to honors. Some of them are even butchers. Here, however, they turn their imperfections to good account; for they procure food and other things for the Elect, whose lot without them would indeed be heroic. Nor do they observe the seal of the bosom; for they marry. They try, however, to limit the evil effects that result.

They have one serious inescapable obligation — never to be the direct instrument of giving food to anyone not of their faith.

To do so is to deliver the divine substance in the food into the hands of devils. If a starving man appeals to them they can give him money — but not food. On the other hand they do well to bring food to the Elect who pray for them. When they die the Auditors do not go directly to the Kingdom of Light. They acquire new bodies in the cycle of existence. If they have lived well according to their state, they will merit to become members of the Elect in their new life and so will enjoy release in due course. If they have lived badly, they will become a plant or tree and have the further disadvantage of being able to hear the word of God without being able to do anything about it. An Elect, however, by eating the plant may free them. But if they have been so bad as to deserve to become an animal, then they have little hope of salvation; for no Elect may eat of an animal.

The Wicked are not all equally culpable: some err in ignorance; others by imprudence; others still through malice. The first have only to be shown their mistake and they will reform and be forgiven. The second group are more culpable, but even they are forgiven; for the Manichees follow Christ's injunction to forgive him who repents even seventy times seven. The third group are lost for ever.

All mankind will appear for the Last Judgment when those who belong to the Devil will be told to depart to him. That judgment will take place only when all those who dedicate themselves to God have entered the Kingdom of Light. Then there will be an immense conflagration. Whatever divine substance remains will be collected into the realm of Light and the two Kingdoms of Good and Evil will, as in the beginning, be separate and apart once more.

From the foregoing it is possible to see how, in spite of the enormous difference in the doctrines which they professed, Manichees who were content to remain Auditors could seem to differ little in practice from ordinary Christians. In a sense, it might seem that to become a Manichee was to depart little, if at all, from being a Christian.

5

THE ARDENT MANICHEE
AND HIS FRIENDS

ITHIN A FEW DAYS, as we have seen, of his reading of
Cicero's *Hortensius*, Augustine was enrolled as an
Auditor among the Manichees. The episode is presented in a most dramatic way in the *Confessions*, from which one
might understand that the *Hortensius* did really work a conversion
to philosophy in a day, and that, as a result, he joined the
Manichees who professed to teach truth which could be perceived
by reason, and who still retained in reverence the name of Christ.
But in point of fact, the *Hortensius* is at most a symbol of the dawn
of adult reasoning, and the Manichees had long been destroying
whatever confidence he had in the religion of his mother. Their
constant appeal to reason and reason only would have been enough
in itself to cause the mental climate, so to speak, in which the reading of the *Hortensius* became significant. This in effect is the same
as saying that in all of this Augustine gradually succumbed to the
proselytism of the Manichees. That this is so can be indicated in a
variety of ways.

In his *On the Usefulness of Believing,* for example, he tells us
that the Manichees were accustomed to point out to Christians
that they (the Christians) had a superstitious fear of using their
reason, while they (the Manichees) had no such fear but, on the
contrary, believed only what they already understood. This, says
Augustine, was the sole reason for his becoming a Manichee. So

impressed was he with their alleged objectivity and devotion to truth that at the time he never once questioned the accuracy of their account of various points of Christian doctrine: later he was aghast at his simplicity. If he had reflected for a moment he would have realized that his own acquaintance with Christian teaching was incomplete and immature. But he was bemused by the Manichean talk of Truth.

One might argue, however, that he fell under the spell of the Manichees because the *Hortensius* had already converted him to the pursuit of rational truth. It was not so. In *Sermon* 51 he reveals the whole situation to us. There we are told that the discrepancies between the Evangelists in their accounts of the genealogy and birth of the Savior — a stock Manichean objection, as we have seen — were a great stumbling-block for Augustine at this time. The *Confessions* do not mention this, and unwary readers have been led to believe that it was only the style of the Scriptures, so far inferior, in his mind, to the style of Cicero, which led Augustine to reject them. Readers should have taken warning from Augustine's earlier remarks about the *Hortensius*: that he was interested at this point less in style than in matter and truth. It can hardly have been a coincidence that the principal reason he gave immediately after his reading of the *Hortensius* for rejecting the Scriptures was one of the alleged rational arguments much used by the Manichees. The reasoning the *Hortensius* is supposed to have provoked in him was the reasoning of the Manichees.

In the *Confessions* Augustine sketches briefly some more of the Manichean criticisms of Christianity which bit by bit drew him from his allegiance, such as it was, to the religion of his mother, and adds some of the teachings to which he now gave assent.

> I was, as it were through sharpness of wit, persuaded to assent to foolish deceivers, when they asked me: "From whence is evil?" "Is God bounded by a bodily shape, and has hairs and nails?" "Are they to be esteemed righteous, who had many wives at once, and killed men, and sacrificed living creatures?" (3:12) I scoffed at Your holy servants and prophets. (3:18)

These three criticisms left a deep impression on Augustine's mind. He found no ready answer to the problem of evil, or the nature of God in whose image man was made, or the variation in the dispensation that allowed the Patriarchs to have many wives and do things that no longer met with approval. There would come a day when he would hold the view that evil was nothing but a privation of good, that God was incorporeal, and that God's positive dispensation "in varying times prescribed not every thing at once, but apportioned and enjoined what was fit for each" (3:14). Of the three problems the last was of least significance and cannot long have occupied his mind. But the others were for him two of the greatest intellectual difficulties of his life. They were difficulties brought to his notice by the Manichees.

The Manichees had their own answers, as we have seen, to these problems. Evil was a positive reality. God was corporeal. The stories in the Old Testament about the Patriarchs and their many wives should, along with most of the rest of the Old Testament, be treated with contempt. Augustine accepted these solutions and thereafter became so inured to considering God and creation in such a material way that subsequently it was more difficult than we can easily understand for him to conceive of God as a spiritual substance.

Gradually he accepted other Manichean tenets, their ideas about the sun and moon, and "the five elements, variously disguised, answering to five dens of darkness" (3:11). He began to believe that:

> a fig wept when it was plucked, and the tree, its mother, shed milky tears. But if that fig (plucked by some other's, not his own, guilty hand) was eaten by some Manichean saint, and mingled with his bowels, he would breathe out of it angels. Yes, there would burst forth particles of divinity, at every moan or groan in his prayer. These particles of the most high and true God would have remained bound in that fig, unless they had been set at liberty by the teeth or belly of some "Elect" saint! And I, unhappy, believed that more mercy was

to be shown to the fruits of the earth, than to men, for whom they were created. For if a hungry person, not a Manichean, should ask for that fig, that morsel would seem as it were condemned to capital punishment, which should be given to him. (3:18) Those things I did believe. (3:11)

We must accept Augustine's word for it. He did subscribe to the Manichean beliefs. He agreed with their criticisms and was enthusiastic for their teaching.

They set before me in those dishes, glittering fantasies; it would have been better to love this very sun (which is real to our sight at least), than those fantasies which by our eyes deceive our mind. Yet because I thought them to be You, I fed on them; not eagerly, for You did not in them taste to me as You are; for You were not these emptinesses, nor was I nourished by them, but exhausted rather. (3:10)

The test of his belief in Manicheism is partly the length of time, ten years, he remained a member of the sect, partly the fact that for a time at least he engaged in active proselytism on its behalf so that his very presence became obnoxious even to his mother — but also partly the important consideration that he never advanced from the grade of Auditor to that of Elect. Later he was to say, as in the text just quoted, that he had fed on the Manichean doctrines, but not eagerly; and again, that he was not convinced of Manicheism, but preferred it to other Systems which he attacked with hostility. In yet another place he significantly says that though he was not in the beginning convinced, he hoped that he would yet understand all.

One can conclude without much risk of error that he did embrace Manicheism with enthusiasm and hope at the outset, but that its hold upon him weakened as the years went by. One thing is quite certain: its teachings made his ultimate conversion more difficult and deeply affected his mind and work.

❦

Within a year of his "conversion" to Manicheism Augustine returned to Thagaste, to find that his mother, strong in her Faith, refused him entrance to her house on account of the blasphemies of his errors. The estrangement must have given great pain to both of them, but the one was as stubborn and resolute as the other. Monica sought refuge in tears and the counsel of her friends and spiritual advisers. She was eventually vouchsafed a dream wherein it was revealed to her that her son would yet return to the Faith:

> Your faithful one, wept to You for me, more than mothers weep over the bodily deaths of their children. [...] You heard her, and despised not her tears, when streaming down, they watered the ground under her eyes in every place where she prayed; yes, You heard her. For whence was that dream whereby You comforted her? [...] For she saw herself standing on a certain wooden rule, and a shining youth coming towards her, cheerful and smiling upon her, herself grieving, and overwhelmed with grief. But he asked her the causes of her grief and daily tears, and she answered that she was bewailing my perdition. He bade her rest contented, and told her to look and observe, "That where she was, there was I also." And when she looked, she saw me standing by her on the same rule. (3:19)

Augustine was impressed by the dream when he was told of it, but was even more impressed by his mother's unshakable interpretation of it in her own favor. As a result of the dream Monica agreed to take him into her house, and he consented to live with her and share her table.

Until then, however, he had been welcomed into the family of his patron and true friend, Romanianus. We do not know if Augustine had brought back with him to Thagaste his young son and faithful mistress; but if he did, we can be sure that Romanianus welcomed them too; for he was both generous and wealthy.

In the *Against the Academics*, a work dedicated to Romanianus, Augustine gives us some idea of the kind of life which his patron now shared with him. They lived in a luxurious house in the greatest of ease. They hunted, feasted, played dice, and from time to time engaged themselves in serious conversation. Nevertheless, Romanianus looked after his own estate with great care, protected the interests of many clients, and conferred upon his fellow citizens gifts and benefits — public games and spectacles, for example — such as had never been seen by them before. For these services he was respected by all as a most generous patron. His name was inscribed in bronze by the municipality; honors and extraordinary powers were heaped upon him; and statues were erected to him. Augustine shared in the reflected glory.

With this friend he lived for some time after his return from Carthage, his rhetorical education completed. It was but natural that Augustine should go to him, for he had already shown friendship towards Augustine and had even helped in paying the expenses of his education. From such few vague indications as we have — as for example the ages of their children, and the ease of their relations with one another — one gets the impression that Romanianus cannot have been very much older than Augustine. Augustine freely assumed the right to look after Romanianus' mind and soul; while Romanianus undertook to provide for his friend's material needs. Thus Augustine first persuaded Romanianus to become a Manichee and later a Christian. Romanianus now threw his house open to Augustine and later promised his resources to provide for the needs of Augustine and his friends when they contemplated setting themselves up as a community of philosophers.

On this occasion Romanianus treated Augustine as a brother. "In our town you made me by your patronage, friendship, and the throwing open of your house to me, almost as distinguished and important as yourself" (*Against the Academics* 2:3). Augustine found himself, in fact, in a position which must have been flattering to his self-esteem. A mere youth, he was paid every tribute of respect and affection. His many victories in argument over the Christians, some of whom he won over to Manicheism, endeared him all the more to his friends, who did not fail to pay court to him, and bind him fast in the bonds of their friendship. The accumulation of successes and friends gradually committed him to a more complete and ardent advocacy of Manicheism than he felt within himself. He could not disappoint his friends.

One friendship of this period caused him great joy and in the end great sorrow. He had begun to teach in Thagaste but was living with his mother:

> In those years when I first began to teach rhetoric in my native town, I had made one my friend, very dear to me. We shared pursuits, he was my own age, and, like myself, was in the first opening flower of youth. He had grown up as a child with me, and we had been both school-fellows and play-fellows. But he was not then my friend as afterwards. Nor even then were we true friends, as true friendship is; for it cannot be true, unless You cement them together, cleaving them unto You, by that love which is shed in our hearts by the Holy Spirit, which is given to us. Yet was it very sweet, ripened by the warmth of kindred studies: for, from the true faith (which he as a youth had not soundly and thoroughly imbibed), I had warped him also to those superstitious and pernicious fables, for which my mother wept over me. With me he now erred in mind, nor could my soul be without him. But behold, You were close on the steps of Your fugitives, at once God of vengeance, and Fountain of mercies, turning us to Yourself by wonderful means. You took that man out of this life, when he had hardly completed one whole year of my friendship, sweet to me above all sweetness of my life.
>
> Who can recount all Your praises, which he has felt in his own self? What did You do then, my God, and how unsearchable is the abyss of Your judgments? For a long time, he was very ill with a fever, and he lay senseless in a death-sweat. His recovery being despaired of, he was baptized, without his knowing it. Meanwhile I little regarded this, and presumed that his soul would retain rather what it had received from me, not what was done on his unconscious body. But it proved far otherwise, for he was refreshed and restored.

As soon as I could speak with him (and I could, as soon as he was able, for I never left him, and we hung very much upon each other), I tried to joke with him, as though he would joke with me at that baptism which he had received, when utterly absent in mind and feeling, but had now understood that he had received. But instead he shrunk from me, as from an enemy. With a wonderful and sudden freedom he urged me, if I would continue to be his friend, not to use such language to him. I was astonished and amazed, and decided to suppress all my emotions until he should get better, and his health was strong enough for me to deal with him, as I would. But he was taken away from my frenzy, that with You he might be preserved for my comfort. A few days later, in my absence, he was attacked again by the fever, and so departed.

At this grief my heart was utterly darkened; and whatever I beheld was death. My native country was a torment to me, and my father's house a strange unhappiness; and whatever I had shared with him, lacking him, became a distracting torture. My eyes sought him everywhere, but he was not granted to them. I hated all places, because they did not have him; nor could they now tell me, "he is coming," as when he was alive and absent. I became a great riddle to myself. (4:7-9)

There is no justification for putting only the worst possible construction on this friendship — as some writers have done. The friendship was sincere and ardent, and the death of his friend must have been all the more painful to Augustine because of that friend's sudden aversion from Manicheism into which Augustine himself had led him. Augustine must have felt not only a sense of great loss, but also of betrayal. He may even have felt less confidence in his new religion.

It is perhaps time to consider briefly one of the remarkable features of Augustine's character — his capacity for making friends.

He was always surrounded by friends and their friendship always imposed certain restraints and obligations on him. As a boy he followed in friendship; as a man, he led. When he was a young boy he attempted to be as wicked as his companions so as not to disappoint them. His experience with the Manichean friends of his early manhood involved him more than, of himself, he was willing to be involved: he speaks of that friendship as a bond of little strands wound many times around his neck. In due course he was to lead many of his friends, who relied greatly upon him, to Christianity, and subsequently, as priest and bishop, a countless number to salvation. In his friendships he sometimes received, but always he gave.

How can one explain the attraction he exerted on those who met and knew him? How explain the affection which they felt and continued to feel for him? It is hardly necessary to say that he did not win people's hearts through any obvious *bonhomie*. It would seem that at least when he was a boy he was more reserved and serious-minded than his fellows. Some personal charm he must have had. But greater than this must have been his instant and moving sympathy for others and his desire to make common cause with them. What else there was in this power which drew others to him we can hardly know. But we know enough. We know that he was loved. Not every reserved, clever, ambitious and successful young man is surrounded by a band of loyal and devoted friends.

Augustine was well aware of this gift of his for friendship. Sometimes he refers to it as a kind of weakness. "And what was it that I delighted in, but to love, and to be loved? But I kept not the measure of love" (2:2). And again, referring to the theft of the pears: "Yet alone I would not have done it: such was I then, I remember, alone I never would have done it. I loved then in it also the company of my accomplices, with whom I did it. [...] O friendship too unfriendly! You incomprehensible inveigler of the soul" (2:16). And yet again, of his coming to Carthage:

> I did not love yet, but I wished to love. Out of a deep-seated desire, I reproached myself for not desiring more. I looked

for what I could love, in love with loving, and I hated both safety and a path without snares. For within me, I was starving for that internal food, Yourself, my God; yet, though starving I was not hungry. […] I fell headlong then into the love, in which I longed to be ensnared. My God, my Mercy, with how much bitterness did You out of Your great goodness besprinkle for me that sweetness? For I was both beloved, and secretly won the chains of enjoyment. I was with joy fettered with sorrow-bringing bonds, that I might be scourged with the red-hot iron rods of jealousy, and suspicions, and fears, and angers, and quarrels. (3:1)

It can truly be said that Augustine was passionate, that he was even too passionate. His, however, was no simple passion. One must not suppose that it expended itself fully on lust and anger or other violent emotions and experiences. Of this kind of passion he doubtless had his share. Nevertheless his passion was on the whole less violent, but more sustained; less disturbing but more insistent; less an appetite of the senses, but more a hunger of the heart. "For within me, I was starving." (3:1)

There was hardly any time in Augustine's life when this love of love did not fix itself on God. His own heart, he could well say, was restless always. The passion became more and more spiritual and more concerned directly with the Creator as life went on; but in the earlier days, and especially in the flower of his youth, the passion was less spiritual and often spent itself upon the creature. Hence in these days he had both joy and sorrow.

Apart from Romanianus and the friend whose death moved him so deeply, the names of others of his friends of this time have come down to us.

The first of these is Alypius, a native of Thagaste and a relative of Romanianus. He came of distinguished and perhaps wealthy parents, who at one stage did not altogether approve of his consorting with Augustine. But the young man attended his classes at Thagaste and later, after a period of comparative frivolity, at Carthage. Subsequently he preceded Augustine to Rome and accompanied him to Milan and Cassiciacum. He was influenced by Augustine into becoming a Manichee and eventually a Christian. He was a lawyer by profession, but soon his whole life was devoted to his friendship with Augustine. In the end he became bishop of his native town and in that capacity gave great help to Augustine in his work in Africa. Of him it could truly be said that he was the *fidus Achates* of Augustine.

Another was Nebridius, a serious young man of great intellectual capacity and, in spite of his friendship with Augustine, of much independence. And then there were Honoratus and Fortunatus and many more. Most, if not all, of them followed Augustine into Manicheism and many of them also followed him into Christianity. But some remained Manichees and among them was Fortunatus with whom Augustine held a famous discussion at Hippo.

It is to be remarked that all these friends of Augustine were upright young men, living decent lives and seeking for the truth wherever it was to be found. It is quite unlikely that their characters and manner of life do not reflect also that of Augustine who was the center of their friendship. We must indeed put out of our minds any idea that at this or any other time Augustine and his friends were anything but good-living (by the standards of their time and place) and rather serious. Just as Vincent the Rogatist gave such testimony of Augustine, so Augustine in his turn gives good testimony of his friends. In particular he praises the chastity and integrity of Alypius and the singular goodness of Nebridius, both of whom became his closest friends and for both of whom he had a most touching affection.

Those who have tasted the joys of an intellectual life lived in the close companionship of friends, all bent on the same ultimate goal, all contributing in some way to the delight of discovery, all responsive to a feeling of sympathy and affection, will know something of the satisfaction and pleasure and excitement of the life which Augustine was now living. His lot, moreover, was cast in a pleasant place, in a place of honor and a place of comfort. A

life full of promise lay before him and beckoned to him to advance
and claim what could be his.

This feeling of optimism and strength must have had more
to do with his early departure from Thagaste than any feeling of
sadness over the death of his well-loved friend. In the *Confessions*
he dwells at length upon this latter motive, and on it only. "And
thus from Thagaste, I came to Carthage." But in the *Against the
Academics* only the other motive is mentioned:

> When I returned to Carthage with a view to advance in my
> profession, and when I revealed my hopes and my plan not
> to any of my family but to you [Romanianus], although you
> hesitated a little because of that deep-seated affection of
> yours for your own home town — for I had already begun
> teaching there — nevertheless, when you found you could
> not overcome a young man's ambition for what seemed to
> him to be best for him, you turned with a measure of be-
> nevolence truly wonderful from opposing my plan to sup-
> porting it. You provided for my venture all that was neces-
> sary. Once again you, who had there looked over, as it were,
> the cradle and very nest of my studies, supported me now
> in my first efforts when I ventured to fly alone. (2:3)

Both motives doubtless weighed with him; nor is it likely that
they were the only ones. Life is compounded of joy and sorrow, of
trivialities and things of greater issue. Augustine had had his sorrows and setbacks in Thagaste: he had been from time to time perhaps shaken in his allegiance to Manicheism, as on the occasion
of his mother's dream and his dying friend's repudiation of the
Manichean teachings. But he had also had his success and joy. Even
as a Manichee a notable triumph had come his way. It had encouraged him greatly and confirmed him in his chosen allegiance:

You gave her [Monica] another answer, by a priest of Yours, a certain bishop brought up in Your Church, and well studied in Your books. This woman entreated him to consent to talk with me, refute my errors, unteach me ill things, and teach me good things (for this he was accustomed to do, when he found persons fitted to receive it). He refused, wisely, as I afterwards perceived. For he answered that I was as yet unteachable, being puffed up with the novelty of that heresy, and had already perplexed many unskillful persons with captious questions, as she had told him. "Let him alone for a while," he said, "only pray to God for him. He will of himself by reading find what that error is, and how great is its impiety." At the same time he told her, how he himself, when a little one, had by his seduced mother been consigned over to the Manichees. He had not only read, but frequently copied out almost all their books, and had (without any argument or proof from anyone) seen how much that sect was to be avoided; and had avoided it. When he had said this, she would not be satisfied, but continued to urge him, with entreaties and many tears, that he would see me and talk with me. He, a little displeased with her importunity, said: "Go your way and God bless you, for it is not possible that the son of these tears should perish." (3:21)

Augustine for the moment had triumphed. But it is well to note that a man skilled in such matters should have accurately forecast the course that he was yet to run. There was nothing miraculous in it. It was a question of time.

Meanwhile Augustine was well content with his life as a Manichee and with his friends. They assembled to recite their prayers, which they said facing the sun during the day and the moon at night. They listened together to the reading of the holy books. They knelt before the dignitaries of their sect to receive their benedictions, and to these same dignitaries they carried the food and sustenance which they were not allowed to procure for themselves. They practiced the Manichean chastity, avoiding as far as they could the birth of children and the postponement of the return of divinity to its rightful home.

In Carthage he could hope to lead a fuller life as a Manichee and if ever he were to realize the worldly ambition entertained for him from an early age by his parents, teachers and friends, and which he himself had always cherished, he would have to go there. African rhetors had advanced to the highest positions in the Roman imperial service. First, however, they had established themselves in Africa — in Carthage. Romanianus agreed with him and, apparently, helped him to be appointed, it would seem, to a public office there as a master of Rhetoric.

6

THE SUCCESSFUL RHETOR
AND HIS DOUBTS

WHEN AUGUSTINE began to teach in Carthage in 374, he had already placed his foot firmly on the first rung of the ladder by which men of his day climbed to the pinnacles of power and distinction in the Roman Empire. Glittering were the prizes within the reach of this young African. Worldly ambition had always been present to Augustine's mind; but we tend to think of his progress in religion rather than his successes in his career. Nevertheless from the time of his earliest promise in the children's school in Thagaste right up to the year of his conversion, ambition made ever-increasing demands upon his time and thought.

The careers of many of his recent predecessors and actual contemporaries encouraged his highest hopes. Ausonius is in this period the outstanding example of a successful rhetorician. For about thirty years of his life this son of Bordeaux was grammaticus and rhetor in his native city. Having become tutor of Gratian, he himself gained high offices and helped various members of his family to all the principal magistracies of the West. Ausonius became quaestor, Prefect of the Gauls, Pretorian Prefect and, finally, Consul in 379. His father was made Prefect of Illyria. His uncle, formerly a rhetor in Toulouse, was installed in high office in Constantinople. His son, Hesperinus, became Proconsul of Africa in

376 and later Pretorian Prefect of Italy. His son-in-law, Thalassius, was Proconsul of Africa in 378. So much in the days of Augustine could one rhetor from Bordeaux do for himself and his relations. He was not the only one. Others were promoted through the influence of Symmachus who actually recommended Augustine for the highest secular post he ever held — a chair of rhetoric in Milan, the seat of the Imperial Court. Neoterius, who started life as a simple clerk, became a Prefect and eventually Consul under the patronage of Symmachus. Palladius, who came to Rome about 378, with Symmachus' help became Master of the Offices. Symmachus helped Pacatus, who came to Rome about 389 and recited a panegyric before Theodosius, to be made Proconsul of Africa in 390. Priscianus, Marinianus, Theodorus and his brother Lampadius were all advanced through the help of Symmachus about the same time. Indeed, one gathers from the correspondence of Symmachus himself, that this aristocrat, *littérateur* and important public man regarded it as part of his duty to help on promising young rhetors, were they from Bordeaux, Toulouse, Trèves, or Carthage.

From the very beginning of his career in Carthage, which was to last for about nine years, Augustine took every possible step to distinguish himself above his colleagues. Thus even as a bishop deploring the vanity of his earlier life he seems to take pride in his intellectual efforts of those days:

> And what did it profit me, when I was about twenty years old, that a book of Aristotle, which they call the ten *Categories*, fell into my hands […], and I read and understood it unaided? When I conferred with others, they said that they barely understood it with very able tutors, who not only orally explained it, but drew many things in the sand. After all this, they could tell me no more of it than I had already learned, reading it by myself. […] And what did it profit me, that I could read by myself and understand all the books I could procure of the so-called liberal arts? […] Whatever was written, either on rhetoric, or logic, geometry, music, and arithmetic, I understood by myself without much difficulty

or any instructor. […] I did not feel that these arts were attained with great difficulty, even by the studious and tal-
ented, until I tried to explain them to such people. I found
that my best student was the one who followed me not altogether slowly. […] How did I benefit from my skill in those
sciences and all those difficult volumes, unraveled by me,
without aid from human instruction? (4:28-31)

One could easily get the impression from these words of Augustine that he had read not only very widely, but also very deeply.
He mentions only one book, Aristotle's *Categories*, of course, but
he also says that he read whatever was written on rhetoric, logic,
geometry, music, and arithmetic. We shall not err in supposing that
he meant whatever was written in Latin; nor shall we err in supposing that all that added up to relatively little in the end.

The education of the day aimed at producing a man who was
both eloquent and "learned." The learning, however, was of a very
utilitarian character, for it was made up of what was most useful
for speaking. In actual fact it was little more than a knowledge of
the art of oratory itself with all its technicalities, and of such data
about various subjects as were likely to prove useful to the speaker.
It was mostly a thing of the classroom; as Marrou says, it was for
teachers and their promising pupils. Men rarely got beyond the
stock-in-trade of the schoolroom, and a good sample of the kind
of discussion conducted even by men of great secular position and
presumed learning, can be seen in Macrobius' *Saturnalia*. Men discussed grammar and the rules of rhetoric right up to old age.

The quality of this finished education is well seen in the *lettre
d'art* and in the occasional verse of the day. We have no verses written by Augustine in fulsome compliment to a friend; but many of
his letters, even when he was an old ecclesiastic and at heart little
concerned to indulge in vain and flattering addresses to his friends,
bear all the marks of rhetorical composition: they abound in exaggerated formality and compliment, but they signify little more than
that Augustine conformed to the conventions of his time.

Nevertheless Augustine to some extent also defied these conventions. He did in fact try to resist the insincerity of rhetoric, and also deepened his knowledge. He was doing something unusual when he read Aristotle's *Categories*. What he was doing was so unusual that he could not but be amazed at the audacity and success of his performance. We must not, however, suppose that the extent and profundity of his reading was remarkable — except only by the standard of most of his contemporaries. After his conversion, and especially when he was writing *On the Trinity* and the *City of God,* he did make a study of available material which by any standard was wide and deep. But while still a young rhetor at Carthage, although he read more widely and deeply than his fellows, he did not very greatly surpass them in his knowledge of grammar, or of mythology, history, physical science and philosophy. He probably read the *Encyclopedia* of Celsus, Livy, Lucretius, Eutropius, some translations from the Greek such as Cicero's and Chalcidius' rendering of Plato's *Timaeus,* Apuleius' translation of the *Phaedo,* and Victorinus' translation of Aristotle's *On Interpretation* and *Topics;* but above all, the works of Varro, Seneca, Apuleius, and especially Cicero, who, when all is said, is the main source of his information in the earlier days.

His industry enabled him to score at least two important successes within a few years of his return to Carthage. One was his book *On the Beautiful and Fitting* which will be discussed presently. The other was victory in important rhetorical competitions:

> I remember also, that when I had decided to compete for a theatrical prize, a sorcerer asked me what I would give him to win. But I, detesting and abhorring such foul mysteries, answered: "Though the garland were of imperishable gold, I would not suffer a fly to be killed to gain it for me." For he was to kill some living creature in his sacrifices, and by those honors to invite the devils to favor me. (4:3)

Let it not be thought that Augustine had too little interest in the outcome of the contest. The reason for his refusal was that the killing of a living creature in such conditions ran counter to

Manichean teaching. Moreover, the Manichees had their own sorcerers, the "Mathematicians" or "astrologers."

> These imposters then, whom they style Mathematicians, I consulted without scruple; because they seemed to offer no sacrifices, nor to pray to any spirit for their divinations. (4:4)

Augustine put great faith in these astrologers as indeed did all devout Manichees — for did not the sun and moon and stars have an important part in the teaching, and did not Mani himself encourage them to have recourse to astrology? If he was not successful through the influence of the astrologers in the contest just referred to, he was successful in another similar one as great, if not greater. But if the astrologers helped him to win, they were soon to find him falter in their support.

The occasion was a competition at which the Proconsul himself, Vindicianus, who held office in Africa in 377, presided. Augustine was victorious and was crowned by Vindicianus with a garland in the great theater amidst a vast concourse. As a result of this meeting Augustine became a friend of the Proconsul, who, when he learned that the young rhetor was given to astrology, advised him to abandon such a futile pursuit. Augustine was moved by the sincerity of Vindicianus' advice, which moreover corresponded with the constant entreaties of his friend Nebridius; but he still could not abandon a practice in which he and the Manichees put such trust. This success, however, was of the utmost importance for his worldly career. Through his assiduous (as he tells us) cultivation of the Proconsul he procured the *entrée* to the highest official circles in Africa. Thus it was perhaps that he came to know Flaccianus, who was to become Proconsul of Africa in 393. It is possible that in this way his first contact was made with Symmachus, who was later to procure for him his post in Milan and who also was Proconsul at Carthage.

All this had happened within three years of taking up his work as rhetor at Carthage and when he was only twenty-three years of age. Within another three years he had added the second distinction — that of the publication of his *On the Beautiful and Fitting,* which he mentions in the following terms:

> But what moved me, O Lord my God, to dedicate these books to Hierius, an orator of Rome? I did not know him by sight, but loved him for the fame of his learning which was eminent in him, and for some words of his I had heard, which pleased me. But more did he please me, because he pleased others, who highly extolled him. They were amazed that out of a Syrian, first instructed in Greek eloquence, should afterwards be formed a wonderful Latin orator, and one most learned in things pertaining to philosophy. [...] That orator was of that sort which I loved, as wishing to be myself such. I erred through a swelling pride. [...] I loved him more for the love of his commenders, than for the very things for which he was commended. [...] And it was important to me, that my discourse and labors should be known to that man. If he approved of them, I would have been the more kindled; but if he disapproved, my empty heart, void of Your solidity, would have been wounded. (4:21-23)

The gesture of the dedication to this successful rhetor, personally unknown to Augustine, is clear in intent: where Hierius had arrived, there Augustine very much wanted to be. Within yet another three years, in fact, he did depart for Rome. It was no unpremeditated resolution.

It is unfortunate that we do not know more about this first book of Augustine's. As we have seen, he seems to have been content when he was writing the *Confessions* to remember little of it himself although at the time of its composition he admired it greatly:

> I wrote *On the Beautiful and Fitting,* I think, in two or three books. You know, O Lord, for it is gone from me; for I do not have it. This work has strayed from me, I know not how. [...] And yet the *Beautiful and Fitting,* on which I wrote, I dwelt on with pleasure, and surveyed it, and admired it, though no one joined me in admiring it. (4:20, 23)

His forgetfulness in later years, and his enthusiasm at the time can be accounted for. Apart from the fact that it is not unknown, even in modern times, for a writer to forget completely the very existence of an earlier work of his own, publication in Augustine's day was often very casual, and an author might easily have a doubt as to the exact form in which a work of his became available to the public. His forgetfulness may have been in no way feigned. As has been said, however, he had a fondness for appearing to be rather indefinite in his expressions and this may be a case in point. And as for his early enthusiasm — *On the Beautiful and Fitting* as revealed in his account of it in the *Confessions*, was at once an ambitious rhetorical work and a public expression of his Manichean faith. It is significant that even in 380 he still felt, in spite of some misgivings, fairly optimistic about his chosen belief.

He reveals the genesis and some of the main ideas of the work in the following account which, in spite of its length, may be of interest. His friends may have had some part in stimulating his thoughts:

> To my friends I said: "Do we love anything but the beautiful? What then is the beautiful? And what is beauty? What is it that attracts and wins us to the things we love? For unless there were in them a grace and beauty, they could by no means draw us to them." And I noted and perceived that in bodies themselves, there was a beauty, from their forming a sort of whole; and again, another beauty from apt and mutual correspondence, as of a part of the body with its whole, or a shoe with a foot, and the like. [...] My mind ranged through corporeal forms. The "Beautiful" I defined and distinguished as what is so in itself and the "Fitting" as the beauty which is in correspondence to some other thing: and this I supported by corporeal examples. And I turned to the nature of mind, but the false notion which I had of spiritual things did not let me see the truth. Yet the force of truth of itself flashed into my eyes, and I turned away my panting soul from incorporeal substance to lines, and colors, and bulky magnitudes. And not being able to see these

in the mind, I thought I could not see my mind. In virtue I
loved peace, and in vice I abhorred discord; in the first I observed a unity, but in the other, a sort of division. And in
that unity, I conceived the rational soul, and the nature of
truth and of the chief good to consist. But in this division I
miserably imagined there to be some unknown substance of
irrational life, and the nature of the chief evil, which should
not only be a substance, but real life also, and yet not derived from You, O my God, from Whom are all things. That
first I called a Monad, as a soul without sex; but the latter I
called a Dyad: anger in deeds of violence, and lust in vicious-
ness; not knowing of what I spoke. For I had not known or
learned that neither was evil a substance, nor was our soul
that chief and unchangeable good. (4:20, 24)

The passage quoted is a little reminiscent of Plotinus' famous
essay *On Beauty* (*Ennead* 1:6), which Augustine read at the time
of his conversion: it would seem that when writing these lines towards the year 400, he allowed himself to echo Plotinus' phrases.
It also reveals Augustine's direct or indirect indebtedness to Plato's
Phaedo, and to the Neo-Pythagoreans whose doctrine, according
to Porphyry, on the question of the Monad and Dyad was similar
to that of the Manichees. His indebtedness to the Stoics is even
more evident; for they regarded the soul as a particle of the divine
substance having corporeal attributes but possessing a certain principle of unity, which is responsible for the remarkable harmony to
be found within all things and for the equally remarkable way in
which all things fit in with and are adapted to one another — hence
they spoke of the world as a cosmos, a mighty organism.

It is, however, the Manichean influence upon this treatise
which is most evident, and here most important. They too taught
that the soul was a very subtle body which was part of God. But
they especially asserted that evil is a real substance separate from
God: "For I had not known or learned, that neither was evil a substance, nor our soul that chief and unchangeable good." These two
persuasions were stubbornly held by Augustine up to the time of

his conversion, and while he held them he was a Manichee. Augustine must have enjoyed considerable peace of mind from his coming to Carthage in 374 up to the publication of his book *On the Beautiful and Fitting* in 380. He can have had no serious doubts about his religious beliefs. Indeed in the *Confessions* he time and time again deplores the way in which he had abandoned himself to unholy doctrines. His successes in his profession and the notoriety which they earned for him must have induced in him a feeling of optimism and high hope for his future career. But sweeter than all to him was the company of his friends, old and new, pupils and patrons — and of these many, but not all, were Manichees:

> What restored and refreshed me chiefly was the solace of friends, with whom I loved what instead of You I loved [Manicheism]. And this was a great fable, and protracted lie, by whose adulterous stimulus, my soul, with itching ears, [cf. 2 Tm 4:3] was being defiled. But that fable would not die to me, as often as any of my friends died. There were other things we did which more took up my mind: to talk and joke together; to do each other favors; to read together gracefully-written books; to fool around or be earnest together; to disagree at times without discontent, as a man might debate with his own self; and even with the seldomness of these disagreements, to season our more frequent agreements; sometimes to teach, and sometimes to learn; to long for the absent with impatience, and welcome the coming with joy. These and similar expressions, proceeding out of the hearts of those who loved and were loved in return, by the face, the tongue, the eyes, and a thousand pleasing gestures, were so much fuel to melt our souls together, and out of many make but one. (4:13)

His peace of mind was soon to receive a succession of rude jolts, partly to his intelligence, partly to his moral feeling, and partly to his personal position.

His reading in philosophy, especially in physical science,

gradually made him realize that the Manichean doctrine on these matters was not as probable as at first it had seemed, and eventually he found himself convinced one day that it was not even as probable as that of the lay philosophers, as reported, for example, in the De astronomia of Apuleius, or the Disciplinarum libri of Varro, or Cicero's translation of Aratus' Phaenomena, or the other precise accounts of the physical theories held by the various schools. One could collect from Augustine's later books against the Manichees a whole list of the objections which began to occupy his mind at this stage with regard to the questions not only of physics but also of morals and his own personal position. It will suffice here to indicate some of those which had most effect upon him and are stressed in the account he gives in the Confessions.

He was immensely impressed by the accurate calculations of these lay scientists, who could foretell precisely, for example, when an eclipse would take place:

> Much they have found out; they foretold, many years before, eclipses of those luminaries, the sun and moon — what day and hour, and to what extent — nor did their calculation fail; and it came to pass as they had foretold. [...] Many truths concerning created things I retained from these men, and saw the reason thereof from calculations, the succession of times, and the visible testimonies of the stars. I compared them with the words of Mani, who in his frenzy had written at length on these subjects, but I did not discover any rational account of the solstices, or equinoxes, or the eclipses of the greater lights, nor anything of this sort which I had learned in the books of secular philosophy. But I was commanded to believe; and yet it did not correspond with what had been established by calculations and my own sight, but was quite contrary. (5:4, 6)

Augustine asked himself why Mani had bothered to dogmatize on physics, about which he knew nothing? And if Mani deliberately taught falsehood in one particular, might not his whole teaching be false?

Who asked Mani to write on these things also, a skill in which was no element of piety? [...] But since he impudently dared to teach things he was ignorant of, he plainly could have no knowledge of piety. (5:8)

Augustine becomes very wroth in the *Confessions* at Mani's presumption in this and other matters. It is safe to say, however, that at the actual time, when his belief in the physics of the Manichees was first shaken, he was probably more sad than angry; more willing to learn than to denounce. After all, the Manichees had attracted him by their profession of appealing to his reason only. Were they to be found wanting in the one thing that mattered? The situation was not clear. His Manichean advisers confessed to him that they could not deal with his intellectual difficulties, but they immediately went on to assure him that there was one who could — Faustus of Milevis. Augustine would meet him. Until then he must obviously believe what later he would understand.

Another intellectual doubt had also arisen, partly through his interest in astrology which Manicheism had encouraged. Astrology naturally led to astronomy and the more he knew of the latter, the less confidence he had in the former. Outside influences, such as the advice of Nebridius, Vindicianus and Flaccianus, had been working on him, but he gave up all belief in astrology when he became convinced that horoscopes were of no value whatever: that any apparent accuracy was purely a matter of chance. This conviction was borne in upon him as a result of a conversation which he held, either in Carthage at this time or in Milan before his conversion, with a certain Firminus.

Astrology, therefore, greatly weakened its hold upon his mind or was abandoned altogether, and with it departed also more of his faith in Manicheism. For many years yet Augustine might still feel at the back of his mind that part of the apparent success of astrology and demonology — for he had at least some slight acquaintance with those who sought favors in the cult of demons — could be explained through the operation of evil spirits who, being spirits, knew the future. In the main, however, he gave up these pursuits and interests, although, as in the past, so now, his anxiety about his career must have tempted him greatly to indulge in these practices. In the meantime he clung to his Manichean belief, pinning all his faith on the coming of Faustus.

Faustus did come, about the year 383. Augustine says that he had longed to see him "for almost all of those nine years, wherein with unsettled mind" he had been a Manichee. Now, however, the need was critical and the interview almost decisive:

> When he came, I found him a man of pleasing discourse, and who could speak fluently and in better terms, yet still could say only the selfsame things which they were accustomed to say. But what good was the neatness of the cup-bearer to my thirst for a more precious draught? […] I found him first utterly ignorant of liberal sciences, except grammar, and that but in an ordinary way. […] I began to despair of his opening and solving the difficulties which perplexed me. […] For he knew that he did not know these things, and was not ashamed to confess it. […] But all my efforts by which I had intended to advance in that sect, came utterly to an end, once I came to know that man. I did not detach myself from them altogether; but as one finding nothing better, I had decided to be content meanwhile with what I had in whatever way fallen upon, unless by chance something better should dawn upon me. (5:10-13)

Even though Augustine still called himself a Manichee, and still thought of God as corporeal and of the same nature as his own soul, and of evil as a principle independent of God, nevertheless his faith was shaken. Manicheism no longer had his complete loyalty and soon he was to take notice of moral delinquencies among its adherents which, once his faith was weakened, took on a serious character. These charges of heinous conduct and immorality which Augustine preferred against the Manichees in many of his works, and notably in *On the Morality of the Manichees*, find but slight mention in the *Confessions*, and it is just as well. They are exaggerated and in part provoked by the Manichees' report concerning himself; that he failed to live up to the chastity of the Manichean life and had therefore abandoned it. Nevertheless, he did witness at Carthage how some of the Elect behaved in a way little in accord with their professed abhorrence of women. He noticed that they went unpunished; and when he asked for an explanation he was told that if they were punished they might desert and report the whole sect — which was proscribed — to the state officials. Rumours moreover were rife not only of various scandals in the sect in Carthage, but also of disagreements and disedifications at Rome. Such scandals are always unsettling; when one's faith is faltering, they can have an effect out of all due proportion.

Within the company of his friends Augustine not only did not find support; he found instead an argument against Manicheism which he could in no way rebut. It was Nebridius who advanced it. What could the principle of Darkness do, he asked, against the principle of Light? It could either injure it or not injure it. If it could injure it, then the principle of Light was no real God. If it could not injure it, then the principle of Light did wrong in entering into conflict with it and so imprisoning in darkness part of itself. The argument seemed to Augustine to be irrefutable. Likewise he was troubled by the inadequacy of the answer given by Faustus, it would appear, to an objection against the existence of the Manichean principle of Evil. Faustus "proved" its existence by asking: What would a man do if one put a scorpion in his hand? Would he not draw back from the evil — the existing substantial evil? Augustine was shocked at the puerile "proof" and disconcerted to discover that Faustus did not give that reply to the objector but only to the Manichees in private. From this Augustine concluded that the Manichean leaders had no confidence in their own arguments and that their followers were truly children.

Moreover, Christianity was beginning to attract his more serious attention. Not only was his mother vigilant to exercise every pressure, direct or indirect, upon him in its favor, but he was particularly impressed by the showing of a Christian, Helpidius, in a controversy with his own co-religionists.

One can say that the first steps towards his final conversion were taken here.

Perhaps the most uncomfortable feeling of all for the Manichean Augustine was one of isolation. He and his friends were a mere handful in the midst of a vast population which did not share their belief. While he felt strong in his faith, he felt happy in belonging to a privileged minority. When he began to doubt the privilege, the feeling of being in the wrong must have been difficult to dismiss. It was easy to bear reproach when one believed. When one no longer felt secure, it became almost impossible to suffer the endless charges of monstrous practices which were constantly levelled against the Manichees. Even the State had outlawed them. Diocletian in 296 had decreed that their leaders be burned along with their books; that the followers be decapitated or condemned to the mines; and that their property be confiscated for the Treasury. In 372, Valentinian had prohibited them from meeting under pain of a fine or banishment and confiscation. In May, 381, Theodosius had taken away civil rights from them, and in March, 382 had ordered the ultimate punishment for those of them that attempted to live in community. It was owing to this last decree, doubtless, that Faustus fled to Africa and that Augustine was enabled to have his famous meeting with him. The Manichees later on charged Augustine with deserting them through fear of persecution. It is hardly likely that Augustine was so fainthearted. Nevertheless, when the hand of every man was against him as a Manichee, and when he had in any case lost confidence in his religion, he must have felt very insecure and unhappy. This feeling of isolation must have entered deeply into his spirit, for in his early books, both in favor of Christianity and against Manicheism, he greatly stresses how men were flocking to the one, and how the other was left with little following.

All the same in 383 he was still a Manichee. In that year he made up his mind to go at last to Rome, where, it had been arranged, he was received in Manichean circles. There can be no doubt but that an important motive for doing so was to improve his position, which in effect he did. The reason given by Augustine for his departure from Carthage, namely that the pupils there were very unruly, doubtless also influenced his action. The charge that he was fleeing from persecution of the Manichees in Africa cannot be substantiated, nor is it likely; for he could have met with persecution in Rome too. It is probably true to say that he was happy to escape from the scene at once of his early vigorous apostolate for Manicheism and his later sorry disillusionment: he would be able to live a more independent life even among Manichees in Rome.

It would seem that Augustine left rather suddenly. He had not acquainted his friend and patron Romanianus of his projected departure, and in fact had in closing down his school in Carthage to some extent abandoned the education of Romanianus' children which had been entrusted to him. In this he hardly behaved with propriety. He did worse. He deceived his mother. What caused him to behave so meanly to those two, to whom he was so closely bound and obliged? What sudden impulse or sudden circumstance drove him to do this thing to them? Impulse it must have been, for no circumstance that we can reasonably conjecture could explain his sudden and irresponsible deceit. It looks as if he wanted to escape from everybody and everything he knew; to be free from all ties and in a new country. One has the impression that he felt himself as it were suffocating and had suddenly to fight for air. His action was done in the end without deliberation. The great struggle to be master of his own mind had commenced, and now a period begins when storms of soul follow hard on one another.

There may seem to be a reminiscence of Dido and Aeneas, if not of Ariadne and Theseus, in the following passage; but it is best to take it as the description of something that actually took place:

> But why I went from Carthage, and went to Rome, You knew, O God, yet showed it neither to me, nor to my mother, who grievously bewailed my journey, and followed me as far as the sea. But I deceived her, as she was holding

me by force, that either she might keep me back, or go with me; I feigned that I had a friend whom I could not leave, till he had a fair wind to sail. And I lied to my mother, and such a mother, and escaped. […] Refusing to return without me, I scarcely persuaded her to stay that night in a place very near our ship, where there was a chapel in memory of the blessed Cyprian. That night I secretly departed. […] The wind blew and swelled our sails, and withdrew the shore from our sight; and she on the morrow was there, frantic with sorrow. […] And yet, after accusing my treachery and hardheartedness, she betook herself again to intercede to You for me, went to her accustomed place, and I to Rome. (5:15)

7

MOOD OF SCEPTICISM

A S Augustine came in from Ostia across the flat brown countryside towards Rome in the autumn of 383 he must have been full of expectation to catch a glimpse of the seven hills, the towering temples, and above all, perhaps, the Capitol and the Forum. Here had been the center of the civilization which he was educated to admire; here had been the very heart of the mighty Empire which he was so willing to serve. As he approached the city he felt the thrill we all feel when first we see with our eyes and tread with our feet sites long known to us from our reading and study. It was comparatively easy for him to see in his mind's eye Cicero making his way down to the Senate-house, or Caesar as Pontifex Maximus engaged in some religious rite. But he would think especially of Cicero, that great orator whose books were the instruments of his daily toil.

Soon, however, the busy life of the present Rome would have intruded upon his attention. Even in modern times when such large areas of ancient cities are set apart as oases of the past, the visitor will soon be absorbed in the whirling life of the people around him. How much more must this have been so in the case of Augustine when the past was not so completely marked off from the present, either in space or time; when men still sat in their shops on the slopes of the Palatine or transacted their business not far from the *lapis niger*?

Augustine would scarcely have had time to commune with

the past and, sensitive though he must have been to such things, mark the difference of atmosphere between this city and his own Carthage, the difference in the food and clothes and attitude towards life, before he found himself listening to the advice and answering the questions of the Manichean friends who had received him in Rome. They would have asked him about Faustus and discussed with him the life that lay before him.

Almost immediately upon his coming to Rome he fell violently sick and believed himself to be in imminent danger of death. He did not ask for baptism. It would certainly have caused him some embarrassment to do so, for he was lodged in the house of a Manichean Auditor and was in communication with some of the Elect, and even with a Manichean bishop. But he cannot seriously have had any desire for Christian baptism: for the moment he allowed himself to be regarded as a Manichee.

By the members of the sect he was accepted without question. They gave him all the help they could in his profession. When he recovered from his illness, therefore, with help from the Manichees he opened a school of rhetoric in the city where Cicero had once delivered his orations.

Unhappily his experience with Roman students was not more fortunate than with the Carthaginians. In Carthage they were unruly. In Rome they would not pay their fees — they removed to another master. Augustine or his friends would, doubtless, have discovered a way of dealing with this situation; but as he stayed at Rome no more than a year in all, he and they had no opportunity to do so.

In the meantime, his allegiance to Manicheism had weakened even more. In fact, to use his own words, he had now not only despaired of making progress in it, but was both lax and careless, even for one who held it *faute de mieux*. His observation of the conduct of his co-religionists had sharpened greatly, and in Rome he found reason for being shocked. One story in particular caused him much pain. The rumor was that one of the novices to the grade of the Elect, whose duty it was to consume the offerings which the Elect could not manage to eat, so distended his stomach in the performance of his office that he burst asunder and died. Augustine could hardly believe so revolting a story; but he knew that it was a sacrilege for such excess food to be dealt with by any other method. We may take it, then, that Augustine's Manichean period begins to draw rapidly towards a close sometime in the year 384, that is to say when he was nearly thirty years of age, and had been a member of the sect for some ten years.

There are men, who, having spent all their early manhood in the bosom of a religious society such as the Manichees and then departed from among their fellows, never recover from their experience of that first buoyant happiness and the later sad despair. Their lives afterwards are often inert and without much interest; for they nurse the wound they fancy they have received. Augustine was not of the number of these. We have seen that he gradually became a Manichee, for apparently good reasons, and even more gradually ceased to be one for apparently even better reasons. There were critical times in the beginning and especially at the end, but fundamentally there was nothing sudden or inexplicable about his accepting Manicheism or rejecting it.

The truth of the matter is that Augustine was psychologically robust, being both courageous and honest. The experience of Manicheism deepened his understanding of religion, philosophy, and his own character. Many men as robust psychologically as he was have also a certain outward softness, a manifest sensitivity, an overflowing sympathy, affection and enthusiasm which invite one to suppose that they have not the strength to encounter a great trial. In fact they are as finely-tempered steel and can bear many a shock which would shatter one more gross than they. Men have always supposed some contradiction between the writer of the melting words of the *Confessions* and the relentless opponent of the Donatists; they have been attracted by the one and repelled by the other. Have they not done more than what passes for justice to the one, and less than justice to the other? Augustine never changed: he was always fine and sensitive, strong and firm.

When eventually he rejected Manicheism, he threw it off, as though it were a cloak which he had outgrown. There was nothing sudden about this, nothing dramatic. Given his courage, energy of spirit, intelligence and honesty, the process was but a natural one — as the bishop whom his mother had consulted had known.

It would be a mistake to suppose that Manicheism left no mark on him. The metaphor of the cloak must not be pushed as far as that. Men carry around with them the marks of their previous experience. Who cannot recall some person who betrays in his appearance, carriage, or conversation something of his past? And these are only the outward manifestations of an impression that reaches to the deepest parts of the soul. It was sometimes said of Augustine that he never ceased to be a Manichee; and in a sense this is true. The problems he chose to deal with, but above all his method of dealing with them, reveal this.

Augustine had embraced Manicheism with a high optimism and a large generosity. He had given it every opportunity to win him for itself. In his disillusion what more natural than to expect him on the one hand to think once again of the religion in which he was brought up, and on the other to harbor notions of utter scepticism about all religion and all philosophy?

We have the testimony of his *Confessions* that at this time both ideas occurred to him. He could hardly have been in Rome for very long without coming up against the evidences of that Christianity in which he had been nurtured. Everywhere he went he was reminded of the martyrs of the past and the authority of the present. We may recall that Helpidius had already set him thinking on the possibility of defending the Christian Scriptures after all. We may be sure that Monica had been quick to sense the growing change within him and had redoubled her prayers and entreaties until it may be he felt impelled to fly from her and Africa. Now in Rome he confesses that at times he had a wish to consult with some Christian skilled in the Scriptures:

Yet at times truly I wished to discuss these points with someone very well skilled in those books and to learn what he
thought about them: for the words of one Helpidius, as he
spoke and disputed face to face against the said Manichees,
had begun to stir me even at Carthage. (5:21)

Even at this stage he felt the need of expert guidance such as
Ambrose later in his sermons was to give him. His interest in
Ambrose, therefore, cannot have been solely in his eloquence: it
was not by accident that his words impressed Augustine; Augustine was seeking to be impressed. Nevertheless his notions of Christian teachings, mostly derived from the Manichees at this time,
were such that his wish to consult a Christian expert, however
significant for us, remained for the present a mere velleity.

Perhaps his very coming to Rome, added to all his disappointments with Manicheism, provoked in him the mood of scepticism.
Rome would have represented for him more Cicero than either
Christ or Mani. When he thought of Cicero and the problem of
truth, he may have begun by thinking of the *Hortensius* and the
exhortation to discover truth, but knowing Cicero as he must have
known him, he had to end by thinking of the *Academica* and the
declaration that truth cannot be found:

There began to arise a thought in me that those philosophers whom they call Academics, were wiser than the rest,
because they held that men ought to doubt everything, and
held that no truth can be perceived by man. (5:19)

If his preoccupation with the Academics immediately after
his conversion in the autumn of 386 is of any particular significance, it must mean that he pondered over their arguments during his first sojourn in Rome some two years earlier. When at the
ending of his life in his *Retractations* he came to describe briefly
the purpose of his first extant book, *Against the Academics*, he wrote
as follows:

Before I was baptized, I wrote first the *Against the Academics*

> or *On the Academics*. My purpose was to rid my mind of the
> arguments of the Academics with the most cogent reason-
> ing I could muster. For they cause many to despair of finding
> truth. These arguments were troubling me also. (1:1)

Augustine was quite disturbed by the arguments of the Academics, when he came to consider them. Nevertheless he was never
a convinced Academic: his own temperament did not take easily
to scepticism; and it was the nature of this scepticism to be sceptical of itself as well as everything else.

A word must here be said about the New Academy. It received its name because of its relations with the "Old" Academy,
that is to say, the Academy founded by Plato. From this Academy
it had sprung, but, as the name implies, it had also marked itself
off from the original body. The Old Academy was the Academy
of Plato, his pupils, and their successors from the time of its foundation in Athens about 385 B.C. until the time of Arcesilas (315-
241 B.C.). In general, its doctrine was positive. Although it placed
no confidence whatever in the perceptions of the senses, it did put
absolute trust in intellectual cognition. Arcesilas, in denying the
possibility of any knowledge, gave the Academy, over which he
presided at the time, a sceptical turn, and, accordingly, was considered to have founded a "New," "Second," or "Middle" Academy. Carneades (214-129 B.C.) in systematizing the negative criticism of the Middle Academy and developing a technique whereby
he was enabled to argue convincingly for both sides of any problem, was considered to have advanced the Academy even more
upon the road of scepticism, and was, therefore, regarded as the
founder of the "Third" or "New" Academy. Cicero at times professed that he was a follower of the New Academy, and his
Academica was written as an outline and defense of its position.
The influence of the New Academy persisted spasmodically until
the fifth century A.D. One should add that there were occasional
attempts made within the New Academy to return to the teaching of the Old. The most notable of these was that of Antiochus
(130-68 B.C.).

One can be quite satisfied that Augustine's acquaintance with the tenets of the New Academy is adequately represented in Cicero's *Academica*, for his own *Against the Academics* deals almost solely with the arguments to be found there. These arguments are neither exciting nor original, and it will be sufficient for the present purpose to outline the conclusions arrived at by the New Academy as represented in the *Academica*. Augustine sets them down in the following list of propositions: (1) Man can be wise. (2) That percept only can be comprehended which manifests itself by signs that cannot belong to what is not true. (3) The Academic teaching is limited to matters within the range of philosophical enquiry. (4) Since no such signs as are required by (2) are found, nothing can be perceived. (5) As a result of (4), the wise man will never assent to anything. (6) But since (5) logically leads to complete inaction, one must act according to what seems probable.

When Augustine came to refute these conclusions in 386 he found himself in a very advantageous position. He had been convinced by the Platonists that sense-knowledge is not knowledge at all, and that the only knowledge that counted, intellectual knowledge, was independent of the senses at least in its higher and further operations. Consequently the whole case of the Academics against knowledge, being entirely directed against knowledge derived from the senses, became irrelevant. He had learned from Christianity that Christ was Truth. To accept Christ was to possess all Truth. In this way also the arguments of the Academics were circumvented. But he does, for all that, attempt to combat them on their own ground and, when he quotes their arguments and conclusions, although we cannot be sure that he is revealing to us those which had had most effect upon himself, he is at least letting us know the points where he thought the New Academy might seem, but in fact failed, to convince.

These points are therefore of great interest; for they help to show the individual quality of his mind. It will not surprise us to discover that his principal weapon of both defense and attack is dialectical. He conducts his argument almost entirely in the sphere of logic only.

Thus for example with regard to the first of the propositions quoted above: man can be wise. Augustine agrees with this proposition, but asks: How else can man be wise except by the possession of wisdom? To say that man can be wise is implicitly to admit the possibility of his possessing the knowledge which is wisdom. He pretends that by this mere quip he had brought down the Academic house of cards. For good measure, however, he will proceed with the argument. The second and third propositions he is willing to accept. Of the last three, the first is the fundamental one; for if it were disproved that, "nothing can be perceived," then the motive for withholding assent and following only the probable would disappear. The crucial point, therefore, is to prove that something could be perceived, in the full technical sense of perception as set out in the second proposition: something that could not be not-true.

Cicero had maintained that "nothing could be perceived" in any of the three great branches of philosophy as it was then conceived: Physics, Ethics, and Logic. Augustine is certain that he not only could know truth in one of them, but could make true propositions in all three. For example, in Physics he can state without fear of error that "The number of worlds is one or not one." "That number (whatever it be) is finite or infinite." "The world either always was and will always be, or was not always but will always be, or always was but will not always be, or was not always and will not always be." These disjunctive propositions comply with the requirements of the postulate: they simply cannot be false. They are therefore true. If Augustine is asked to elect for one member of the disjunction, he refuses: he cannot do that with certainty. In so far as the disjunction is perfect and exhausts possibility, the disjunctive proposition is true. Augustine is willing to admit that judgment is suspended as to the truth of each member of the proposition. But the vital thing is that he has been able to assert a proposition, indeed, a whole series of propositions, which are true. If it be argued that perhaps there is no world, and that his propositions become invalid, his argument is still untouched. He is not concerned now with the ontological verification of the "impression" he calls "world." It is about the "impression" he can affirm: "one or not one." He is equally certain that six such "worlds" added to one such "world" amounted to seven such "worlds." The state of the percipient, moreover, had nothing to do with the verity of such propositions. Augustine could make similar true propositions about Ethics and Logic.

Cicero had anticipated this line of argument. The truth attainable by logic — which is all Augustine cares to defend — Cicero had said was useless and unreliable: (1) it was confined to itself as an object; (2) it was made insecure by fallacies — by the "sorites"[1] for instance; (3) disjunctive propositions in particular give no truth; (4) the necessity of a particular consequent following upon a particular antecedent was denied by the "mentiens" — ("if you say that you are lying and speak the truth, you are lying; but you do say that you are lying and speak the truth; therefore you are lying").

Augustine takes notice — but hardly sufficient — of these criticisms of Cicero. (1) Logic might not tell one anything about Physics or Ethics, but it did give some truth. That was sufficient to refute the principle that "nothing could be perceived." (2) Objections from fallacies (and the "sorites") could be disposed of or should be ignored as being beyond the knowledge possible to us. (3) The disjunctive proposition is not useless. Cicero had taken the example: "Hemarchus will either be alive tomorrow or not alive," and, following Epicurus, had made the criticism: "If I admit either of the two to be necessary, it will follow that Hemarchus must either be alive tomorrow or not alive; but as a matter of fact in the nature of things no such necessity exists." Augustine replies clearly and definitely that neither member of the disjunction is to be affirmed; the truth lies in the nexus of disjunction. "But elect for one of them," says the Academic. "No, I will not. You invite

---

[1] "Sorites": "the heap." If you remove all but a few, or the last, of the grains of sand in a heap, is it still a heap?

me to renounce what I do know, and affirm what I do not know."
In disjunctive propositions one possessed truth. (4) The "mentiens"
was contemptible. It could easily be dealt with.

Although only one side of the argument of the *Against the
Academics* has been given, and certain other important considerations and biographical material which will come up for discussion at a later stage have been omitted, enough has been said to
suggest that Augustine in 386, and *a fortiori* in 384, was not a very
serious philosopher, however favorably he might compare with his
contemporaries. His rhetorical training and preoccupation with
dialectics had at one and the same time diverted his interest from
the more fundamental questions even of epistemology, and at the
same time rendered him peculiarly immune from attack precisely
on the deeper issues. Augustine could no more be a sceptic than
he could be a professional philosopher. His forte was religion, not
philosophy. His mood of scepticism was undoubtedly disturbing,
but it was also short-lived.

Outwardly he was still a Manichee, living with Manichees
in the greatest friendship.

> Yet I lived in more familiar friendship with them, than with
> others who were not of this heresy. I did not defend it with
> my former eagerness, but my intimacy with that sect (Rome
> secretly harboring many of them) made me slower to seek
> any other way: especially since I despaired of finding the
> truth in Your Church. [...] For when my mind endeavored
> to return to the Catholic faith, I was driven back, since that
> was not the Catholic faith, which I thought to be so. (5:19,
> 20)

The Manichees had their share even in helping him to get
his appointment in Milan:

When therefore they of Milan had sent to Rome to the prefect of the city to furnish them with a professor of rhetoric for the city, and send him at the public expense, I applied (through those very persons, intoxicated with Manichean vanities, to be freed from which I was to go, neither of us knowing it) for the position. Symmachus, then prefect of the city, tested me by setting me some subject, and so he sent me. (5:23)

It is interesting to speculate whether or not Augustine owed his appointment among other reasons to his not being a Christian. If so, then, as he himself suggests, there was a certain irony, or call it Providence, in his going as a definite non-Christian whence he would return one of the most ardent and most powerful Christians that the world has known. At any rate, by the autumn of 384 there had been a strong pagan reaction against the earlier pro-Christian policy of Gratian: one pagan after another had asserted his power and had been invested with authority. The greatest and most influential of these was this very Symmachus, who now sent Augustine to Milan. He had, during the summer of 384, conducted a strong defense of the pagan cults in the episode of the Altar of Victory. He was the great opponent of the Christian Ambrose. When therefore Augustine came to Milan, he came under the highest pagan patronage. His purpose was to reap the rich rewards of a now established career. He was commended doubtless to Symmachus' friend, Bauto, the most powerful man in the Empire, in whose honor Augustine was shortly to deliver a panegyric.

8

AMBROSE AND AMBITION

WHEN AUGUSTINE in his *Confessions* comes to tell of his arrival in Milan, at that time the seat of the Imperial Court, he says nothing immediately of Bauto or his career, but quite simply: "To Milan I came, to Ambrose the bishop." Was it that from the moment he came there Ambrose had so greatly dominated his life and Christianity reclaimed him for itself — or was it that when Augustine was writing his *Confessions* he was taking pains to provide a welcome answer to the query of Paulinus, which in the first instance had been addressed to Alypius but was equally appropriate if addressed to himself: had Ambrose brought him to the Faith? Augustine frequently refers to Ambrose as one of the chief human instruments in his conversion, while at the same time conveying the impression that he had no intimate acquaintance with him. The problem is to discover how intimate or how distant were their relations and trace the influence of Ambrose upon Augustine.

Courcelle in his *Recherches sur les Confessions de saint Augustin* (p. 78 ff.) has microscopically examined the contacts, actual and possible, of these two. From his investigation he feels that he has established — or nearly established — that Ambrose provided Augustine with the synthesis of Neo-Platonism and Christianity which, on the intellectual side, brought him to the Faith. Their relations, however, were not close: the work was done through Ambrose's Christian-Neo-Platonist sermons.

Such a view is original and not impossible. If established, it would simplify the problem of Augustine's conversion; it would eliminate all question of his having been for any period of time, however short, a follower of the Neo-Platonists to the exclusion of Christianity. His own efforts in discovery would be reduced to a minimum. It is clearly necessary, therefore, to examine as closely as is here possible this new and interesting thesis.

On coming to Milan, Augustine paid a call on Ambrose to conciliate him, perhaps, or at any rate out of mere courtesy. This is the proper interpretation, doubtless, of the text in the *Confessions:*

> That man of God received me as a father and showed me
> an episcopal kindness on my coming (*suscepit me paterne,*
> *peregrinationem meam satis episcopaliter dilexit*). Thenceforth
> I began to love that man. (5:23)

Augustine must have been surprised at the reception given to him by Ambrose. He had come, it would appear, on the recommendation of the enemies of Ambrose and to the enemies of Ambrose. Nevertheless, Ambrose welcomed him.

What is the explanation of this welcome, which surprised Augustine himself? Were there Christians in Milan who knew Augustine in the days of his Manichean fervor in Africa, and possibly during the later period when his Manicheism was not so fervent and when he had been moved by the arguments of Helpidius? Were there Christians too who knew him at Rome and had seen that he was scarcely any longer a Manichee and could never be a pagan? Such persons would have known that Augustine might soon become a Christian. Again it is not impossible to suppose that Monica had indirectly approached the clergy of Rome to keep an eye upon her son, who now showed a disposition to return to the fold. We can believe that the holy men of Rome received many exhortations and instructions from the widow in Africa, and that they were invited to prepare for Augustine's coming to Milan. Whatever the explanation, Ambrose did welcome Augustine with a degree of warmth which could hardly have been expected.

Nevertheless, Augustine did not open his heart to Ambrose on the occasion of this first visit. He contented himself for the moment with going to hear Ambrose preach.

> Thenceforth I began to love him, at first indeed not as a teacher of the truth (which I utterly despaired of in Your Church), but as a person who was kind to me. And I listened diligently to him preaching to the people, not with the intention I should have had, but as it were, testing his eloquence, whether it lived up to its reputation, or flowed fuller or lower than was reported. I hung on his words attentively; but of the matter I was as a careless and scornful looker-on. [...] But together with the words which I would choose, there came also into my mind the things which I would refuse; for I could not separate them. And while I opened my heart to admit "how eloquently he spoke," there also entered "how truly he spoke"; but this came by degrees. (5:23-24)

Courcelle has argued that Augustine had no closer contact with Ambrose than this during the whole of his first six months in Milan, corresponding to the first six months of the year 385. There was the first official visit. There were the sermons in public. That was all.

The sermons had a very definite effect. Ambrose's exposition of the Scripture was quite other than that which Augustine had been led by the Manichees to suppose it must be: it commended itself entirely to his intelligence. One could be a Christian, he now knew, without ceasing to use one's reason. Augustine was particularly impressed with Ambrose's figurative explanation of many places of the Old Testament:

> And with joy I heard Ambrose in his sermons to the people, oftentimes most diligently recommend this text [2 Cor 3:6] for a rule: "The letter kills, but the spirit gives life"; while he drew aside the mystic veil, laying open spiritually what, according to the letter, seemed to teach something unsound. (6:6)

One is naturally curious as to whether one can read today any of those sermons of Ambrose which were listened to with such eagerness by Augustine? In a sense it makes little difference to the present enquiry, since almost any of Ambrose's explanations of the Old Testament would illustrate that method of his which so appealed to Augustine. Nevertheless to be able to read even one of those sermons to which Augustine listened might prove helpful in tracing the development of Augustine's thoughts at the time.

Courcelle examines this question with his usual thoroughness and imaginative insight. His conclusions are striking, and if accepted, decisive. He attempts to prove that Augustine could have heard, and therefore presumably did hear, the *Hexameron*, which according to him, was preached by Ambrose on the six days of Holy Week, 30 March-4 April, 386, and *On Isaac and the Soul*, preached, again according to him, also in 386. Courcelle argues that these sermons show not only the definite and specific influence of certain of Plotinus' *Enneads*, notably that *On Beauty*, but also a clear synthesis of Christianity and Neo-Platonism. Augustine listened to these and other sermons like them and quite simply became, in due course, a Christian-Neo-Platonist such as Ambrose was. Subsequently Ambrose introduced Augustine to Mallius Theodorus, a lay and distinguished Christian-Neo-Platonist author, who, in turn, introduced to him the Platonist, that is Neo-Platonist, books which he says he read: they were mainly a few *Enneads* of Plotinus and a book or two of Porphyry's. Finally Augustine consulted the old priest Simplicianus, another Christian-Neo-Platonist, former instructor of, and later successor to, Ambrose in the see of Milan, on the Christian-Neo-Platonist synthesis. Simplicianus finally satisfied him, and there ends the story, at this stage, of Augustine's connection with Neo-Platonism.

The significant point in this version is that Augustine came under the influence of Neo-Platonism and Christianity at the same time and through the instrumentality of a Christian, namely Ambrose. There is, therefore, no question of his having been influenced first by Neo-Platonism independently of Christianity, and then after an interval by Christianity either as a dominant or inferior or equal partner in a philosophical-religious synthesis. All happened at the same time and Christianity was supreme. Ambrose, the principal agent in the affair, guaranteed that.

The thesis is attractive; but it is not proved. Even Courcelle himself does not altogether discourage our lack of confidence in it by his final remarks in the relevant chapter: "Perhaps, but his arguments regarding the date of *De Isaac* and of *De bono mortis* are not fully convincing,[1] since it would seem to be less sure that Ambrose read the *Enneads* and preached Plotinian doctrine. To pretend that these sermons came later, following Augustine, would cause one to imagine that Augustine had revealed Plotinus to Ambrose. Which would seem absurd." (138)[2]

Even if, however, one cannot as yet feel convinced that Ambrose presented Augustine with a ready-made synthesis of Neo-Platonism and Christianity, one must not fail to give due prominence to the enormous influence, according to Augustine himself, he did have upon him. He went very far, in fact, towards solving two of the difficulties that had perplexed him for many years.

The major difficulty was his belief, which he owed to the Manichees, that God was corporeal: "And he said: let us make man to our image and likeness" (Gn 1:26). Ambrose invoked here a text from St. Paul which he was fond of quoting in all his sermons: "the letter kills, but the spirit gives life" (2 Cor 3:6). Another principle employed by Ambrose, this time taken, perhaps, directly or indirectly from Porphyry, was that, when there was question of God or the human soul, there should be no thought of body. Clearly, then, the text from Genesis was figurative and did not refer to any image or likeness in body, but rather in soul. That is to say, the text did not support the view that God was corporeal. That the

---

[1] C. Mohrmann, *Vigiliae Christianae*, October, 1951, pp. 249-254, does not accept Courcelle's dating of these works. Neither does Theiler: see below.

[2] W. Theiler, *Gnomon*, 25 (1953), pp. 113-122 rejects Courcelle's thesis in detail. His position is as follows: Ambrose's Neo-Platonism belongs to the stock-in-trade of asceticism and does not affect the traditional view that, if anything, he was hostile to philosophy; in any case it was derived from Philo, Origen, Basil, Gregory of Nyssa, and Porphyry rather than Plotinus; there is nothing absurd in the idea that Augustine should "reveal" Plotinus to Ambrose. See now G. Madec, *Saint Ambrose et la Philosophie*, Paris, 1974.

Christians should not only allow, but commend a figurative interpretation of Scripture was to Augustine a revelation of the greatest consequence. This fact alone shows us how dominated his mind had been by the Manichees. His whole attitude towards Christianity must now have changed profoundly.

The second difficulty which had greatly troubled Augustine over many years again owed much of its intensity to the Manichees: the problem of evil. Here too Ambrose, as Huhn[3] has demonstrated, had a favorite argument, which in fact was aimed precisely at the Manichean view that not we, but rather the evil in us, was responsible for the evil done by us. Ambrose would have none of this. He insisted that the source of our evildoing was in our own free will:

> But this raised me a little into Your light, that I knew as well that I had a will, as that I lived: when then I willed or did not will anything, I was most sure, that *no other than myself* willed or did not will, and I began to see that there was the cause of my sin. (7:5)

When he had been at Carthage, Augustine tells us,[4] he had been shaken in his Manichean belief on this point and had begun to favor the view that evil was no positive thing but rather, as for example Apuleius of Madauros (where he had been at school) had said in his *De doctrina Platonis*, a privation or lack of good. Now, however, he was further dissuaded from the Manichean view by Ambrose's preaching. Ambrose may have been indebted to Plotinus (*Ennead* 3:2:10) for his view; but Plotinus is far from being the only, or indeed likely, source.

Here then one finds that Ambrose, while preaching on two of his own favorite topics, for neither of which he needed to go directly to any Neo-Platonist source, had, while not finally disabusing Augustine of his views, almost succeeded in doing so. For good measure he also impressed Augustine by the soundness of his plea for restraint and understanding in judging the Law and the Prophets

---

[3] J. Huhn, "Ursprung und Wesen des Bösen und der sünde nach der Lehre des Kirchenvaters Ambrosius," *Forsch. z. Christ. Lit. u. Dogmengeschichte*, XVII, 5, 1933, pp. 33 ff.

[4] *On the Morality of the Manichees* 2.

and the older dispensation: on this point too, Augustine had been troubled by the Manichean polemic. It is difficult to realize how profoundly all this affected Augustine's attitude towards Christianity, especially when represented before the world by a bishop who was not only enlightened and sympathetic, but to himself, while remaining distant, friendly.

Nevertheless, Augustine made no advances to Ambrose: "As it happens that one, who has tried a bad physician, fears to trust himself with a good one" (6:6), so he resisted Ambrose but, significantly, not Christianity. He resumed, what he had dropped in his nineteenth year, his status as a catechumen: "I determined so long to be a catechumen in the Catholic Church, until something certain should dawn upon me, to show me where I should steer my course" (5:25). This was a great change, one very much underrated by biographers, and Ambrose was the chief human agent in it.

To return, however, to the question of the further actual contacts of Augustine and Ambrose at this time — these were brought about by neither of them, but by Monica, who contrived them; and the subject of their conversation was not the synthesis of Neo-Platonism and Christianity, but rather two small items of local church discipline. That Augustine wanted very much to consult Ambrose about his own affairs — as he emphasizes in the *Confessions* — and refrained from doing so when he was at least once, if not twice, provided with the opportunity, can be explained, one supposes, in a number of ways. Did he, for example, display in this instance an uncharacteristic restraint; or is it not more likely that he felt he had not enough reason to look to Ambrose for that union of philosophical and religious teaching for which his soul yearned?

On her arrival in Milan, towards the summer, it would seem, of 385, Monica discovered that two of her favorite religious exercises were not practiced in Ambrose's diocese — fasting on Saturday, and the custom of bringing food and wine to the tombs of the martyrs. Being a woman of zeal and one not easily satisfied — but perhaps she had an *arrière pensée* — she insisted that Augustine would consult no less a person than Ambrose on these two points on her behalf.

Ambrose satisfied Augustine on the question of the custom of bringing food and drink to the martyrs' tombs: there was danger of abuse and confusion with the pagan cult of their dead. On the other point — not mentioned in the *Confessions*, but set out at length in two letters (36:14: about A.D. 395 and 54:2: about A.D. 400) — Ambrose gave no reason beyond local custom and his own practice. In reply to Augustine's query he asked: "What greater instruction can I give you than my own practice?" He saw, however, that Augustine expected some reason. Augustine had plainly misunderstood him and seemed to think that Ambrose was merely exercising his authority in an arbitrary fashion. Accordingly the bishop went on to explain that he himself, wherever he was, followed the local practice, whatever it was. Augustine was satisfied and approved of the wisdom of Ambrose's procedure.[5]

Whether or not these two points were raised by Augustine separately or together, informally at the end of a sermon or formally at a private interview, they point to the fact that Augustine and Ambrose, although they may not have had close and intimate contact with one another, did keep up the relatively friendly relations on which they started. Augustine was apparently still not vitally interested in Christianity, and showed no wish to become more intimate with the bishop. Ambrose, therefore, was content to congratulate him on having such a mother and turn a blind eye on his own apparent indifference. This was the extent of their acquaintance up to the summer of Augustine's conversion.

His want of real interest in the Christian life of Milan is well instanced by his not having firsthand knowledge of two major events in which Ambrose was deeply involved. His own mother, moreover, was very much engaged in one of them, and almost certainly in the other also.

The one was the siege, in February, 386, of Ambrose and his flock in a basilica which the Empress Justina wished to give to the Arians. To prevent this, Ambrose had installed himself in the basilica and it was then that, surrounded outside by soldiers, the faith-

---

[5] Courcelle's interpretation of this scene is forced and not convincing (*Recherches*, p. 90).

ful had for the first time sung hymns and psalms after the manner
of the eastern Churches. Monica took a prominent part in all this.
The whole city was excited by the event — but Augustine was as
yet "unwarmed," as he says "by the heat of Your Spirit." (9:15)

The other was equally stirring: the discovery of the remains
of the martyrs Gervasius and Protasius in June, 386, and their translation for veneration:

> Then You by a vision showed to Your forenamed bishop,
> where the bodies of Gervasius and Protasius the martyrs lay
> hid (whom You had in Your secret treasury stored uncor-
> rupted so many years), whence You might seasonably pro-
> duce them to repress the fury of a woman, but an Empress.
> For when they were discovered and dug up, and with due
> honor translated to the Ambrosian Basilica, not only those
> who were vexed with unclean spirits (the devils confessing
> themselves) were cured. A certain man, who had for many
> years been blind, a citizen, and well known to the city, asked
> and heard the reason of the people's confused joy, sprang
> forth, and asked his guide to lead him there. Led there, he
> begged to be allowed to touch with his handkerchief the bier
> of Your saints, whose death is precious in Your sight. When
> he had done this, and put it to his eyes, they were immedi-
> ately opened. Then the fame of this spread, then Your praises
> glowed and shone, then the mind of that enemy, though not
> turned to the soundness of believing, was yet turned back
> from her fury of persecuting. [...] And yet then, when the
> odor of Your ointments was so fragrant, I did not run after
> You. (9:16)

Augustine frequently refers to this event especially in the last
ten years of his life, when he had overcome an earlier distrust for
contemporary inventions of martyrs and miracles: but he never
states or implies that he took any part in the affair. Indeed, we know
that some of the details he gives us are incorrect — that they derive from inexact and popular report and not from firsthand evidence. Ambrose's part in the affair and the affair itself were the

more striking not only because of the circumstances of the siege in which it happened, but also in view of the fact that only four months before the discovery and translation of the martyrs, an imperial edict had prohibited all such translations or distribution of their relics. Yet Ambrose defied the prohibition on both points.

At the time Augustine must have been rather sceptical of the whole business; for although the enemies of the bishop did not think of explaining away the martyrs Gervasius and Protasius as Castor and Pollux (as some moderns have attempted to do), still they refused resolutely to be impressed by the account of their revelation to Ambrose in a dream or vision, or by the miracles, or by Ambrose's assertion that old men remembered the time when on the tomb of the newly discovered and unknown saints their names were clearly legible.

Augustine, therefore, even within a few months of his conversion, was still not greatly interested in Ambrose's personal affairs or the events that loomed large in the life of the Church in Milan. It would be a mistake, nevertheless, to suppose that he was equally indifferent to Christianity itself. Even as a Christian bishop he was distrustful of miracles, and considered the rapid spread of Christianity the greatest miracle of his time. In any case his interest in Christianity was more an individual and personal one, and more intellectual.

He was, even still, rather perplexed about the nature of the soul and how one could conceive of spiritual substance. Ambrose's sermons had commended to him a non-material view; but he was so wedded to material notions that he sought to learn something of spiritual substance in dreams and visions. Thus, for example, he had a lively interest in the visions which his mother had in connection with his future marriage. They were unsuccessful and more like nightmares than revelations! He doubtless discussed these matters with his friends Nebridius and Evodius, who also were now in Milan with him and with whom he was still to have much discussion on these topics. He was also very puzzled to hear at this time of a father appearing in a dream to a young man who had been called upon to pay again a debt which his father had already discharged:

his father supplied him with all the information necessary to prove that the debt had been paid. It seemed that a soul divested of the body could be aware of human affairs and even be moved by them. His mind was changed on this point when on his return to Africa he discovered that while he was actually in Milan his own image had appeared in a dream to a teacher, once his pupil, who had some difficulty in preparing his class for the morrow! He had been entirely unaware of this appearance and of the help he had given!

Perhaps through some mutual acquaintance, or through his interest in the question of the nature of the soul, on which Theodorus had already written; by some means or other, he became acquainted with Flavius Mallius Theodorus, the foremost Christian Platonist of the day, a man of influence, destined to be consul in 399.

At the moment Theodorus had temporarily retired from public life to an estate in the country and was engaged in writing on philosophical subjects. He was about the same age as Augustine and had been born in Milan of parents who were not wealthy. He had passed, as had Augustine, through the rhetorical schools and legal profession into the service of the Empire. Soon Augustine was to dedicate to him his treatise *On the Happy Life* (386), and to refer to him in another dialogue of the same date. With this man Augustine became acquainted, and with him had many serious conversations.

Here, then, was a second great figure whom, if he was reluctant to consult Ambrose, Augustine could have consulted about the intellectual justification of Christianity. But in this case, too, Augustine does not seem to have availed himself of the opportunity.

Courcelle suggests that Ambrose sent Augustine to see Theodorus and that Theodorus gave to Augustine some of the *Enneads* of Plotinus translated into Latin by Victorinus. There is no proof whatever that anything of the sort took place.

Was Augustine likely to address Theodorus, even formally, with the words: "having read a few books of Plotinus in whom *I am told,* you are interested"[6] if it was Theodorus who actually gave him the very books in question? If the words imply anything on this point, they imply that Theodorus did *not* give him those books. Moreover, Courcelle's theory supposes that when Augustine was publishing the *Confessions* in 400 he was so displeased at Theodorus' resumption of a worldly career by becoming consul in 399, that he refers to Theodorus as one "puffed up with most unnatural pride" (*Confessions* 7:13). This surely is too much. Augustine may have regretted thinking too well of Theodorus in the earlier days, and his attitude to philosophers did not improve as the years went by, but even when an old man he referred to Theodorus in no such terms, but rather as a learned and Christian man.[7]

From Ambrose or Theodorus, therefore, so far as our present information goes, Augustine does not seem to have learned anything of a Christian-Neo-Platonist synthesis: that came to him, he himself says, on the reading of certain books. But Ambrose at least, with whom he had friendly — and distant — relations, had brought him so far towards Christianity that he was again a catechumen; and, having removed some of his difficulties and taught him to respect Christian teaching, had left him well disposed for the revelation which was very soon to come. Thus far had he advanced in the month of June, 386.

There is a strong tendency in writings on the conversion of Augustine to ignore altogether, or say very little of, the worldly career which at this stage in his life was at its most successful and held its highest promise. When he was writing the *Confessions* he was naturally more interested in portraying his intellectual and moral experiences, and we in reading them have the same interest. Nevertheless his preoccupation with his career and material

---

6 *On the Happy Life* 4.

7 *Retractations* 1:1:2.

gains not only absorbed much of his thought but contributed not a little to his mental agitation and perplexity. His interest in a worldly career had grown recently as a natural consequence of his mood of scepticism: the less he had wished to think, the more he had directed his energies towards the world.

Success was now within his grasp:

> See, it is no great matter now to obtain some honorable office, and then what should we more wish for! We have many powerful friends; if nothing else is offered, and we are in much haste, at least a minor governorship may be given us; and a wife with some money, so that she does not increase our burdens, and this shall be the limit of our desire. (6:19)

This was no wishful thinking on the part of Augustine. His calculations would seem to have been exact.

That he could expect something more than a governorship of a minor province if he bided his time is probable enough. He had a store of powerful friends, such as Symmachus and, one can suppose, the effective ruler of the Empire, Bauto. He cultivated them with a view to his own aggrandizement:

> The mornings our students take up; what do we do during the rest? [...] When then will we pay court to our great friends, whose favor we need? [...] When will we refresh ourselves, unbending our minds from this intenseness of care? (6:18)

The feverish intensity and anxiety of his mind at this time is well shown in a famous episode which can be connected either with his panegyric for the consulship of Bauto on 1 January, 385, or, if Augustine delivered two such public panegyrics, that in honor of the young Emperor, Valentinian II, delivered possibly on 22 November of the same year. The feverishness of his anxiety is well seen in the following passage:

> I panted after honors, gains, marriage; and You derided me. In these desires I underwent very bitter crosses. [...] How

wretched was it! [...] How unhappy was I then, and how You dealt with me, to make me feel my unhappiness on that day, when I was preparing to recite a panegyric to the Emperor, in which I was to utter many a lie, and lying, was to be applauded by those who knew I lied. My heart was panting with these anxieties, and boiling with the feverishness of consuming thoughts. For, passing through one of the streets of Milan, I observed a poor beggar, then, I suppose, drunk, joking and joyous. I sighed, and spoke to the friends around me, of the many sorrows of our madness; since with all such efforts of ours, as those in which I then toiled — dragging along, under the goading of desire, the burden of my own wretchedness, and, by dragging, augmenting it — we yet looked to arrive only at that very joyousness, which that beggar had already reached before us, who perhaps should never attain it. For what he had obtained by means of a few begged coins, the same was I scheming for by many a toilsome turning and winding: the joy of a temporary felicity. For although he in fact did not have the true joy, yet I with my ambitious designs was seeking one much less true. And certainly he was joyous, I was anxious; he was free of care, I was full of fears. But if anyone had asked me, would I rather be merry or fearful? I would answer, merry. Again, if he had asked, would I rather be such as the beggar was, or what I then was, I should choose to be myself, though worn with cares and fears; but out of wrong judgment, for was it the truth? For I should prefer myself to the beggar, because I was more learned than he, seeing I had no joy in it, but sought to please men by it; and that not to instruct, but simply to please. (6:9)

Success was at hand, and its very certainty argues most strongly for the sincerity of his conversion; for when that intervened, he gave up all thoughts of worldly advancement. But to be consumed with anxiety for a success, the cup of which one may dash from one's lips the moment when it is proffered, is little solace, if indeed it is not an added aggravation, in one's toil. "We must not lightly abandon them [worldly hopes], for it would be a shame to return again to them." (6:19)

The other worldly interest was marriage. Here once more the motive of ambition was prominent. Augustine had with him in Milan his faithful mistress, the mother of his son Adeodatus. It must be supposed that in her Augustine found much of what he demanded in a wife. At any rate, when she was "torn from his side," as he puts it, his heart, "which clung to her, was torn and wounded and bleeding" (6:25). But Augustine — or was it Monica? — wanted more than a mistress could give, and so she was sent back to Africa, leaving their son with Augustine. Thus a hindrance to baptism, in which his mother was interested, and to a career / marriage, in which they were both interested — had been removed.

> Continual effort was made to have me married. I wooed, I
> was promised, chiefly through my mother's pains. (6:23)

Eventually a suitable girl, one who would not increase his charges, was found for him; but there was the serious disadvantage that he had to wait for two years before he could marry her. Here again it must have been disconcerting to have to strive for a prize and suffer inconvenience when one felt that one might never accept it.

Some writers have elaborated the pathetic scene of Augustine's dismissal of his mistress. On the one side we see the faithful, tearful woman sadly separating from the man and son whom she loved above all else and to whom she had given the best years of her life, and vowing to know no other man but Augustine. On the other we look upon the strong-minded and jealous mother standing behind a regretful and weak-willed but ambitious son.

It is quite idle, however, to conjure up such a picture. We must think of fourth-century Africa, where some women, whatever were their personal attractions and qualities, could not, because of their low condition — even if they were Christians — expect marriage with a man of Augustine's position. Women did not claim equality of opportunity among themselves and still less equality of rights with men. Some women could expect to marry Augustine; others — and Augustine's mistress was clearly one of these — never.

Not only had Augustine no duty to marry his mistress. Such an idea never entered his head — nor for that matter hers, one may suppose. Was he then bound to retain her as she was? There could never have been any such obligation. If he contemplated a suitable marriage or baptism or both, he had, in fact, a duty to remove her. This is exactly what happened. The most and, in view of their close association over a decade and a half and the bond of their son, the least she or we could expect from him is that he should not dismiss her with indifference. This he did not do. On the contrary he felt her loss most bitterly. If Augustine had not told us of their mutual love and sad separation, who would have known of her existence or been able to darken the character of Augustine? Is Augustine to be blamed because he had to put her away and tells us of his sorrow in doing so? She was well loved by him for many years: she gave birth to his son, shared the life of his youth, and abided in his memory.

What with his mind tortured with thoughts of honors, money and marriage, and the feeling that he might yet renounce all of them — and these were only some of his problems — Augustine was troubled: "I had a feeling," he tells us, "that all was not well with me" (6:10). His health was beginning to fail so that he began to fear that he would soon die. The drama of his story becomes more tense. This overworked, ambitious man, with failing body and mind distraught; thinking of position and wealth and marriage; fearful of death and uncertain of all things; disillusioned in religion in the past, distrustful and yet not altogether without hope for the future; with friends as always about him — not to lend any support in his trial, but rather to send him forward to his agony alone — this man encounters a series of, to him, blinding discoveries that have elevated his conversion almost to that of St. Paul and have edified, when they have not perplexed, the world.

9

NEO-PLATONISM FOR THE FEW: THE ASCENT OF THE SOUL

I T MAY COME as a surprise to many admirers of Augustine to learn that a large number of important scholars have maintained that Augustine in 386 was converted not to Christianity but rather to Neo-Platonist philosophy. This view has in recent years been greatly weakened, so that the comparative silence of writers in English on the matter has saved their readers much rather useless controversy.

The controversy, however, was not altogether useless; for it focused attention on the *intellectual* as distinct from the *moral* conversion of Augustine, and thereby our knowledge of Augustine's mental experience at the time of his conversion has been greatly enriched.[1]

There have always been found — as there always will be found — men who impugn the sincerity and truth of Augustine's account of his conversion as set out in the *Confessions*. They must win sympathy, for the *Confessions* is indeed a difficult book. Such an one was Jean le Clerc (1657-1736) who, on the internal evidence of the *Confessions* itself, assailed its truth. In more recent times came Naville, Boissier, Harnack and Loofs, all of whom a few years before the end of the 19th century pointed out what they considered

---

[1] For a brief account of this controversy see J. O'Meara, ed. and ann., *Against the Academics*, Ancient Christian Writers series, Vol. 12, 1950, pp. 19 ff.

to be a grave discrepancy between the account of his conversion given by Augustine in his *Confessions*, written twelve to fourteen years after the event, and that given and implied in his earliest extant writings, the *Dialogues* composed by him at Cassiciacum, a villa some distance outside Milan, within two to four months of the event itself. The one was written by a Christian bishop to exalt the grace of God; the other was written by one whose chief enthusiasm was for philosophy. Harnack, for example, contended that the *Dialogues* do not bear out the idea of a radical conversion to Christianity. Loofs even maintained that in 391, five years after his "conversion," Augustine was still nothing more than a Neo-Platonist with a tincture of Christianity. The *Confessions* in short misrepresent what actually happened.

But more was yet to come. Gourdon in 1900 said that there was flagrant contradiction between the *Dialogues* and the *Confessions*: "In 386," he held, "Augustine underwent a crisis in which he was converted to a good moral life and Neo-Platonic philosophy. That was all." Gourdon put Augustine's sincere conversion to Christianity as late as 400, when he had already been a Christian bishop for five and a priest for nine years. It may be said, in passing, that paradoxical as Gourdon's view in these latter points may seem, it is not impossible, as anyone well acquainted with the ecclesiastical history of the period must know.

By far the best exponent of this point of view, however, is Prosper Alfaric, who in his imposing book *L'évolution intellectuelle de saint Augustin* allowed himself the following remarks:

> When he [Augustine] was baptized, he attached such little importance to this rite that in his writings of that time, where he speaks often of himself and of all that interests him, he never makes the faintest allusion to it. (p. viii) Morally as well as intellectually he was converted to Neo-Platonism rather than the Gospel. (399) He regards Catholicism as a lower form of wisdom, of good only for minds that are weak or not yet mature. (515) If he had died after he had written the *Soliloquies*, we would not have regarded him as anything

but a convinced Neo-Platonist, with a tincture, more or less, of Christianity. (527)

In point of fact none of these assertions is wholly true. One can no more demand of Augustine to speak in the *Dialogues* of "all that interests him" than one could of any writer of a philosophical manual to tell of his marriage or the birth of his children. Augustine does actually allude in no very faint manner to his baptism in the *Dialogues*.[2] There is even great exaggeration in much of what Alfaric has to say; as, for example, that "if Plotinus makes Plato relive, so does Augustine Plotinus" (518); or "For Augustine Christ is the Plato of the mob" (525). Anyone even a little less acquainted with the *Dialogues* than Alfaric — and less prejudiced — would know that these statements are nothing less than gross exaggerations.

Others were found to defend the traditional view, but some of these accorded less to Neo-Platonism in the conversion of Augustine than is warranted by a scrupulously fair interpretation of both the *Dialogues* and the *Confessions*. Prominent among these were Portalié, Boyer and Norregaard.

In more recent years, because of the increased knowledge that resulted from this protracted controversy, a more informed opinion generally prevails in which, while it is admitted that Augustine's conversion to Christianity was sincere and complete, due emphasis is placed on the part played in it by Neo-Platonism. Augustine was convinced at the time that Neo-Platonism and Christianity were two approaches to the same Truth. In this he was deceived; but realization of this came later.

No sooner, however, had one controversy begun to die down than another, a lesser one, arose. Granted that Augustine was influenced by Neo-Platonists, who were the Neo-Platonists and what were the books in question? The list could be narrowed down to two: Porphyry and Plotinus. Theiler[3] said that Porphyry only

---

[2] *On Order* 2:27.

[3] W. Theiler, *Porphyrios und Augustin*, Halle, 1933.

was in question. Henry[4] said Plotinus only. This controversy also has abated, and no scholar would nowadays deny that both Porphyry and Plotinus played their parts.

The only question that remains is as to the extent and nature of the influence of Plotinus and Porphyry. Before an attempt is made to solve that difficult problem, something must first be said of Plotinus,[5] his disciple Porphyry, and Neo-Platonism.

In Porphyry's words: "Plotinus, the philosopher our contemporary, seemed ashamed of being in the body. So deeply-rooted was this feeling that he could never be induced to tell his ancestry, his parentage or his birthplace. He showed, too, an unconquerable reluctance to sit to a painter or a sculptor. 'Is it not enough (he said) to carry about this image in which nature has enclosed us? Do you really think I must also consent to leave, as a desirable spectacle to posterity, an image of the image?'"

So wrote the faithful follower of the great man. We do know, however, that Plotinus was born in A.D. 204-5 in Egypt, probably at Lycopolis and died sixty-five years later near Rome. There is doubt about his nationality; though he was born in Egypt, his name is Roman and his literary language at least is Greek. He studied under Ammonius Saccas at Alexandria, and later joined an ill-fated expedition of the Emperor Gordian against Persia — from a desire to acquaint himself with Eastern thought: Puech has pointed out that Mani and Plotinus could actually have met in battle! Finally, at the age of forty, he settled down in Rome as a teacher of philosophy. He is represented as a man of great personal charm and goodness, an unwearied seeker of truth, an inspiring lecturer, and something of a spiritual director — an ascetic who was also a humanist and a humanitarian. He published no written work before he was fifty. His collected essays, as edited by Porphyry, form the six books known as the *Enneads* (sets of nine treatises). His last words were: "I am striving to give back the Divine in myself to the Divine in the All." As he spoke, it is related, a snake crept under

---

[4] P. Henry, *Plotin et l'Occident*, Louvain, 1934.
[5] For Plotinus, see D.J. O'Meara, *Plotinus* (Oxford, 1993, 1995).

the bed on which he lay and slipped away into a hole in the wall: at the same moment Plotinus died.

Porphyry[6] was born at Tyre, or possibly Batanea in Palestine, about A.D. 232, studied under Longinus at Athens and became the faithful disciple of Plotinus, whose biography he wrote and whose works he edited about 300, some five years before his own death. He was a very prolific writer, dealing with philosophical commentaries, history, biography, metaphysics, psychology, moral philosophy, philosophy of religion, rhetoric, mathematics, astrology, poetry and letters. The most distinguished Porphyrian scholar of modern times, Bidez, says: "In the whole extant work of Porphyry there is not a thought or an image which one can confidently affirm to be his own." His aim in fact was to be, not an original thinker, but an interpreter and popularizer of the philosophical and religious doctrines of others and above all of Plotinus. Eunapius describes him as a Godsend to a generation who found Plotinus difficult and enigmatic both in style and doctrine. We must not, however, allow our present persuasion — as represented, for example, in Bidez' judgment — on the relative merits as thinkers of Plotinus and Porphyry to distort our vision of the position as it presented itself to the men of the fourth century. His was the chief name in philosophy at the time. As Courcelle[7] finely says: "There was only one philosophy, the Neo-Platonic: and the master of men's minds was Porphyry."

If it be asked, for example, which of the Neo-Platonists received the most extensive notice from Augustine, the answer is unhesitatingly Porphyry. This of course may be due to the exigencies of polemic or greater acquaintance. If it be asked which of them was most highly praised by him — and this is much more significant — the answer again is Porphyry.

This appreciation is in striking contrast to that given of Plotinus. While Augustine speaks of Porphyry as the "most noble

---

[6] For Porphyry, see A. Smith, "Porphyrian Studies since 1913," *Aufstieg Und Niedergang Der Römischen Welt*, New York 1987, vol. 36.2.

[7] *Les lettres grecques en Occident*, Paris, 1948, p. 394.

philosopher of the pagans," "so great a philosopher," "whose reputation is widespread," "the most learned of the philosophers,"[8] he praises Plotinus not, so to speak, in his own right as a philosopher, but as having understood Plato better than others, and as being almost Plato come to life again. There can be no doubt that Augustine did value Plotinus' work very highly. This, however, does not detract from his rather special esteem for Porphyry — an esteem truly remarkable in a bishop of that day. St. Jerome affords a lively contrast. To him Porphyry is "stupid, impious, a blasphemer, not right in the head, accursed, impudent, a sycophant, a calumniator of the Church, a mad dog barking against Christ."

Neo-Platonism as a system purported to be a revival of Platonism, but was in fact a synthesis of Platonic, Aristotelian, Stoic, and Pythagorean elements. It dominated the pagan philosophical world from the middle of the third to the beginning of the sixth century A.D. It was at once a set of doctrines and a way of life. The central doctrine was that only the intelligible really is. Intelligence, since it seemed to be necessarily dual, inasmuch as it implied in its very notion not only a subject that "intellects" but also an object that is "intellected," could not be the primary principle, and had to have its source, therefore, in a unity that was not intellectual, and that, therefore, by definition, was not. This principle received the name of the One, or the God which is beyond being. It is, as it were, the unmarked center of a circle.

Related to it by emanation is Intelligence, which is and which alone is. This is the second principle. There is a third principle called the Soul. It arises, as it were, on the fringe of being, of Intelligence: it is a link between Intelligence and Material things. Now we are all of the order of Intelligence, but we find ourselves in composition with Matter. Our true life is the life of Intelligence, of Nous, of immediate intuition of all truth, and not the life of discursive reason. We need but recollect ourselves and remember that we are Gods, and already we *are* Gods. Matter does make this almost impossible for some of us, and difficult for nearly all of us.

---

[8] See J. O'Meara, *op. cit.*, p. 161 f.

Hence our effort must always be directed to purgation, to ridding ourselves as far as possible of the Matter which is the vesture of our decay, and to asserting the Godhead in us, until we are altogether freed from the body and resume our union with the All-Intelligent, from which we can rise ultimately to the mystical union with the One, the Good, or, as he is sometimes called, the Father.

There is general agreement nowadays that Augustine in 386 read among other treatises of Plotinus that *On Beauty* (*Ennead* 1:6) and also at least the *Return of the Soul*[9] of Porphyry. He was profoundly impressed by the teaching he believed he found in these treatises on the destiny of mankind. For the *few*, who were capable of it, return to the Father could be achieved through the ascetic purgation of the soul and the exercise of the highest powers of "reason": it was an ascent, or return, of the soul to God, which manifested itself at its highest point here below as ecstasy. For the *many*, who were incapable of purgation or the higher use of reason, there had to be, it was contended, some universal way of authority, which if they followed they would reach the Fatherland.

For the moment it will suffice to speak of Augustine's interest — a personal one — in the Neo-Platonic way of life for the few: the way of ascent and ecstasy. Its most famous formulation is that found in Plotinus' *On Beauty*, some of which may be quoted in the inspired translation of Stephen MacKenna:

> Therefore we must ascend again towards the Good, the desired of every Soul. Anyone that has seen This, knows what I intend when I say that it is beautiful. Even the desire of it is to be desired as a Good.
>
> To attain it, is for those that will take the upward path, who will set all their forces towards it, who will divest themselves of all that we have put on in our descent: so, to those that approach the Holy Celebrations of the Mysteries, there

[9] This appears to be a descriptive title; cf. p. vii and p. 151, n. 4.

are appointed purifications and the laying aside of the garments worn before, and the entry in nakedness — until, passing, on the upward way, all that is other than God, each in the solitude of himself shall behold that solitary-dwelling Existence, the Apart, the Unmingled, the Pure, that from Which all things depend, for Which all look and live and act and know, the Source of Life and of Intellection and of Being.

And one that shall know this vision — with what passion of love shall he not be seized, with what pang of desire, what longing to be molten into one with This, what wondering delight! If he that has never seen this Being must hunger for It as for all his welfare, he that has known must love and reverence It as the very Beauty; he will be flooded with awe and gladness, stricken by a salutary terror; he loves with a veritable love, with sharp desire; all other loves than this he must despise, and disdain all that once seemed fair.

This indeed is the mood even of those who, having witnessed the manifestations of Gods or Supernals, can never again feel the old delight in the comeliness of material forms: what then are we to think of one that contemplates the Absolute Beauty in Its essential integrity, no accumulation of flesh and matter, no dweller on earth or in the heavens — so perfect Its Purity — far above all such things in that they are non-essential, composite, not primal but descending from This?

Beholding this Being — the Choragos of all Existence, the Self-Intent that ever gives forth and never takes — resting rapt, in the vision and possession of so lofty a loveliness, growing to Its likeness, what Beauty can the soul yet lack? For This, the Beauty supreme, the absolute, and the primal, fashions Its lovers to Beauty and makes them also worthy of love. And for This, the sternest and the uttermost combat is set before the Souls; all our labor is for This, lest we be left without part in this noblest vision, which to attain is to be blessed in the blissful sight, which to fail of is to fail utterly. For not he that has failed of the joy that is in color or in visible forms, not he that has failed of power or of honors or of kingdom has failed, but only he that has failed of only This, for Whose winning he should renounce kingdoms and command over earth and ocean and sky, if only, spurning the world of sense from beneath his feet, and straining to This, he may see.

It is evident from the following, and two other lengthy passages[10] from the seventh book of the *Confessions*, that Augustine nearly sixteen years later is deeply moved at the mere recollection of how the Neo-Platonic ascent of the Soul so impressed him in 386 as to invite him to aspire to it:

Yet there dwelt with me a remembrance of You; nor did I doubt, that there was One to Whom I might cling, but that I was not yet able to cling to You: for the corruptible body presses down the soul, and the earthly tabernacle weighs down the mind that muses upon many things. And I was most certain that Your invisible works from the creation of the world are clearly seen, being understood by the things that are made, even Your eternal power and Godhead. For examining why I admired the beauty of bodies celestial or terrestial; and what aided me in judging soundly on things mutable, and saying, "This ought to be thus, this not"; examining, I say, why I so judged, seeing I did so judge, I had found the unchangeable and true Eternity of Truth, above my changeable mind. And thus by degrees, I passed from bodies to the soul, which perceives through the bodily senses; and thence to its inward faculty, to which the bodily senses represent things external, which is the limit reached by the faculties of beasts; and thence again to the reasoning faculty, to which what is received from the senses of the body, is referred to be judged. When my reasoning faculty found itself also to be a variable thing, it raised itself up to its own understanding, and drew away my thoughts from the power of habit, withdrawing itself from those troops of contradictory phantasms. This was so that it might find what that light was, by which it was sprinkled, when, without all

---

[10] 7:16, 26.

doubting, it cried out, "That the unchangeable was to be preferred to the changeable." Thus also it knew the Unchangeable, which, unless it had in some way known, it had had
no sure ground to prefer it to the changeable. And thus with
the flash of one trembling glance it arrived at That Which
Is. And then I saw Your invisible things made understandable by the things which are made. But I could not fix my
gaze on this; and being struck back in my weakness, I was
thrown again on my usual habits, carrying along with me
only a loving memory of this, and a longing for what I had,
as it were, perceived the odor of, but was not yet able to feed
on. (7:23)

Three times he lingers with the recollection, a bishop inter-
spersing now quotations from the Scriptures with the words of
Plotinus which ever remained in his memory. The question arises
as to whether or no Augustine, on first reading Plotinus, had received, or attempted some mystical experience such as had been
granted to the author of the *Enneads* a number of times. One will
not readily believe that the ecstasy of contemplative union with
the One was accorded him at this early date: the question will have
to be asked at a later stage if Augustine had any mystical experiences at all before the death of Monica. Writers have contended,
however, that on this first reading of Plotinus he attempted such
ecstasy, perhaps more than once. Some imply that he succeeded
and others that he failed. Henry[11] is so bold as to say that Augustine was a born mystic — *un mystique né*. He goes on to add that in
this he took after his mother, for she too was a mystic. The reading of Plotinus, therefore, illumined his intelligence, flowed over
into his emotions, and gave rise to strong mystical aspirations. The
ecstasy, Henry claims, was relatively successful. Not everyone,
however, will grant in advance that Augustine was a mystic in a
specialized signification of the term; and much less perhaps will it
be granted for Monica.

---

[11] P. Henry, *La vision d'Ostie*, Paris, 1938, p. 88.

Courcelle[12] is equally bold. He believes that Augustine on reading Plotinus' treatise *On Beauty* which, he alleges, Ambrose had paraphrased for him, felt confident on a whole series of occasions that he could forthwith elevate himself to the vision of God according to the dialectical methods of Plotinus. But though he did ascend in his mind to Being, the result was a disappointing failure because of his poor moral state. It may seem to many that Courcelle attributes an optimism too naive to the barely initiated and as yet unpurged Augustine.

Theiler[13] as usual supposes that Porphyry, and not Plotinus, is behind the scenes. In fact, according to him, there were no attempts at ecstasy at all. Augustine at the time merely pondered on Porphyry's doctrine of the ascent of the soul in so far as it threw light on his own difficulties — the problem of evil, for example. Later, however, in writing the *Confessions* Augustine employs as a literary device a Porphyrian soul-ascent *motif,* in which he now includes Scriptural quotations, his mature thoughts on the difference in teaching between Christianity and Neo-Platonism, and an attack on the gross polytheism of Porphyry. Although, Theiler believes, there was no attempt at ecstasy, and, of course, neither success nor failure, still the account in the *Confessions* reflects — apart from the accretions mentioned — a mental activity that had taken place.

It is impossible on the evidence he submits, and for other reasons, to dismiss Theiler's case for Porphyry here, and one may also feel reluctant to dismiss the case for Plotinus. One is not compelled to do either; for in the *Confessions* Augustine at this point speaks not of a book, or books of Plotinus or Porphyry, but rather three times of certain Platonist (that is Neo-Platonic) books — which would allow for separate works of both Neo-Platonists. Neither should one minimize the striking nature of the mental experience in question, for even Augustine's earliest reference to it conveys the strong impression that the experience was out of the ordinary.

---

[12] *Recherches*, pp. 157 ff.

[13] *Gnomon*, 25 (1953), p. 120.

Incidentally even in his earliest works — although hardly as soon as his first reading of the books in question — Augustine already attacked Porphyry for reasons similar to those later given in the *Confessions* and had already worked out at least some of the differences between Christian and Neo-Platonic thought which are there set out.[14]

There can be little doubt but that he would have liked to experience Plotinian ecstasy and took whatever steps he could to that end; but on the whole it is best to rule out here all question of any true ecstasy or mystical experience. The reading at least, of Plotinus' treatise *On Beauty* and Porphyry's *Return of the Soul*, was for Augustine a highly exciting discovery of a new range of ideas and possible experiences, which gave promise of solving his intellectual difficulties and involved a strengthening asceticism in his way of life. That, and a feeling of elevation and of an ascent of the spirit is, however, not properly ecstasy.

This interpretation of the alleged mystical experiences is borne out by the earliest text referring to the matter and dating from within a few months of the occurrence.

> But lo! when certain books full to the brim, as Celsinus says, had wafted to us good things of Arabia, when they had let a very few drops of most precious unguent fall upon that meagre flame, they stirred up an incredible conflagration — incredible, Romanianus, incredible, and perhaps beyond even what you believe of me — what more shall I say? — beyond even what I would believe of myself. What honor, what human pomp, what desire for empty fame, what consolations or attractions of this mortal life could move me then? Swiftly did I begin to return entirely to myself. (*Against the Academics*, 2:5)

This passage is echoed closely in the *Confessions* apropos of his reading of the *Hortensius* of Cicero. As it would be idle from the language employed about that experience to suppose that there had been question of ecstasy or something mystical following on the

---

[14] See pp. 202 f.

reading of the *Hortensius*, so it would be to suppose the same for the later reading of the Neo-Platonists. Innumerable are the instances from ancient and modern literature, whether philosophical, religious, or literary, of books making such deep impression on men's lives, and the treatise of Plotinus *On Beauty* is only a little more likely to have such an effect than, say, the *Symposium* of Plato or even the *Somnium Scipionis* of Cicero. It may not be amiss, moreover, to add that some of the alleged echoes of Plotinus' *On Beauty* in the text just quoted, as also in the passages in the *Confessions* describing the alleged ecstasies, may belong as much to the stock in trade of general Platonic literature as to either Porphyry or Plotinus.

The reading of the Neo-Platonists, then, left Augustine in a state of spiritual elevation. The earlier exaltation induced by the reading of Cicero's *Hortensius* was far transcended. The materialist rationalism of the Manichees had slipped away from him for ever. The passing mood of scepticism had but sharpened his appetite for the spiritual doctrine which now flooded his intellect and overflowed into his emotions. Not long before this he had desired to form with his friends a community devoted entirely to the pursuit of philosophy: in this they may have been following the example of some Manichean friends at Rome, or even Plotinus himself, who had planned such a community.

> And many of us friends conferring about, and detesting the turbulent turmoils of human life, had debated and now almost resolved on living apart from business and the bustle of men. This was to be thus obtained: we were to bring whatever we might each procure, and make one household of all. [...] We thought that there might be some ten persons in this society, some of whom were very rich, especially Romanianus our townsman. [...] But when we began to consider whether the wives, which some of us already had, others hoped to have, would allow this, all that plan, which was being so well molded, fell to pieces. (6:24)

The desire for such a life was now even more compelling. This desire was later fostered by the example of Christian monasteries, and finally realized partly in his semi-philosophical semi-religious retreat in the country for some months before his baptism, and more fully in his religious settlement in Thagaste. What ended in a seminary, began as a philosophical project.

"Conversion" to philosophy was at this period not an uncommon thing.[15] Nock remarks:

> Any philosophy of the time set up a standard of values different from those of the world outside and could serve as a stimulus to a stern life, and therefore to something like conversion when it came to a man living carelessly. It is said that Polemo when drunk and garlanded went into Xenocrates's lecture-room, was moved to abandon his earlier ways, and devoted himself so eagerly to philosophy that he became next head of the school. Again, in one of Lucian's *Dialogues of Courtesans* (X), we read how a teacher of philosophy has forbidden Drose's lover to come to her, promising that his pupil would after training in hardship, be happy and virtuous. The philosophy which addressed itself to the world at large was a dogmatic philosophy seeking to save souls. (*Conversion*, p. 173)

This, then, was the stage to which the Neo-Platonist books had brought him. He aspired to a life not only free from worldly cares and preoccupations, but given wholly to the contemplation of the immaterial One, the Good, the Father. Such a life involved an ascetic purgation of the soul of all the unnecessary defilements which arose from its being imprisoned in the body. He could not expect that he would immediately be granted an ecstatic vision of the One; nor was it in fact granted him. He could aspire to it and make himself less unworthy of it: this he attempted to do. He had the assurance of the Neo-Platonists that, whereas the mass of mankind were incapable of this lofty contemplation and purgation and had to be led to God by the way of authority, a few, among whom he was one, could arrive at the Vision of the Father through reason alone. Such assurance he was later to call presumption.

---

[15] See A.D. Nock, *Conversion*, Oxford 1933.

10

NEO-PLATONISM FOR THE MANY: THE UNIVERSAL WAY

F OR A LONG TIME Augustine held the view that the Neo-Platonists, observing that the mass of men were incapable of raising themselves to a life of purgation and intellectual contemplation, supposed that there must be some Mediator between the Father and mankind, some commanding authority, some universal way of the soul's deliverance. They examined the claims of Christ, whom they judged to be an excellent man, but whom they rejected because of his birth of a virgin and death on a cross, and because Christianity, they felt, was destined to be wiped out in the persecutions that it encountered. The clearest text referring to this topic comes from the *City of God*: Porphyry is the Neo-Platonist who is exclusively mentioned:

> But Porphyry, being under the dominion of these envious powers [i.e., demons], whose influence he was at once ashamed of and afraid to throw off; refused to recognize that Christ is the Principle by whose Incarnation we are purified. [...] [This was] a great mystery, unintelligible to Porphyry's pride [...] And this we carnal and feeble men, liable to sin, and involved in the darkness of ignorance, could not possibly understand, unless we were cleansed and healed by Him, both by means of what we were [men], and of what we were not [righteous]. [...] You [Porphyry] say, indeed, that ignorance, and the numberless vices resulting from it, cannot be

removed by any mysteries, but only by the *patrikos nous*, that is, the Father's mind or intellect conscious of the Father's will. But that Christ is this mind you do not believe; for Him you despise on account of the body He took of a woman and the shame of the cross. [...] You [Porphyry] proclaim the Father and His Son, whom you call the Father's intellect or mind, and between these a third, by whom we suppose you mean the Holy Spirit. [...] In this, though your expressions are inaccurate, you do in some sort, and as through a veil, see what we should strive towards; but the incarnation of the unchangeable Son of God, whereby we are saved, and are enabled to reach the things we believe, or in part understand, this is what you refuse to recognize. You see in a fashion, although at a distance, although with filmy eye, the country in which we should abide; but the way to it you know not. Yet you believe in grace, for you say it is granted to few to reach God by virtue of intelligence. [...] You make no doubt that in this life a man cannot by any means attain to perfect wisdom. [...] Oh, had you but recognized the grace of God in Jesus Christ our Lord and that very incarnation of His, you might have seemed the brightest example of grace. But what am I doing? I know it is useless to speak to a dead man — useless, at least, so far as regards you, but perhaps not in vain for those who esteem you highly, and love you on account of their love of wisdom or curiosity about those arts which you ought not to have learned. [...] This is the vice of the proud. It is, forsooth, a degradation for learned men to pass from the school of Plato to the discipleship of Christ, who by His Spirit taught a fisherman to think and say: [there follow the opening words of the Prologue to St. John's Gospel]. [...] [They] are ashamed of the medicine, which could heal them. And, doing so, they secure not elevation, but a more disastrous fall.

Then comes Porphyry's account of his search for a universal way of delivering the soul:

[Porphyry] does not say that this way does not exist, but that this great boon and assistance [...] has not come to his

knowledge. And no wonder; for Porphyry lived in an age
when this universal way of the soul's deliverance — in other
words, the Christian religion — was exposed to the persecutions of idolaters and demon-worshippers, and earthly
rulers, that the number of martyrs or witnesses for the truth
might be completed and consecrated. [...] Porphyry, being
a witness of these persecutions, concluded that this way was
destined to a speedy extinction, and that it, therefore, was
not the universal way of the soul's deliverance, and did not
see that the very thing that thus moved him, and deterred
him from becoming a Christian, contributed to the confirmation and more effectual commendation of our religion.
(10:24-32. A.D. 415-417. Translated by Marcus Dods,
Nicene and Post-Nicene Fathers series.)

Although this is the clearest statement of Augustine's notions
on the Neo-Platonic search for a Mediator to lead the mass of mankind to the Father and their rejection of Christ, it is far from being the only one. It was a topic to which he often returned and it
was a topic which goes back to the time of his conversion.[1] One
can go further and say that this idea played a vital part in that conversion.

It is important to establish the connection of this topic, as
fully articulated in the *City of God,* with his actual conversion and
the works which he composed before his baptism. There is only
one convincing way of doing so and that, unfortunately, is to give
a selection of the relevant texts going back to the very beginning.
In this way the clear connection can be established, the various
elements in it demonstrated, its importance in Augustine's own
conversion made clear, and the source of its inspiration in Porphyry
made manifest. While one should not attach too much importance
to it, one might notice in passing the recurrence of identical or
similar phraseology in these passages.

---

[1] For a discussion of this topic see J. O'Meara, *op. cit.*, especially the notes. Cf. also the
author's "Neo-Platonism in the Conversion of Saint Augustine," *Dominican Studies*, Oct.-
Dec., 1950, pp. 331 ff., and "A Master-Motif in St. Augustine," *Actes du Premier Congrès
de la Fédération Internationale des Associations d'Etudes Classiques*, Paris, 1951, pp. 312ff.

There is, for example, a letter of 410 in which we read of:

that example of divine humility, which in the fullness of
time was furnished by our Lord Jesus Christ — that one
example before which, even in the mind of the most head-
strong and arrogant, all pride bends, breaks, and dies. The
Platonist school of philosophers felt it necessary to submit
with pious homage to Christ and to apprehend the Incarnate Word of God. Then flourished at Rome the school of
Plotinus which had as scholars many men of great acuteness and ability. But some of them were corrupted by curious inquiries into magic, and others, recognizing in the Lord
Jesus Christ the embodiment of Truth and Wisdom, passed
into his service. (*Letter* 118:17-33)

Here there is question not of Porphyry only but of other
Platonists as well. But who will deny that Porphyry is in Augustine's
eyes the most prominent member of the school of Plotinus, that
scholar of great acuteness and ability who was corrupted by curious inquiries into magic and did not recognize in Christ the embodiment of Truth and Wisdom?

And surely Porphyry was in Augustine's mind as he referred
to his favorite topic in *On the Trinity* (A.D. 400-416):

Therein is our true peace and firm bond of union with our
Creator, that we should be purified and reconciled through
the Mediator of life, as we had been polluted and alienated,
and so had departed from Him, through the mediator of
death. For as the Devil through pride led man through pride
to death; so Christ through lowliness led back man through
obedience to life. [...] [The Devil] puffs up man the more,
who is eager for power rather than righteousness, through
the pride of elation, or through false philosophy; or else en-
tangles him through sacrilegious rites, in which, while cast-
ing down headlong by deceit and illusion the minds of the
more curious and prouder sort, he holds him captive also to
magical trickery; he promises too the cleansing of the soul,
through those initiations which they call *teletai,* by trans-

forming himself into an angel of light, through divers machinations in signs and prodigies of lying. [...] In no wise therefore are souls cleansed and reconciled to God by sacrilegious imitations, or curious arts that are impious, or magical incantations; since the false mediator does not translate them to higher things, but rather blocks and cuts off the way thither through the affections, malignant in proportion as they are proud, which he inspires into those of his own company; which are not able to nourish the wings of virtue so as to fly upwards. (4:13,15, translated by A.W. Haddan, Nicene and Post-Nicene Fathers series.)

Next there comes a passage from the *Confessions*, where the topic is treated not only in its general aspect as referring to all mankind, but in its particular application to Augustine himself. It is a most significant text for the present purpose and will have to be quoted at length:

And You willed first to show me, how You resist the proud, but give grace to the humble, and by how great an act of Your mercy You had traced out to men the way of humility, in that Your Word was made flesh, and dwelt among men. You procured for me, by means of one puffed up with most unnatural pride certain books of the Platonists, translated from Greek into Latin. And in them I read, not indeed in the very words, but to the very same purpose, enforced by many and various reasons, that: "In the beginning was the Word and the Word was with God, and the Word was God." [Jn 1:1] [...] For I traced in those books, that it was in many and various ways said, that the Son "was in the form of the Father, and thought it not robbery to be equal with God," [Ph 2:6] because naturally He was the Same Substance. But that "He emptied Himself taking the form of a servant, being made in the likeness of men, and found in form as a man, humbled Himself and became obedient unto death, the death of the cross," [Ph 2:7-8] [...] these books do not have. [...] But such as are lifted up in the lofty walk of some would-be sublimer learning, do not hear Him saying "Learn of Me, for I am meek and lowly in heart." [Mt 11:29] "Although they knew God, yet they do not glorify Him as God, nor are thankful, but grow vain in their thoughts; and their foolish heart is darkened; professing that they were wise, they became fools." [Rm 1:21-22]

And therefore I read there also, that "they had changed the glory of Your incorruptible nature into idols and various shapes, into the likeness of the image of corruptible man, and birds, and beasts, and creeping things" [Rm 1:23]; namely into that Egyptian food, for which Esau lost his birthright, [...] turning in heart back towards Egypt. These things I found here, but I did not feed on them. [...] For it pleased You, O Lord, to take away the reproach of being younger from Jacob. [...] You called the Gentiles into Your inheritance. And I had come to You from among the Gentiles; and I set my mind upon the gold which You willed Your people to take from Egypt, seeing that it was Yours, wherever it was. And to the Athenians You said by Your Apostle, that "in You we live and move, as one of their own poets had said." [Ac 17:28] And truly these books came from Athens. [...]

And being admonished by them to return to myself, I entered into my inward self, You being my Guide, and I was able, for You had become my Helper. And I entered and beheld with the eye of my soul (such as it was), above the same eye of my soul, above my mind, the Light Unchangeable. [...] And You beat back the weakness of my sight, streaming forth Your beams of light upon me most strongly, and I trembled with love and awe. I perceived myself to be far off from You in the region of unlikeness, as if I heard Your voice from on high: "I am the food of grown men; grow, and you shall feed upon Me." [...]

And yet I did not press on to enjoy my God; but was borne up to You by Your beauty, and soon borne down from You by my own weight. This weight was carnal custom. Yet there dwelt with me a remembrance of You; nor did I doubt that there was One to Whom I might cling, but was not yet able to cling to You. [...] I saw Your invisible things made understandable by the things which are made. But I could not fix my gaze on this; and being struck back in my weakness, I was thrown again on my usual habits. [...]

Then I sought a way of obtaining strength, sufficient to enjoy You; and I did not find it, until I embraced that Mediator between God and men, the Man Christ Jesus, [...] calling unto me, and saying, "I am the way, the truth, and the life," and mingling that food which I was unable to receive, with our flesh [...] that Your wisdom might provide milk for our infant state. For I did not hold to my Lord Jesus Christ, I, humbled, to the Humble; nor did I know yet to where His infirmity would guide me. [...]

But having then read those books of the Platonists, and from them been taught to search for incorporeal truth, I saw Your invisible things, made understandable by those things which are made. [...] Of these things I was assured, yet too unsure to enjoy You. I prated as one well skilled; but had I not sought Your way in Christ our Savior, I would have proved to be, not skilled, but killed. For now I had begun to wish to seem wise, being filled with my own punishment, yet I did not mourn, but rather scorn, puffed up with knowledge. For where was that charity building upon the foundation of humility, which is Christ Jesus? Or when should these books teach it to me? Upon these, I believe, You therefore willed that I should fall, before I studied Your Scriptures, that it might be imprinted on my memory, how I was affected by them. Thus afterwards when my spirits were tamed through Your books, and my wounds touched by Your healing fingers, I might discern and distinguish between presumption and confession; between those who saw where they were to go, yet did not see the way, and the way that leads not only to behold but to dwell in the beatific country. [...] It is one thing, from the mountain's wooded top to see the land of peace, and to find no way to get there, and in vain to go through unpassable ways, opposed and beset by fugitives and deserters, under their captain the lion and the dragon [the Devil; cf. 1 P 5:8; Rv 12:9]; and it is another thing to keep on the way that leads there. (7:13-27)

Here we have a blend of his own preoccupation with the ascent of his own spirit and the salvation of all mankind, with the clear indication that at first he too did not accept Christ's Incarnation, but for a time followed the Neo-Platonists and, one can say, Porphyry in their pride. He too shared Porphyry's view that Christ was an excellent man, but that was all. The significance and importance of all this will appear presently.

The next relevant text is from *On the True Religion* (A.D. 386-390):

> If after so much outpouring of blood and burnings and crucifixions of martyrs the Churches spread but the more fruitfully even to the barbarians; if so many now embrace this way, that one time desert islands and the solitudes of many lands are filled, why do we still yawn listlessly from yesterday's inebriation, and seek guidance in the entrails of slaughtered cattle? Let those who hold that it is a good and desirable thing [to contemn the world and to submit the soul to God to be purged by virtue] recognize, and yield to God through whom all peoples have now been persuaded to believe. Let them bow down to Him; nor let them be prevented by curiosity or vainglory from seeing the difference between the proud conjectures of a few and the manifest salvation and reformation of mankind. (2:7)

A number of other texts can be given without comment:

> This much I now dare to say quite plainly to you that, if we keep with all steadfastness to the course which God has commanded us and we have undertaken to hold, we shall arrive by way of the Power and Wisdom of God at the Highest Principle of all things. [...] And truly then shall we despise those who scoff at the human nature taken by the most powerful, eternal and unchangeable Son of God, to be an exemplar and the first fruits of our salvation, and at his birth of a Virgin, and the other miracles recounted in his connection. [...] And death, the absolute flight and escape from this body, which before was feared, will be desired as the greatest boon. (*On the Greatness of the Soul* 76, A.D. 388)

For when we are puzzled by the obscurity of things, there is a twofold way which we follow, either "reason" or, at any rate "authority." Philosophy holds out the promise of a rational account; but few indeed are those whom it sets free. These it compels not only not to despise those mysteries, but alone to understand them as they need to be understood. True, and, so to speak, genuine Philosophy has no other task but to teach that the Beginning of all things is without beginning, and how great is the Intelligence which therein remains, and what without any deterioration emanated from thence in order to our salvation. The mysteries — worthy of all reverence, freeing, as they do, mankind through a convinced and unshakable Faith — proclaim this Beginning to be one God omnipotent, and to be the Tripotent Father, Son, and Holy Spirit. Moreover these mysteries proclaim also how great a matter it is that so great a God has deigned for our sakes to assume and wear even this body of our kind; and this, in proportion as it seems more vile, the fuller it is of mercy, and the further and more deeply removed from any pride of clever folk. [...]

Authority, however, is partly human, partly divine; but the true, solid and highest authority is that which is called divine. In this, one has to guard against the subtle wiles of the living creatures of the air [i.e. "demons"]. These have — through certain divinations and some teachings in matters pertaining to bodily senses — been very readily accustomed to deceive souls. [...] All these things with greater secrecy and firmness are committed to us by the sacred rites in which we are initiated, wherein the life of good men is most readily purged, not by the tortuous windings of dialectic but by the authority of the mysteries. (*On Order* 2:16,27, A.D. 386)

You, Alypius, have told us who it is that can point out Truth. For you said that only some Deity could reveal to man what Truth is. There has been nothing in our conversation which has given me more delight, nothing more profound, nothing more probable, and — if only that Deity be present to us, as I trust He is — nothing more true. For even the renowned Proteus is introduced as an image of Truth. Truth, I say, is represented in poetry as Proteus, whom no man can lay hold of, if being deceived by false images, he slacken or unloose the knots of comprehension. There are indeed such images which essay to deceive and make sport of us, even when we have already seized upon Truth and hold it, so to speak, within our hands. I cannot find words to express how highly I prize this benefit — namely that my most intimate friend agrees with me not only on human probabilities but also about religion itself. (*Against the Academics* 3:13, A.D. 386)

Finally:

But as to that which concerns erudition, doctrine and morals, since there have been very acute and very clever men who taught in their disputations that Aristotle and Plato agree with one another — at last after many generations and many conflicts there is strained out, as it were, one system of true Philosophy. For that Philosophy is not of this world — such a philosophy our sacred mysteries most justly detest — but of the other, intelligible, world. To this intelligible world that very subtle reasoning would never recall souls blinded by the manifold darkness of error and stained deeply with the slime of the body, had not the Most High God in a certain compassion for the masses bent and submitted the authority of the Divine Intellect even to the human body itself. By whose precepts and deeds souls are awakened and are able, without the strife of disputation, to return to themselves, and see once again their Fatherland. (*Ibid.*, 3:42)[2]

One can hardly deny the identity of the theme, so many instances of which have just been given, from its first occurrence in a work dating from the time of his conversion, through all the other

---

[2] Augustine connects Porphyry explicitly with the *Soliloquies*, a work contemporary with the *Against the Academics*, in *Retractations* 1:4:3. See J. O'Meara, *op. cit.*, p. 181 f.

works mentioned, right up to its explicit and emphatic association with Porphyry alone of all Neo-Platonists in the *City of God*. There the theme is connected by Augustine specifically with Porphyry's *Return of the Soul*, a work which both Courcelle and Theiler, for example, are agreed in holding to have been one of the Neo-Platonist books read by Augustine before his conversion. The evidence of the series of passages just quoted, apart from some further detailed evidence, points strongly to the conclusion that as in the *City of God*, so in the *Against the Academics*, and the *Confessions*, Porphyry is *the* Neo-Platonist associated with this theme in Augustine's mind. If Augustine does not say of Plotinus in the *City of God* that he posited the necessity of a Mediator, to purify and elevate men and lead them, not by reason, but by the universal way of authority, to the Father; and that Plotinus rejected Christ as that Mediator because of his taking human flesh, and because the Christian religion was through persecution doomed to extinction; and that Plotinus fell into this error because of his pride and subjection to demons — neither does he do so in the *Against the Academics* or the *Confessions*. Moreover, he could hardly have done so; for the topic fits Plotinus not at all, but Porphyry down to the last detail.

One should not insist too much on the point, but it is only right that Porphyry's part in Augustine's conversion should be clearly recognized. A careful study of the texts quoted will, perhaps, compel belief that in all of them and particularly the text from the *Confessions*, Augustine was thinking of Porphyry — but not to the exclusion of others. It is very unlikely that a name associated emphatically above all others with a clearly recognizable topic when it is presented in one place should have no connection whatever with that topic when it occurs in another place. When the topic occurs in the *Confessions* it is not, indeed, explicitly related to Porphyry. Significantly, nevertheless, the topic is not related to any other author — not to Plotinus, for instance — but rather to the "Platonists" and that emphatically, three times.[3] It would be entirely unreasonable to conclude that Porphyry was excluded.

There are in any case among many others two indications in the passage from the *Confessions*, which strongly suggest that Porphyry was in Augustine's mind.

The first indication comes from the phrase: "You procured for me, by means of one puffed up with most unnatural pride certain books of the Platonists, translated from Greek into Latin"; subsequently we are told that Marius Victorinus was the translator. In the context of the theme of this passage the phrase almost certainly means that the "one puffed up with most unnatural pride" is Porphyry. For Augustine the proud man *par excellence* is Porphyry. He speaks of him in this way always. We know that Victorinus did translate some of Porphyry into Latin: his *Isagoge*. We have no certain knowledge that he translated one word of Plotinus, although he may well have done so. We know, moreover, that Victorinus, as Porphyry before him, had paid cult to demons. We should not be put off by the words: "You procured for me by means of one…," as if they implied that the books were given to Augustine by someone who was not their author. Augustine is addressing God and stressing that in His Providence He was using a proud instrument for Augustine's good: "You procured for me, by means of one puffed up with most unnatural pride…." Courcelle's suggestion that Mallius Theodorus is meant, is directly contradicted by all the evidence and has been rightly dismissed by Theiler.

The second arises from the words: "And therefore I read there also, that they had changed the glory of Your incorruptible nature into idols and various shapes. […] I set my mind upon the gold which You willed Your people to take from Egypt, seeing that it was Yours, wherever it was." The people in question, whom he also characterizes as "Egyptians," are clearly the Neo-Platonists. This is confirmed by his repetition of the same context in his *On the Trinity* where, however, he mentions the Platonists by name and

---

adds, significantly, the words: "They fell into the power of demons that deceived them." Exactly the same thing is found in his *On Christian Doctrine*, where again he adds that they perversely and injuriously abused in the cult of demons what truth was vouchsafed to them. As we have seen, Porphyry is *the* Neo-Platonist whom Augustine castigates for his cult of demons.

It has been suggested that the exclusive mention of Porphyry in the *City of God* is due to the fact that, as Augustine was there arguing against the errors of the Neo-Platonists, he naturally directed his attention against that Neo-Platonist who most attacked Christianity — Porphyry. It is also suggested that as the "Vision of Ostia," about which more will be said later, shows the influence of Plotinus, so the passage from the *Confessions* quoted in this chapter is more likely to refer to him than Porphyry.

But the argument here does not rest only on the exclusive mention of Porphyry in the *City of God*: it rests on all the texts and such parts of them as can be shown to refer to Porphyry and not to Plotinus. What is said of Porphyry in the *City of God* could not be said of Plotinus at all — and that is a capital point — and could be said if not of Porphyry only, at least of Porphyry especially. Again so little is Augustine acquainted with Porphyry's famous *Against the Christians* that Courcelle[4] asserts that he never knew it at all: this seems improbable, and Dyroff's view that he did know it seems sound — but at least one cannot presume too easily on his thinking of Porphyry as the principal anti-Christian controversialist. And as for the "Vision of Ostia" — even if the influence of Plotinus is there dominant, it is clearly a fallacy to argue that on that account alone it is probable that his influence dominates in the passage from the *Confessions*: the two episodes differ greatly. In point of fact Theiler shows good reason for denying that in the "Vision of Ostia" the influence of Plotinus is dominant.

Finally no scholar will now deny that Augustine read Porphyry's *Return of the Soul* in 386. This is the very book men-

---

[4] *Les Lettres grecque en Occident*, p. 165. P. Beatrice believes that no such title or work existed, and that the reference is to the *Philosophy from Oracles* (*Return of the Soul*).

tioned by name in the *City of God* in the context of the passage quoted. It would be hazardous to deny that it is behind every one of the passages mentioned in this chapter, including the passage from the *Confessions*.

Augustine, as it happens, shows a greater acquaintance with Porphyry than with any other Neo-Platonist. As at the beginning of his writing career when he projected a series of works introductory to philosophy, so at the end, when he wrote his *Retractations* he followed, perhaps, the example set by Porphyry. In adopting, except for his first few works, the dialogue form of question and answer (or "catechism dialogue"), he may also have imitated Porphyry. In later life at least he knew Porphyry's *Life of Plotinus*, *Philosophy from Oracles* and *Letter to Anebo* (an Egyptian priest), and may have known Porphyry's work proving that the philosophies of Plato and Aristotle were really the same.[5]

Be that as it may the important thing here is to keep to what Augustine says in the *Confessions*. He read certain books of the Neo-Platonists — Plotinus and Porphyry. In *On the Happy Life* there is an uncertain reading which *may* mention Plotinus only. But apart from the uncertainty of the reading, and the fact that the mention of Plotinus is not necessarily exclusive of Porphyry, Plotinus and Porphyry — because of their relation as master and principal interpreter — can easily be confused. Henry, who of all others at one time would exclude Porphyry from having anything to do with the conversion of Augustine, himself cites a case in Macrobius' *Saturnalia* where something is attributed to Plotinus where clearly it should have been attributed to Porphyry.[6]

Augustine spoke the literal truth when he said — not as Courcelle supposes, that Ambrose discovered Neo-Platonism to

[5] *Against the Academics* 3:42, quoted on p. 148.

[6] *Plotin et l'Occident*, p. 154 ff.

him; nor as Henry supposed, that he read Plotinus only; nor as Theiler supposed, that he read Porphyry only — that he discovered Neo-Platonism through his own reading of certain books of the Platonists, who were, one may confidently say, Porphyry and Plotinus.

Plotinus' essay *On Beauty* informed him of a spiritual Trinity and dispelled forever his Manichean notions of a corporeal deity. Other essays of Plotinus equally dispelled his Manichean view of evil as a substance. Plotinus, moreover, summoned him from amongst the many to aspire through purgation and the higher operation of his intelligence to union with the One.

Porphyry's *Return of the Soul* also spoke to him of the Trinity and of purgation and union. Further it alone told him of the necessity of a Mediator for the many, and encouraged his old Manichean prejudices against the birth of Christ of a virgin and his death on a cross, and in favor of demonology.

For an interval, then, however short, Augustine followed Porphyry in his pride: "Had I not sought Your way in Christ our Savior, I would have proved to be, not skilled, but killed. For now I had begun to wish to seem wise, […] puffed up with knowledge. Upon these [books], I believe, You therefore willed that I should fall before I studied Your Scriptures, that it might be imprinted on my memory, how I was affected by them [that is, made proud]. Thus afterwards when my spirits were tamed through Your books, and my wounds touched by Your healing fingers, I might discern and distinguish between presumption and confession." The interval of Platonist presumption, when Augustine felt himself one of the few, and rejected Christ as the way of authority for the many, was quickly succeeded by submission to Christ and a lifetime of confession. The full meaning of the title *Confessions* can be found especially here.

At this point, however, he was still a Platonist full of presumption.

11

SUBMISSION OF INTELLECT[1]

T HE INTERVAL BETWEEN Augustine's "conversion" to Neo-Platonism, and his conversion to Christianity cannot have been great. His final surrender to the latter came, it would appear, about the first week in the August of 386,[2] and this was preceded by a succession of events, each of them bringing him closer and closer to the acceptance of Christ. Although one cannot date precisely his reading of the Neo-Platonist books, the generally chronological order of the account in the *Confessions* and the impression one gets from the text itself suggests that his purely Neo-Platonic period was of short duration.

His intellectual submission to Christianity was occasioned by his reading of St. Paul, which was due to his curiosity to discover if there was accord between St. Paul's teaching and the teaching of the Neo-Platonists:

> Very eagerly then I seized the sacred writings of Your Spirit, and chiefly the Apostle Paul. Then those difficulties vanished away, in which he once seemed to me to contradict himself, and the text of his discourse disagreed with the testimonies of the Law and the Prophets. And the face of that

---

[1] The separate treatment of intellect and will in this and the following chapter is for convenience in exposition.

[2] See Courcelle, *Recherches*, p. 202.

> pure word appeared to me one and the same; and I learned
> to rejoice with trembling. So I began; and whatever truth I
> read in those other books, I found here amid the praise of
> Your grace. (*Confessions* 7:27)

From this account, and another which will be examined later,[3] we gather that Augustine on his own initiative thought of comparing the Neo-Platonist teaching with St. Paul. No sooner had the idea occurred to him than he put it into execution.

We cannot presume to account for *why* the idea occurred to him at all. We must take his word for it that it did. He himself simply says that the idea came casually to him: "All that I did — let me admit it — was to look back, from the end of a journey, as it were, to that religion...." There would of course be nothing extraordinary in such a thought: after all, had he not been a Christian catechumen for most of his early life and become so again only recently? Had he not been influenced towards Christianity by Ambrose? On a previous similar occasion — when he had read Cicero's *Hortensius* in his nineteenth year — had he not likewise turned to the Scripture?

But perhaps a key to the situation lies in his having been for most of his adult life a Manichee. To the Manichees the Epistles of the Apostle Paul represented the best and purest part of the Christian Scriptures. To them he seemed to maintain their Manichean distinction between the principles of Good and Evil, the spirit and the flesh, the New and the Old Law. They supposed, it is true, that some of his writings had been corrupted by the Christians for their own purposes. But in the main they respected him greatly. Later in Augustine's controversial writings against the Manichees, for example, he frequently quoted texts from St. Paul used by Faustus, or Fortunatus, or Felix, or Secundinus.

Hence, if there occurred to him this idea to confront the Neo-Platonists with the Scriptures, it became in effect, whether we consider his Christian background or more particularly his Manichean

---

[3] See p. 190 f.

background, a question of turning to St. Paul. Then he discovered that St. Paul, contrary to what the Manichees had said, did not contradict himself, and that his text agreed with the testimonies of the Law and the Prophets.

It may be helpful to remark that one of the self-contradictions which the Manichees discovered in St. Paul related to the nature of Christ. In the Epistle to the Romans (1:3) he speaks of him as born "of the seed of David, according to the flesh." But in a later text he says: "Wherefore henceforth, we know no man according to the flesh. And if we have known Christ according to the flesh, now we know him so no longer" (2 Cor 5:16). The Manichees contended that he did right in contradicting himself. They held with him in preferring the second view, while the Christians laid stress on the Word made flesh. The Manichees asserted that Paul's teaching on Christ: "Who being in the form of God, thought it not robbery to be equal to God, but emptied himself, becoming obedient unto death, even to the death of the cross" (Ph 2:6-7) was the true, but now forgotten, teaching of the Church. But in their teaching he had only the *appearance* of being flesh — he feigned to die, to show men that death and the escape of the divine spirit from the flesh was a good thing: he showed the way through death to life.

In the *Confessions* Augustine describes how the Neo-Platonist books spoke to him of the Father, Word and Holy Spirit and of the necessity of a Mediator to lead all men to the Father. In St. Paul he found the same doctrine. The effect on him, of course, was a far greater appreciation of St. Paul, not now, however, in the Manichean interpretation of his teaching, but, as a result of the preaching of St. Ambrose, more in a Christian sense. At this point the lessons he had learned from the preaching of St. Ambrose proved decisive: he now saw that St. Paul did not contradict himself: that his words could be reconciled in a Christian sense and the text of his discourse fit in with the testimonies of the Law and the Prophets.

Thus at this critical stage in the account of Augustine's conversion, Manicheism again claims attention. The *Confessions* itself has made this imperative. Thirteen chapters of book seven are given to the description of the effect on him of his reading of the Neo-Platonist books. In those thirteen chapters, nearly one-third of the account is given up solely to the consideration of how he had eventually solved his Manichean difficulties about the possibility of a spiritual God, the problem of evil, and some theories, held by himself and Alypius, as to the nature of Christ. The good bishop had, doubtless, a polemical purpose in this — but he had a personal reason also for thus dwelling once again upon Manicheism at this stage.

For it was Neo-Platonism that finally delivered him from the two persisting difficulties which had been so deeply ingrained in him by the Manichean teaching of a material God and a principle of Evil. The Neo-Platonist books rid his mind forever of these difficulties and we shall hear no more of them. The Neo-Platonist teaching bridged the gap between a material Manicheism and a spiritual Christianity. His conversion was not from a recent scepticism, which was both superficial and passing, nor from indifference, of which he was psychologically incapable, but from Manicheism and Manicheism only. It is only right, then, that it should reappear in the end to be vanquished for ever.

There are other reasons for its reappearance. Neo-Platonism, or at least that later and less pure version of Plotinus' teaching represented in Porphyry, while being radically opposed to Manicheism, found common cause with it in particular matters in its opposition to Christianity. One important instance is their common opposition to a real Incarnation and a real death of Christ upon the cross. They shared a dislike for the body and a contemptuous disdain for religious "beliefs" while at the same time paying cult to demons.

What more natural, then, than that he should think of them both together in this hour of crisis, when the immaterialism of the one helped him to dismiss the materialism of the other, and when he rejected both together for their pride and superstition?

❧❧❧

Manicheism was to prove an even greater obstacle in the last outstanding difficulty, as he saw it, to his submission to Christianity — the obligation to be chaste. His Manichean period had given him exaggerated notions of standards in chastity. It was not that Christianity was content with less in this matter; but rather that it made less of a fetish of it. For all the frailties of their Elect, and the large concessions made to their Auditors, the Manichees preached in season and out an exaggerated observance of bodily chastity. Their whole doctrine as it revealed itself in practice concentrated on this one point: the evil of reproduction and everything connected therewith. Nor did Neo-Platonism with its emphasis on ascetical purgation in any way tend to counteract the influence of Manicheism in this regard.

His difficulty was further aggravated by his desire to lead a life of philosophy and chastity in community with others. For him Christian chastity seemed almost to demand evangelical chastity. Just as his acceptance of Christ, when it came, was total and without any reserve, so had to be his acceptance of chastity. Here can be seen clearly something of his true character. He was essentially ambitious in his ideals. Whether it was a question of prowess at lessons or play or wickedness when he was young, of Manicheism in his twenties, of worldly success and an improving marriage in his early thirties, or now of philosophy and chastity, the highest ideal was for him the only possible one. He had made up his mind, even before he accepted Christ, to live a life of philosophy in community. Now he was confronted with the challenge of the strictest chastity. The pattern of Augustine's later life was set even before he was converted: there was afterwards no sudden, unexpected or incomprehensible change.

At this point Augustine had arrived at the stage described in his own words:

> I was hedged round about on all sides by You. Of Your eternal life I was now certain, though I saw it in a figure and as through a glass. [cf. 1 Cor 13:12] Yet I had ceased to doubt that there was an incorruptible substance, the source of all

other substance; *nor did I now desire to be more certain of You,
but more steadfast in You.*
The Way, the Savior Himself, well pleased me, but as yet I
shrank from going through its narrow gate. (8:1)

As yet, however, although he saw far enough to know that
he could accept Christ in the Incarnation and chastity as an ideal,
he had fully accepted neither the one nor the other. He was now
in that harrowing but common state of knowing not only what he
ought to do but also that he would do it, and yet feeling himself
unable to take the final step. To a man in such a condition the
decision to do what he knows he will do may be slow in coming;
but when it comes it is taken quickly and sometimes without even
a last convulsion, and the change is radical. It is as if day followed
night, or, to use a simile employed by both Augustine and Newman,
like coming into port after a rough sea. It is as if, the intellect being satisfied, the exhausted will were building up reserves of
strength for the final hour of travail.

The mention of Newman prompts one to instance his experience as some help in understanding that of Augustine in this last
difficult stage. Newman and Augustine differed in many things —
the one was a born celibate who, according to himself, had a weak
hold on material things and wished to be converted alone without the company of others; the other had loved women, and, again
according to himself, had too strong a hold on things material, and
was quite willing to lead others to conversion along with him. Their
conversions, moreover, were not the same in kind; for Anglicanism
and Manicheism are very far indeed from being alike, and while
Augustine had long ceased to be a Manichee in persuasion before
he was converted, Newman claims to have passed directly from the
one stage to the other. Nevertheless the words of the one, describing as they do in language fully comprehensible to us an experience which had after all many points of comparison with that of

the other, may help us to gain a greater insight into Augustine's mental experiences and developments in the few difficult weeks before his conversion.

If one considers the nature of the documents even, the *Confessions* and the *Apologia*, one notices, of course, the element of defense in both: Newman writing twenty years after the event to justify his transfer of allegiance from the Church of England to the Church of Rome; Augustine writing some fourteen years after the event to justify his transfer of allegiance from the Church of Mani to the Church of Christ. Augustine could have used almost the very words which Newman used of himself; "a man, who had written strongly against a cause, and had collected a party round him by virtue of such writings, gradually faltered in his opposition to it, unsaid his words, threw his friends into perplexity and their proceedings into confusion, and ended by passing over to the side of those whom he had so vigorously denounced."[4] The same necessity that determined the topics of the *Apologia* impelled Augustine to elaborate the importance of the Neo-Platonic immaterialism in his abandonment of Manichean materialism, and the absolute importance of his acceptance of the Word made flesh.

Augustine too, *mutatis mutandis*, could have said:

> I will draw out, as far as may be, the history of my mind; I will state the point at which I began, in what external suggestion or accident each opinion had its rise, how far and how they developed from within, how they grew, were modified, were combined, were in collision with each other, and were changed; again how I conducted myself towards them, and how, and how far, and for how long a time, I thought I could hold them consistently. I must show, — what is the very truth, — that the doctrines which I held, and have held for so many years, have been taught me (speaking humanly) partly by the suggestions of Protestant friends, partly by the teaching of books, and partly by the

---

4 *Apologia pro vita sua*, Ed. Longmans, 1924, p. vi.

action of my own mind: and thus I shall account for that phenomenon which to so many seems so wonderful, that I should have left "my kindred and my father's house" for a Church from which once I turned away with dread. (*Apologia*, xxiv-xxv)

It is interesting to note that both fell under the spell of a book in their teens. For Augustine it was Cicero's *Hortensius* with its inculcation of the pursuit of wisdom; for Newman it was a work of William Romaine's. Curiously enough, Newman also betrays a vagueness — similar to that which we have seen in Augustine — even about something that affected him deeply: "When I was fifteen, (in the autumn of 1816,) a great change of thought took place in me. I fell under the influences of a definite Creed, and received into my intellect impressions of dogma, which, through God's mercy, have never been effaced or obscured. [...] One of the first books I read was a work of Romaine's; I neither recollect the title nor the contents, except one doctrine, which of course I do not include among those which I believe to have come from a divine source, viz. the doctrine of final perseverance. I received it at once, and believed that the inward conversion of which I was conscious, (and of which I still am more certain than that I have hands and feet,) would last into the next life, and that I was elected to eternal glory. I have no consciousness that this belief had any tendency whatever to lead me to be careless about pleasing God. I retained it till the age of twenty-one, when it gradually faded away" (4). The impression of the *Hortensius* likewise faded from Augustine's mind.

Both men had, at any rate, in their early days, what Newman calls "Blessings of friends, which to my door *unasked, unhoped,* have come" (15). Both had for a time a belief in demons, "a middle race," as Newman calls them, "neither in heaven, nor in hell; partially fallen, capricious, wayward; noble or crafty, benevolent or malicious, as the case might be. These beings gave a sort of inspiration or intelligence to races, nations, and classes of men. Hence the action of bodies politic and associations, which is often so different from that of the individuals who compose them" (28-29). Both, from being rather intolerant of miracles and such like, ended by being tolerant. As Newman accepted unquestioning the Protestant account of what Rome believed, so Augustine had the doctrine of the Christians from the followers of Mani. Each had a fundamental difficulty to overcome before he could be converted: for Newman it was what he believed to be the Roman cult of the Virgin; for Augustine it was the Christian belief in a spiritual God.

Both seemed to have had a sense of mission — an obligation to take the initiative, and so not withhold from their friends the example at least of their courage and integrity. People around them responded to that sense. If Newman felt sure that he could not die, when stricken with fever at Leonforte, until he had answered the call: *exoriare aliquis* (arise, some avenger) — so could a bishop say to Monica: "It is not possible that the son of these tears should perish." Men felt that these were men of destiny.

Being leaders and men of destiny, they were both capable of a certain fierceness in expression and in action. Of Newman Blanco White was to say: "my heart feels a pang at the recollection of the affectionate and mutual friendship between that excellent man and myself; a friendship, which his principles of orthodoxy could not allow him to continue in regard to one, whom he now regards as inevitably doomed to eternal perdition. Such is the venomous character of orthodoxy. What mischief must it create in a bad heart and narrow mind, when it can work so effectually for evil, in one of the most benevolent of bosoms, and one of the ablest of minds, in the amiable, the intellectual, the refined John Henry Newman!" (48). Similar words were written of Augustine during his life and even since his death. Newman compelled no Donatists to join with him, had no mistress to dismiss, nor did he forsake and cheat his mother at her prayers. But there were actions of his that were judged as hardly.

Augustine too had endured a long *malaise*, a period of moral sickness when he was ill with suspense and able neither to acquiesce in one religion nor go to another, to be content with Mani or throw in his lot with Christ. Newman's words illustrate very well Augustine's somewhat sceptical complaint that having been deceived in Manicheism he feared to be deceived a second time: "My difficulty was this: I had been deceived greatly once; how could I be sure that I was not deceived a second time? I thought myself right then; how was I to be certain that I was right now? How many years had I thought myself sure of what I now rejected? how could I ever again have confidence in myself? As in 1840 I listened to the rising doubt in favour of Rome, now I listened to the waning doubt in favour of the Anglican Church. To be certain is to know that one knows; what inward test had I, that I should not change again, after that I had become a Catholic? I had still apprehension of this, though I thought a time would come, when it would depart" (228). With Augustine also the changes that happened resulted not from outside influences, but from the working of his own mind, and the accidents about him: for no one tried to bully him into the course along which he followed; nor did any books in themselves decide his conversion. He too saw the hand of Providence in apparent misfortunes, when he was driven to take a course of action which otherwise he had feared to take: for Augustine it was some chest trouble which compelled him to give up his teaching in Milan, a circumstance which, he admits, had some influence on his withdrawal to a purely religious and philosophic life; for Newman it was the sudden outburst of indignation caused by his famous Tract: by it he was delivered, as he says, "from an impossible position in the future." What both might have feared to bring about of their own volition was welcomed by both in the end.

There came a time, however, in both their lives when the weariness of waiting and sickness of delayed hope were suddenly and rudely broken into by the reading of certain books. In Newman's case it happened as follows:

> The Long Vacation of 1839 began early. [...] I was returning, for the Vacation, to the course of reading which I had many years before chosen as especially my own. I have no reason to suppose that the thoughts of Rome came across my mind at all. About the middle of June I began to study and master the history of the Monophysites. I was absorbed

in the doctrinal question. This was from about June 13th to August 30th. It was during this course of reading that for the first time a doubt came upon me of the tenableness of Anglicanism. I recollect on the 30th of July mentioning to a friend, whom I had accidentally met, how remarkable the history was; but by the end of August I was seriously alarmed. [...] I found, as it seemed to me, Christendom of the sixteenth and the nineteenth centuries reflected. I saw my face in that mirror, and I was a Monophysite. The Church of the *Via Media* was in the position of the Oriental communion, Rome was where she now is; and the Protestants were the Eutychians. Of all passages of history, since history has been, who would have thought of going to the sayings and doings of old Eutyches, that *delirus senex*, as (I think) Petavius calls him, and the enormities of the unprincipled Dioscorus, in order to be converted to Rome! (114)[5]

Who, we might ask, would have thought of Augustine's going to the anti-Christian Porphyry — or for that matter Plotinus — again some time in the summer, but of 386, in order to be converted to Christianity! Yet so it was.

Newman too — and the coincidence is curious — was thinking of the appalling state in which the mass of mankind was, "the greatness and littleness of man, his far-reaching aims, his short duration, the curtain hung over his futurity, the disappointments of life, the defeat of good, the success of evil, physical pain, mental anguish, the prevalence and intensity of sin, the pervading idolatries, the corruptions, the dreary hopeless irreligion, that condition of the whole race, so fearfully yet exactly described in the Apostle's words, 'having no hope and without God in the world'" (242). Newman also decided that some way of authority, a power invested with the prerogative of infallibility, was necessary to deliver men from the evil plight in which they find themselves. His words are well in the tradition of Platonism: "She [the Church] has it in charge to rescue human nature from its misery, but not

---

[5] *delirus senex*: crazy old man.

simply by restoring it on its own level, but by lifting it up to a higher level than its own. She recognizes in it real moral excellence though degraded, but she cannot set it free from earth except by exalting it towards heaven" (247-248).

As Augustine, so Newman felt drawn to living in community, which he did, again as Augustine, both before and after his conversion. To the periods of Cassiciacum and Thagaste correspond in some way those of Littlemore and Birmingham. Neither of them, again, could really say that he had been converted until it was almost over, although both had little doubt at a relatively early stage as to what would be the outcome. In Newman's words: "Certitude is a reflex action; it is to know that one knows. Of that I believe I was not possessed, till close upon my reception into the Catholic Church. Again, a practical, effective doubt is a point too, but who can easily ascertain it for himself? Who can determine when it is, that the scales in the balance of opinion begin to turn, and what was a greater probability in behalf of a belief becomes a positive doubt against it?" (216). And again: "I felt altogether the force of the maxim of St. Ambrose, "Non in dialectica complacuit Deo salvum facere populum suum;" — I had a great dislike of paper logic. For myself, it was not logic that carried me on; as well might one say that the quicksilver in the barometer changes the weather. It is the concrete being that reasons; pass a number of years, and I find my mind in a new place; how? the whole man moves; paper logic is but the record of it. All the logic in the world would not have made me move faster towards Rome than I did; as well might you say that I have arrived at the end of my journey, because I see the village church before me, as venture to assert that the miles, over which my soul had to pass before it got to Rome, could be annihilated, even though I had been in possession of some far clearer view than I then had, that Rome was my ultimate destination. Great acts take time" (169).[6] There is little of this that is not true of Augustine's conversion too. It helps also, perhaps, to

---

[6] *Non in dialectica complacuit Deo salvum facere populum suum:* Not by means of logic was God pleased to save His people.

avoid overestimating the purely intellectual or "logical" element in Augustine's acceptance of Christianity.

In point of fact conversion came for both of them not in the assent to propositions but in the acceptance of an Authority which guaranteed the truth of mysteries which they could never be expected to understand. Newman had been impressed by the insistence in Butler's *Analogy* on a visible Church, the oracle of truth and a pattern of sanctity. He had himself felt the need for some such authority if men were to be saved. He discovered that logical arguments brought one probability, but then that "the argument from Probability, in the matter of religion, became an argument from Personality, which in fact is one form of the argument from Authority" (19). He illustrates the ultimate role of Authority in his own conversion: "People say that the doctrine of Transubstantiation is difficult to believe; I did not believe the doctrine till I was a Catholic. I had no difficulty in believing it, as soon as I believed that the Catholic Roman Church was the oracle of God, and that she had declared this doctrine to be part of the original revelation" (239). For Augustine, too, conversion was ultimately not a question of understanding, but of submission.

And now, to anticipate the account of the final stage of Augustine's conversion, the comparison may be pursued through a number of quite surprising details. It is hardly likely that Newman should have modelled either his conversion or his account of it on the *Confessions* of Augustine. There may, of course, have been echoes of it in his mind; but the similarity in the experience (allowing for the differences also) is sufficient explanation for the similarity in the occurrences themselves and even the methods and expressions used in describing them. At any rate the parallel is strikingly close.

En passant it may be remarked that one of the difficulties for the modern reader of the *Confessions* is the reduction of the rhetorical, or perhaps mystical, to a bald account of what actually took place. We are told of visions and appearances and voices. What are we to believe? How much can we suppose to be rhetorical or the customary technique of edifying hagiography? We hesitate to believe that all that Augustine says is plain unadorned truth, that, for example, he did see a vision of Continence — and yet at this remove of time and change in outlook and difference of person, we cannot be sure that all such things are but the instruments of literary device.

There is no such difficulty with Newman. He too conjures up visions and voices, and "a spirit rising from the troubled waters of the old world, with the shape and lineaments of the new" (115); he speaks of ghosts and the heavens opening and closing again and sudden visitations, and of a stranger from the bank warning him in a voice of authority and an earnest tone, and then becoming silent. The reader is in no doubt that Newman is but using a figure of speech. When he writes: "I had got but a little way in my work, when my trouble returned to me. The ghost had come a second time," we know exactly what he means. On the whole one can have the same confidence in interpreting similar descriptions in the *Confessions* in the same way.

To resume — perhaps the most surprising point of comparison between the two conversions is outlined, on Newman's side, in the following description: he had just recounted how during the course of a vacation's reading he was seriously alarmed by his first doubt about Anglicanism:

> Hardly had I brought my course of reading to a close, when the *Dublin Review* of that same August was put into my hands, by friends who were more favourable to the cause of Rome than I was myself. There was an article in it on the "Anglican Claim" by Dr. Wiseman. This was about the middle of September. It was on the Donatists, with an application to Anglicanism. I read it, and did not see much in it. [...] But my friend [...] pointed out the palmary words of St. Augustine, which were contained in one of the extracts made in the *Review*, and which had escaped my observation. "Securus judicat orbis terrarum." He repeated these words again and again, and, when he was gone, they kept ringing in my ears. [...] Who can account for the impressions which are made on him? For a mere sentence, the words of St. Au-

gustine, struck me with a power which I never had felt from any words before. To take a familiar instance, they were like the "Turn again Whittington" of the chime; or, to take a more serious one, they were like the "Tolle, lege, — Tolle, lege," of the child, which converted St. Augustine himself. "Securus judicat orbis terrarum!" By those great words of the ancient Father, interpreting and summing up the long and varied course of ecclesiastical history, the theory of the *Via Media* was absolutely pulverized.

I became excited at the view thus opened upon me. I was just starting on a round of visits; and I mentioned my state of mind to two most intimate friends: I think to no others. After a while, I got calm, and at length the vivid impression upon my imagination faded away. What I thought about it on reflection, I will attempt to describe presently. I had to determine its logical value, and its bearing upon my duty. Meanwhile, so far as this was certain, — I had seen the shadow of a hand upon the wall. [...] He who has seen a ghost, cannot be as if he had never seen it. The heavens had opened and closed again. The thought for the moment had been, "The Church of Rome will be found right after all;" and then it had vanished. [...] What gain is it to please the world, to please the great, nay even to please those whom we love, [...] to be applauded, admired, courted, followed, — compared with this one aim, of not being disobedient to a heavenly vision? (116-118)[7]

Newman himself has suggested the comparison of this scene with the *tolle lege* of Augustine's own conversion. It must be admitted that the comparison is close enough. We have the sympathetic presence of friends in the background, interested in and concerned with what is happening to the protagonist; the providential invitation to read a text; the words piercing straight to the heart, to convey the solution or to indicate it in a passage from St. Paul; the dramatic disappearance of all difficulties, the heightened

---

[7] *Securus judicat orbis terrarum:* The world judges with assurance [that they are not good men who, in whatever part of the world, separate themselves from the rest of the world.]

emotion and clarity of vision; and then the eventual calm and the toning down to common day. But it was a different day; for all was changed utterly.

No one nowadays will have difficulty in deciding what is historical in Newman's narrative and what is not. He will not deny that the words were read, that their effect on his mind and emotions was extraordinary, and that a lasting impression of the clarity of his perception and the heightening of his emotions remained with him. The point to be emphasized here is that these three items are historical; the words, the perception, and the heightened emotion. Was it the same in Augustine's case?

Briefly to complete the comparison, one may be allowed to point out that as Augustine, so Newman claimed that with his conversion came immediately "perfect peace and contentment of mind." Not that he never had difficulties — for any honest thinking man who yields to revelation will always find a tension between his reason and his belief: a tension which can benefit both the one and the other. In the cases of both men one can at least judge the sincerity of their conversions or of their descriptions of how these things happened from their acts. As Newman says: "Speak by acts." To both men conversion did seem, as it were, the "coming into port after a rough sea."

To return to Augustine alone — at this point he felt convinced of the truth of Christianity, but as yet could not bring himself to accept it or practice the chastity it demanded. The intellect was satisfied, but the will was inert. Providence, however, soon brought his will little by little through a succession of episodes to the verge of action, until finally it needed but the smallest push to make it act.

He decided to consult Simplicianus, an old priest, acquainted with Neo-Platonism, about his present state and try to discover the "best way for one in my case to walk in Your paths" (8:1). Augustine had begun to feel unhappy merely in not being a Christian:

he felt a great loneliness when he saw Christians fill their churches, while he remained outside. He found no satisfaction in his work, for by now he had given up all hopes of honor and profit. Only the love of woman still held him in bondage:

> But still I was enthralled with the love of woman, nor did the Apostle forbid me to marry, although he advised me to something better, chiefly wishing that all men were as he himself was. [cf. 1 Cor 7:25-40] But being weak, I chose the more indulgent place; and because of this alone, was tossed up and down in everything else. [...] I had now found the goodly pearl, which selling all that I had, I should have bought, and I hesitated. To Simplicianus then I went, the father of Ambrose in receiving Your grace, and whom Ambrose truly loved as a father. To him I related the mazes of my wanderings. (8:1)

Augustine's problem, as he presents it here, is centered on continence. He was satisfied intellectually about Christianity; but he did not feel within himself the power to observe celibacy, and he did not seem to be satisfied with the one without the other.

His interview with Simplicianus forced him to attend to essentials: it was essential to profess the Christian faith. The direction their conversation took was determined by Augustine's telling him of his reading of the Neo-Platonist books which had been translated by Victorinus, who had been a professor of rhetoric at Rome and had become a Christian. Simplicianus congratulated him on his good fortune in having come under the influence of a philosophy which in so many ways accorded so well with Christian teaching. He pointed out the apparent correspondence between the Christian Trinity and the Neo-Platonic Three Hypostases. He stressed, it would appear, that the Platonists themselves saw the correspondence, and quoted the case of one of them who said that the beginning of St. John's Gospel should be written in letters of gold and set up to be read in the highest places in all churches. But he stressed above all the example of Victorinus.

Gaius Marius Victorinus was an African, a rhetor, an exponent of Neo-Platonism, and a convert to Christianity. It was his translation of the Neo-Platonic books which Augustine had read. He had, when he had become a Christian, devoted a good deal of attention to the theology of the Word made flesh. He was one of the first, if not actually the first, to attempt a synthesis of Christianity and Neo-Platonism, although the apparent correspondence between the Neo-Platonic Hypostases and the Christian Trinity had been pointed out already by Amelius, and the possible copying of the one from the other had already been variously explained. Victorinus belonged to the generation before Augustine; but his distinction had been so great — the rare honor of a statue in Trajan's Forum had been paid to him — that his example was sure to impress Augustine when now Simplicianus, who had known Victorinus intimately, told him the story of his remarkable conversion.

As an old man, who had achieved an outstanding reputation for learning, who had instructed so many Senators, who had defended with thundering eloquence the cult of idols, he had become convinced from the study of the Scriptures of their truth and frequently confessed to Simplicianus, in private however, that he was already a Christian. Simplicianus as frequently replied that he could not so regard him unless he saw him "in the church of Christ." Victorinus always retorted by asking "if *walls* make Christians." Victorinus in fact was afraid, in entering a Christian Church, "to offend his friends, proud demon-worshippers." Eventually, however, fearing to be denied by Christ before the holy angels, and gathering strength through study and thought, he became "bold-faced against vanity, and shame-faced towards the truth," and suddenly and unexpectedly said to Simplicianus: "Let us go to the church; I wish to be made a Christian." Forthwith he became a catechumen and not long after asked for baptism, "Rome wondering, the Church rejoicing."

> To conclude, when the hour was come for making profession of his faith (which at Rome they, who are about to approach to Your grace, deliver from an elevated place, in the sight of all the faithful, in a set form of words committed to

memory), the presbyters, he said, offered Victorinus (as was done to those who seemed likely through bashfulness to be alarmed) to make his profession more privately: but he chose rather to profess his salvation in the presence of the whole multitude. […] When, then, he went up to make his profession, all whispered his name one to another with the voice of congratulation. […] And there ran a low murmur through all the mouths of the rejoicing multitude, "Victorinus! Victorinus!" Sudden was the burst of rapture, that they saw him; suddenly were they hushed that they might hear him. He pronounced the true faith with an excellent boldness, and all wished to draw him into their very heart: yes, by their love and joy they drew him there, such were the hands by which they drew him. (8:5)

When Simplicianus had finished, Augustine "was on fire to imitate him." Simplicianus was pleased since "for this very end had he related it." He pointed the moral even closer by going on to add that Victorinus, not content with being a Christian, willingly embraced the sacrifices thereby imposed on him. One was that, since Christians had been prohibited by the Emperor Julian from teaching, he resigned from his profession. In this too did Augustine wish to imitate him, even if there were no longer any obligation on a Christian to do so. But "my will the enemy held, and thence had made a chain for me, and bound me. For of a perverse will, was a lust made; and a lust served, became custom; and custom not resisted, became necessity" (8:10). In other words he felt he could not be chaste and so could not be a Christian.

Courcelle argues that there was more than one interview with Simplicianus and that the chief gain to Augustine was an understanding of the true Christian teaching on the nature of Christ. As against Alfaric, who supposes that Augustine — in order to flatter Simplicianus who had succeeded to the see of Ambrose when Augustine was writing the *Confessions* — had exaggerated the importance of the role played by Simplicianus in his conversion, Courcelle maintains that Simplicianus in fact did more for Augustine than is described in the *Confessions*. Simplicianus — a disciple of the Neo-Platonist Christian Victorinus — had instructed Ambrose: he must, Courcelle argues, have done more to give intellectual guidance to Augustine than Augustine says.

This may be so. But it is better, perhaps, to focus attention on what Augustine himself wishes to tell us about his dealing with Simplicianus. He is mentioned chiefly as a narrator of the story of Victorinus. The point of the story of Victorinus is that Victorinus had not been content to be a Christian at heart, but suddenly and unexpectedly insisted on making the most public profession of his faith. He went even further; he resigned his office. This is not an appeal to the intellect: it is a strong appeal to the will. And Augustine took it as such; for his weakness in the face of this challenge was a weakness in the will, a weakness arising from the flesh. "But that new will which had begun to be in me, freely to serve You [...] was not yet able to overcome my former wilfulness, strengthened by age. Thus did my two wills, one new, and the other old, one carnal, the other spiritual, struggle within me; and by their discord, undid my soul" (8:10).

The appeal to the story of Victorinus did not, so to speak, carry the day. But it served a useful purpose, for it narrowed down the issue to one point — his will on continence.

> Nor did I now any longer have my former plea, that I hesitated to be above the world and serve You, because the truth was not altogether ascertained to me; for now it too was. But I, still under service to the earth, refused to fight under Your banner, and feared as much to be freed of all encumbrances, as one should fear to be encumbered with it. Thus with the baggage of this present world was I held down pleasantly, as in sleep. And the thoughts in which I meditated on You, were like the efforts of those who would awake, but, overcome with a heavy drowsiness, sink back again. [...] I, convicted by the truth, had nothing at all to answer, but only those dull and drowsy words, "presently, presently"; "in a little while." But "presently, presently," had no present, and my "little while" went on for a long while. (8:11)

Providence, however, had something in store for his will.

12

SUBMISSION OF WILL

Q UICKLY THERE CAME another challenge to his will and from the conflict he emerged converted.

He had by this time given up all interest in honors and wealth and was chafing under the necessity of carrying out the obligations of his profession. He tells us that he attended the Church, whenever he was free from the office under the burden of which he groaned. One day he was alone with Alypius, when in came a fellow African, Pontitianus, a Christian highly placed at the Emperor's court. He sat down to talk with them and quite casually opened a book, which lay on the table before them, thinking that it was probably connected with Augustine's profession of rhetoric. When he saw what it was, he smiled and glanced at Augustine, expressing both his joy and at the same time wonder that Augustine should be reading the Epistles of St. Paul. Augustine admitted that he was studying the Epistles very carefully.

In the course of the subsequent conversation Pontitianus told them the story of the Christian Egyptian monk Antony, of whom to Pontitianus' amazement Augustine and Alypius had never heard. Whereupon Pontitianus not only dwelt the more upon that wonderful story, but told them of "the flocks in the monasteries, and their holy ways, and the fruitful deserts of the wilderness" (8:15), about which also they knew nothing. He went on to tell them of a monastery even at Milan, "full of good brethren, outside the city walls, under the fostering care of Ambrose." And of this too they knew nothing — an indication perhaps of how little had been their contact with either Ambrose or the life of the church in Milan.

Finally Pontitianus recounted to them a marvellous event of which he himself had had personal experience. One afternoon when he was at the court at Trier, three others and himself went for a walk in some gardens near the city walls. They were walking two by two. Nothing in particular happened to himself and his companion; but the other pair came upon a cottage in which lived some Christian ascetics. There they discovered a little book, which happened to be the *Life of Antony*, of which Pontitianus had just spoken to Augustine.

> One of them began to read, admire, and kindle at it. As he read, he began to meditate on taking up such a life, and giving over his secular service to serve You. [...] Then suddenly filled with a holy love, and a sober shame, in anger with himself he cast his eyes upon his friend saying: "Tell me, I ask you, what would we attain by all these labors of ours? What do we aim at? What do we serve for? Can our hopes in court rise higher than to be the Emperor's favorite? And in this, what is there not brittle, and full of perils? And by how many perils do we arrive at a greater peril? And when do we arrive there? But if I wish it, I can become a friend of God now at once." So spoke he. And in pain with the birth of a new life, he turned his eyes again upon the book, and read on, and was changed inwardly, and his mind was stripped of the world, as soon became apparent. For as he read, and rolled up and down on the waves of his heart, he stormed at himself a while, then discerned, and determined on a better course. And now being Yours, he said to his friend, "Now I have broken loose from those our hopes, and am resolved to serve God; and this, from this hour, in this place, I begin upon." (8:15)

His companion felt moved to follow him upon the spot. Pontitianus and his friend came upon them, but on departing left them in the cottage, there to remain. Not only that but the former *fiancées* of the new ascetics also dedicated themselves to God.

The group of ascetics at Trier may well have some connection, as has been suggested, with the visit to that place about 336 of the author of the famous *Life of Antony* referred to — St. Athanasius. The further suggestion of Courcelle that one of the two men so converted to a life of asceticism was St. Jerome, has, not without some reason, been put aside by Theiler.

The appeal in this challenge to Augustine is again to his will, but it is more urgent and more intimate. Again it is the example of men who gave up office for a life of Christian asceticism. But there is more urgency in the example. The experience happened apparently without any warning — the men were in fact affianced — and had an immediate and total effect. Furthermore the example told not of the freeing from demon-worship, as in the case of Victorinus, but from the flesh, as represented both in the choosing of celibacy by two couples who had almost been married, and the heroic resistance of St. Antony to the almost overwhelming diabolical assailments against his chastity. The fact that Antony is represented as being only barely able to resist, but resisting all the same, must have been of especial significance for one who felt himself so weak in this matter as did Augustine.

The effect of Pontitianus' story must be told in Augustine's own words, for it is the *dénoûment* of our story:

> And he [Pontitianus] having brought to a close his tale and the business he came for, went his way; and I went into myself. What did I not say against myself? With what scourges of condemnation did I not lash my soul, that it might follow me, striving to go after You! Yet it drew back; it refused, but did not excuse itself. All arguments were spent and confuted; there remained a mute shrinking; and my soul feared, as it would death, to be restrained from its habitual course, by which it was wasting to death.
>
> Then in this great contention of my inward dwelling, which I had strongly raised against my soul, in the chamber

of my heart, troubled in mind and countenance, I turned upon Alypius. "What ails us?" I exclaimed: "What is it? What did you hear? The unlearned start up and take heaven by force, and we with all our learning, but without heart, see where we wallow in flesh and blood! Are we ashamed to follow, because others have gone before, but are unashamed not even to follow?" Some such words I uttered, and my fever of mind tore me away from him, while he, gazing on me in astonishment, kept silence. For it was not my usual tone; and my forehead, cheeks, eyes, color, tone of voice, spoke my mind more than the words I uttered. A little garden there was by our lodging, which we had the use of, as of the whole house; for the master of the house, our host, was not living there. To there had the tumult of my breast hurried me, where no man might hinder the hot contention in which I had engaged with myself, until it should end as You knew, I knew not. I was healthfully distracted and dying, to live; knowing what evil thing I was, and not knowing what good thing I was shortly to become. I retired then into the garden, and Alypius followed on my steps. For his presence did not lessen my privacy, and how could he forsake me so disturbed? We sat down as far removed as might be from the house. I was troubled in spirit, most vehemently indignant that I did not enter into Your will and covenant, O my God, which all my bones cried out to me to enter, and praised it to the skies. And therein we do not enter by ships, or chariots, or feet — no, we do not move so far as I had come from the house, to that place where we were sitting. For, not to go only, but to go in there, it was only necessary to will to go, but to will resolutely and thoroughly; not to turn and toss, this way and that, with a maimed and half-divided will, struggling, with one part sinking as another rose.

Lastly, in the very fever of my irresoluteness, I made with my body many such motions as men sometimes would, but cannot, either because they do not have the limbs, or these are bound with bands, or weakened with infirmity, or are in any other way hindered. Thus, if I tore my hair, if I beat my forehead, if locking my fingers I clasped my knees;

I willed, I did it. But I might have willed, and not done it, if the power of motion in my limbs had not obeyed me. So many things then I did, when "to will" was not in itself "to be able". But I did not do what I both longed incomparably more to do, and which soon after, when I should will, I should be able to do; because soon after, when I should will, I should will thoroughly. For in these things the ability was one with the will, and to will was to do; and yet was it not done. And more easily did my body obey the weakest willing of my soul, in moving its limbs at its nod, than the soul obeyed itself to accomplish in the will alone this its momentous will. (8:18-20)

So deeply had Manicheism entered into his outlook that in this very last act of the drama he has to disabuse himself once again through the deliberate and free movement of his limbs that he is free to will and has not within himself a principle of evil which acts for evil in spite of him. He thinks of how his whole life had manifested this disease in his will: how the *Hortensius* of Cicero had won his intellect to Wisdom, but he had not followed; how he had asked in the very commencement of his early youth for chastity and continence — only not just then. What a fatal disease this was that prevented him from doing what unlearned men could carry out! But he was determined this time to win through. He knew that he *could* will.

Thus I was soul-sick, and tormented, accusing myself much more severely than usual, rolling and turning myself in my chain, until it was wholly broken, by which I now was barely — but still — held. And You, O Lord, pressed upon me in my inward parts by a severe mercy, redoubling the lashes of fear and shame, lest I should again give way — and, not bursting that slight remaining chain, it should recover strength, and bind me faster. For I said within myself, "Be it done now, be it done now." And as I spoke, I all but enacted it. I all but did it, but did not do it. I did not sink back to my former condition, but stayed close by, and took a breath. And I tried again, and was closer, and then still closer to my goal, and almost touched and laid hold of it; and yet did not reach it, nor touch it, nor lay hold of it. I hesitated to die to death and to live to life: and the worse to which I was inured, prevailed more with me than the better, to which I was unused. The nearer the moment approached in which I was to become other than I was, the greater horror it struck into me; yet did it not strike me back, nor turned me away, but held me in suspense.

The very toys of toys, and vanities of vanities, my ancient mistresses, still held me. They plucked at my fleshly garment, and whispered softly, "Do you cast us off? And from that moment shall we no more be with you for ever? And from that moment shall not this or that be lawful for you for ever?" And what was it which they suggested in "this or that," what did they suggest, O my God? Let Your mercy turn it away from the soul of Your servant. What defilements did they suggest! What shame! And now I much less than half heard them — they did not openly show themselves and contradict me, but muttered as it were behind my back, and privily plucked at me, as I was departing, to only look back on them. Yet they delayed me, so that I hesitated to burst my bonds and shake myself free from them, and to spring over to where I was called. A powerful habit continued saying to me, "Do you think you can live without them?"

But now it spoke very faintly. For on that side to which I had set my face, and where I trembled to go, there appeared to me the chaste dignity of Continence. She was serene, yet not relaxedly gay, honestly alluring me to come, and doubt not; and stretching forth to receive and embrace me, her holy hands full of multitudes of good examples. There were so many young men and maidens here, a multitude of youths and people of every age, grave widows and aged virgins; and Continence herself in all; not barren, but a fruitful mother of children of joys, by You her Husband, O Lord. And she smiled on me with a persuasive mockery, as if she would say, "Can you not do what these youths, what these maidens can? Or can they do it either by themselves, and not rather in the Lord their God? The Lord their God gave me to them. Why do you stand with your own strength, and so stand not?

Cast yourself upon Him, fear not, He will not withdraw Himself that you should fall; cast yourself fearlessly upon Him. He will receive and will heal you." And I blushed greatly, since I still heard the muttering of those toys, and hung in suspense. And she again seemed to say, "Stop your ears against those your unclean members on the earth, that they may be mortified. They tell you of delights, but not as does the law of the Lord your God." This controversy in my heart was self against self only. But Alypius, sitting close by my side, in silence waited for the result of my unwonted emotion. (8:25-27)

This passage is undoubtedly rhetorical and contains a conscious echo of the famous literary theme of the choice of Hercules between Virtue and Pleasure. There can be no question whatever but that the appearances of his ancient mistresses with their suggestions on one side, and Continence with her accompanying youths and maidens on the other, is purely fictitious. It is but Augustine's way of dramatizing the crisis and marking the critical choice; either his former ways or Continence. The choice is narrowed even further, for of himself he could never hope to be chaste. It was either himself alone incontinent, or himself with Christ continent: "Can you not do what these youths, what these maidens can? Or can they do it either by themselves, and not rather in the Lord their God? [...] Why do you stand with your own strength, and so stand not?"

The ultimate challenge had come. Would he or would he not accept Christ as the Mediator who would raise him so that he might live a life of virtue? Was he going to follow the Neo-Platonists in their pride, who presumed to rely on reason alone and themselves to practice virtue and arrive at union with the One? Victorinus had not done so. Antony, the desert monks, and the couples of Trier had practiced continence — but only because they had accepted Christ, who had sustained them in their life of asceticism. Would he not also follow their example? He wanted above all to do so — there was really no choice — he lacked only that final act of will and it, he knew, was possible:

But when a deep consideration had from the secret bottom of my soul drawn together and heaped up all my misery in the sight of my heart; there arose a mighty storm, bringing a mighty shower of tears. So that I might pour it forth wholly, in its natural expressions, I rose from Alypius. Solitude seemed to me to be more appropriate for the business of weeping, so I retired so far that even his presence could not be a burden to me. Thus was it then with me, and he perceived something of it; for something I suppose I had spoken, in which the tones of my voice appeared choked with weeping, and so had risen up. He then remained where we were sitting, very astonished. I cast myself down I know not how, under a certain fig tree, giving full vent to my tears; and the floods of my eyes poured out, an acceptable sacrifice to You. And, not indeed in these words, yet to this purpose, I spoke much to You: "And You, O Lord, how long? How long, Lord, will You be angry, for ever? Remember not our former iniquities," [Ps 79:5, 8] for I felt that I was held by them. I sent up these sorrowful words: "How long? How long, tomorrow, and tomorrow? Why not now? Why not is there this hour an end to my uncleanness?"

So was I speaking, and weeping in the most bitter contrition of my heart, when lo! I heard from a neighboring house a voice, as of a boy or girl, I know not, chanting, and often repeating, "Take up and read; take up and read." Instantly, my countenance altered. I began to think most intently, whether children were accustomed in any kind of game to sing such words: nor could I remember ever to have heard the like. So checking the torrent of my tears, I arose; interpreting it to be no other than a command from God, to open the book, and read the first chapter I should find. For I heard of Antony, that coming in during the reading of the Gospel, he received the admonition, as if what was being read, was spoken to him; "Go, sell all that you have, and give to the poor, and you shall have treasure in heaven, and come and follow me." [Mt 19:21] And by this oracle he was at once converted to You. Eagerly then I returned to the place where Alypius was sitting; for there I had laid the volume of the Apostle, when I arose thence. I seized, opened, and in silence read that section, on which my eyes first fell: "Not in rioting and drunkenness, not in debauchery and wantonness, not in strife and envying: but put on the Lord Jesus Christ, and make no provision for the flesh, in its concupiscence." [Rm 13:13-14] No further would I read; nor did I need to: for instantly at the end of this sentence, by a light of serenity infused into my heart, all the darkness of doubt vanished away. (8:28-29)

The conversion of Augustine, of his intellect which could not resist the truth, and of his will which could resist the good, was accomplished.

"Put on the Lord Jesus Christ, and make no provision for the flesh, in its concupiscence." Readers have often been puzzled as to why this text should have such virtue for Augustine at this moment. They have a feeling that, while the reference to concupiscence fitted in with Augustine's account of his own life, the text must have had some special — almost miraculous effect: as if the reading of the text alone completed all in a flash. But Augustine never invested his conversion with the air of mystery or miracle. There was no special virtue in the text itself. It was its appositeness and the special circumstances in which he had read it — the story of Antony, who coming in during the reading of the Gospel, received the admonition as if what was being read was spoken to him: "Go, sell all you have"; the story of the men at Trier; his own determination to will; his knowledge that he ought to submit to Christ — all these made his happening upon this particular text seem so remarkable, so providential, that his assent was given almost without his knowing it. This moment had been so long in coming, had been arrived at through such a series of experiences and meditations, all of them leading directly or indirectly, in a greater or less degree to this end, that even a less apposite text from Scripture would have brought Augustine at that time to the acceptance of Christ. As it was, no text could be found more apposite and more compelling. If Augustine's own words: *securus judicat orbis terrarum*, could work such a change in Newman, what might we not expect from this text in the case of Augustine?

A more mundane instance may help us to see what transformation can be effected by a text. Rousseau in his *Confessions* describes how one day in the summer of the year 1749 he was reading the *Mercure de France* while walking to Vincennes to see his imprisoned friend Diderot. He came upon this question propounded by the Academy of Dijon for a prize: Has the progress of the sciences and arts done more to corrupt morals or improve them? He goes on:

> The moment I read this I beheld another universe and became another man. Although I have a lively recollection of the effect they produced upon me, the details have escaped me. What I remember quite distinctly about this occasion is that when I reached Vincennes I was in a state of agitation bordering on delirium. Diderot noticed it; I told him the cause and read him Fabricius' Soliloquy which I had written in pencil under an oak tree. He encouraged me to give my ideas wings and compete for the prize. I did so, and from that moment I was lost. All the rest of my life and of my misfortunes followed inevitably as a result of that moment's madness.
>
> My feeling rose with the most inconceivable rapidity to the level of my ideas. All my little passions were stifled by an enthusiasm for truth, liberty, and virtue; and the most astonishing thing is that this fermentation worked in my heart for more than four or five years as intensely perhaps as it ever worked in the heart of any man on earth. (Translated by J.M. Cohen. Book Eight: 1749)

Later in a similar context he speaks of himself in these terms, reminiscent perhaps of Augustine's reactions on reading the Neo-Platonist books:

> Exalted by these sublime meditations, my soul soared towards the Divinity; and from that height I looked down on my fellow men pursuing the blind path of their prejudices, of their

errors, of their misfortunes and their crimes. Then I cried to them in a feeble voice which they could not hear, "Madmen who ceaselessly complain of Nature, learn that all your misfortunes arise from yourselves" (Book Eight: 1753).

Few will see supernatural interference in the affairs of poor Jean-Jacques, as he called himself with such sympathetic consideration. Indeed some may say that there is something almost improper in mentioning him at all in connection with this "too sacred almost" scene, as one writer has called it.

Nevertheless the passage from Rousseau may serve a useful purpose in showing how much of Augustine's final crisis could be purely human and, above all, how sudden and complete and relatively lasting a transformation of outlook and even morals can be achieved without any appeal to supernatural grace, without any expectation, and in the twinkling of an eye. For the change in Rousseau was sudden, marked and enduring. That Augustine should emerge from his long prepared conversion not only a convinced Christian but able to practice chastity is surely less wonderful — even if there were no question of grace.

There is a curious recurrence of certain features in the various conversions which have been mentioned. Is it strange that Augustine, Rousseau, Newman should all have had a pitying view of the mass of humanity embedded in its filth and misfortune? Is it strange that some of these conversions should find two friends present together, the two friends at Trier, Augustine and Alypius, Rousseau even and Diderot? Is it strange that some of these conversions should take place suddenly? Is it strange that a few words — a quotation from the Gospel for Antony, *tolle lege* for Augustine, *securus judicat orbis terrarum* for Newman, a topic suggested for an essay for Rousseau — should be the immediate spark to the flame in all these cases? Are they all interdependent so that there is conscious or unconscious derivation in the experiences or the description of them? Or is it not rather that they are all historical, but that the experiences being somewhat similar, naturally have some characteristic marks in common?

Take the point of the suddenness of conversion. The famous transformations of Polemo, Paul, Monica, Alypius, Victorinus, and Augustine — not to mention Rousseau — were all sudden. The suddenness of the conversion of Polemo is fictitious. The suddenness of the conversion of Paul is taken to be historical. What of the others — is the suddenness of them, as told by Augustine, purely literary, and is it based on the fiction of Polemo or the fact of Paul? Or is the suddenness of the change in Augustine historical and that in Monica, Alypius, and Victorinus modelled in a literary way on Augustine's, or Polemo's, or Paul's conversion? Or is the suddenness in all of them — Polemo apart — historical? Surely it is in the nature of conversion that although the whole process may be gradual the realization that it has taken place comes in an instant and causes surprise?

These considerations invite the introduction of a very important question. Did Augustine in fact cast himself under a fig tree and hear the words *tolle lege*?[1] There is no doubt about the reading of the *Mercure de France* by Rousseau, or of the *securus judicat* by Newman: but doubt has been cast on the historicity of the *tolle lege*.

It has been customary to regard this episode as fully historical, that is to say that Augustine did cast himself down under a fig tree, weeping and asking God to deliver him from his bonds; and that he did hear a child's voice from next door singing "Take up and read"; and that thereupon, regarding the words of the child as conveying a command from God, he opened the text of St. Paul.

Various explanations have been attempted to account for the words used by the child[2] — in spite of the text itself which tells us that even Augustine found no ready explanation although he reflected on the matter at the time (a point, by the way, which is considered to endorse the reality of this episode). Le Clerc thought that the child was practicing the imperative mood of the third conjugation, or was repeating a school bidding to one who had not memorized his lesson: "take up and read." Wunderle and Lindau

---

[1] Cf. p. xxv.

[2] Courcelle, *Recherches*, pp. 190 ff. indicates some of these.

suggest some children's game with a boat, in which case the words refer to the lifting and fastening of the anchor. Some suggest that Augustine actually heard something else, but thought that he heard *tolle lege*. Others, getting away from the historicity of the event, see in the words of the child the employment by Augustine of well-known religious practices or literary conceits: Balogh sees here an omen in the words of the child and a consultation of fortune in Augustine's "cutting" of the sacred text; Geffcken points out that the formula *"tolle lege"* is found in Greek literature and Christian hagiography; and Boehmer thinks that the Bible itself, being in a sense the oracle of God, gave rise to the injunction to consult it.

Courcelle has devoted his industry and erudition to the interpretation of this episode. He dwelt at length upon it in his *Recherches* and has since written at least five learned articles to defend his view. Briefly his contention in his *Recherches* is that the whole description is literary and fictitious. In this part of the text he notices echoes of Plotinus; employment of a well-known literary *motif* (Hercules choosing between Virtue and Pleasure); a literary "controversy" between the Vanities and Continence; and certain reminiscences of Persius ("tomorrow, and tomorrow"). He goes on to suppose, therefore, that the "Take up and read" is fictitious also. To support his view on this point he argues that the fig tree is clearly symbolical, since it obviously refers to the fig tree under which sat Nathaniel in the Gospel, and is moreover frequently employed by Augustine himself in his later works as symbolizing the shadow of sin. He seeks confirmation in appealing to a variant reading in the text, where one manuscript has *de divina domo* ("from the house of God": that is heaven) instead of *de vicina domo* ("from a neighboring house"). The conclusion is clear: Augustine heard no voice but the voice "within his heart." The child is one of the children of Continence, referred to earlier, speaking within him and inviting him to embrace chastity.

This interpretation has been quite rightly criticized. Mohrmann[3] has induced Courcelle to have less confidence in his vari-

---

[3] *Loc. cit.*

ant reading *de divina domo*, although he still attempts to avoid the *impasse* by maintaining, with some ingenuity, that even if *vicina* is *written*, *divina* is *meant* and hence arose the confusion. In effect he has abandoned that major portion of his argument without admitting it. Mohrmann has also questioned the literary allusions to Persius. But the more Courcelle is countered, the more inventiveness he displays; and it would be impossible, not to say useless, for us here to follow him through the maze of speculation with which in his various articles he has surrounded the question.[4] He has suggested, for example, among other things, that Augustine in attributing the words "Take up and read" to a child, had in mind the part played by children in connection with the oracle of Apis. One can, however, detect in Courcelle's more recent writing some loss of confidence in his position. He allows not only the possibility that the garden in which the scene occurred is real, but that the fig tree (or at any rate some tree) may be real and even that it is possible (for others, of course) to hold that the *tolle lege* was spoken from the house next door.

Courcelle is on surer ground when he suggests the possibility that the *tolle lege* scene is a doublet of the conversion of the two men at Trier which had just been recounted to Augustine by Pontitianus. He points out that two people, a leader and a follower, are involved in both episodes; that a text plays a vital part in both; and that the leader becomes agitated and eventually resolves to embrace Christian asceticism, and in this his companion follows him. There are a few other minor correspondences, some of them forced, and some of them capable of varied interpretation. In the main, however, the doublet is there. But what does that prove? Certain correspondences have here been pointed out between, for

---

[4] "Note sur le Tolle, lege," *L'année théologique*. No. 39, 1951, pp. 253-260; "L'oracle d'Apis et l'oracle du jardin de Milan," *Revue de l'histoire des religions*, t. CXXXIX, 1951, pp. 216-231; "Les 'voix' dans les Confessions de saint Augustin," *Hermes*, t. LXXX, 1952, pp. 31-46; "Source Chrétienne et allusions païennes de l'épisode du Tolle, lege," *Revue d'histoire et de philosophie religieuses*, t. XXXII, 1952, pp. 171-200; *Leçon Inaugurale*, Collège de France, Dec. 1952, p. 29; "L'enfant et les 'sorts bibliques,'" *Vigiliae Christianae*, Vol. VII, n. 4, Oct. 1953, pp. 194-220.

example, Rousseau's and Newman's experience and that of Augustine; but for all that one is not forced to conclude that there was any necessary connection, much less any imitation either in the experience or its description, and still less that the various descriptions were not historical. Even if there is a connection between the accounts of the conversions of Augustine and the men of Trier, is it not possible that the connection is the other way round, that Augustine, who recounts both here, and who had a fondness for grouping events in patterns and employing similar formulae in their description, made the story of the two men at Trier follow the pattern of his own actual experience? One of these events he knew well; for it was the crisis of his life. The other he merely heard of. Is it to be argued that his account of what he heard is historical, and his account of what he experienced so intensely is unhistorical, on the ground that the description of the second account comes after and is like the first?

The influence of the story of the two men of Trier and especially of the story of the conversion of Antony affected Augustine profoundly. In his account of his own conversion he actually recalls that of Antony and the Gospel text which worked it, immediately before he describes his reading of the text which was to work his own. In short, he had his own conversion in mind when he was describing the conversion of the two men through reading the *Life of Antony*, and he had especially the *Life of Antony* in mind when he himself was being converted. This in effect is to say that the story of that great champion of chastity, joined to the stories of his learned and many unlearned imitators, provoked the final crisis for Augustine: which is quite simply what the *Confessions* says.

So much indeed can one believe in the historicity of the *tolle lege* episode in the *Confessions*, that it is possible to suggest that not only is it untrue to say — as Courcelle says — that no trace of it can be found elsewhere in Augustine's writings, but that deep traces of it are to be found in many significant passages. The experience for Augustine was so unique, intense, and personally vital that it colored other descriptions of the same or similar events.

At an earlier stage the case of the *Hortensius* has been instanced. When, fourteen years after his conversion, he came to describe this event which happened nearly fourteen years before that conversion, he describes it at least partly in terms of the *tolle lege* scene. The effect of the *Hortensius* on him, he says, was *sudden*; it gave him an *incredible* burning desire for wisdom; every vain *hope* became worthless; *unknowing* he was returning to God; he burned to *remount from earthly things* to God; his only objection to the *Hortensius* was that the name of Christ which "my *tender heart*, even with *my mother's milk*, devoutly drunk in," was not in it; he resolved to consult the Scriptures and *"behold,"* he says, *"I see* a thing not understood by the proud, nor laid open to children"; his swelling *pride* shrunk from the lowliness of the Scriptures, and yet "were they such as would grow up in a *little one"*; *therefore* he fell among (the Manichees).

Augustine himself connects the two events; for, in the course of his description of the final episode in his conversion, he reflects how he had previously been "converted" by the *Hortensius* and yet had not been able all along to live up to that conversion; he was still putting off the good life. One cannot deny that when describing the effect of the *Hortensius* he anticipated the outlines and even many verbal expressions which he was to use for the later even more memorable event.

Is it fanciful to see in the expressions referring to "tender heart" and "drunk in with mother's milk" an echo of the child who took part in the *tolle lege* scene? It will be easier to judge when the connection of the description of the garden scene with another text, already quoted, is examined: the passage is from his *Against the Academics*, the very first description of his conversion:

> But lo! when certain books full to the brim, as Celsinus says, had wafted to us good things of Arabia, when they had let a very few drops of most precious unguent fall upon that mea-

ger flame, they stirred up an incredible conflagration — incredible, Romanianus, incredible! What honor, what human pomp, what desire for empty fame could move me then? Swiftly did I begin to return entirely to myself. Actually, all that I did — let me admit it — was to look back from the end of a journey, as it were, to *that religion which is implanted in us in our childhood days* and bound up in the marrow of our bones. *But it indeed was drawing me unknowing to itself.* Therefore, stumbling, hastening, yet with hesitation I seized the Apostle Paul. For truly, I say to myself, those men would never have been able to do such great things, nor would they have lived as they evidently did live, if their writings and doctrines were opposed to this so great a good. I read through all of it with the greatest attention and care. (2:5)

He adds in effect that the reading of St. Paul threw great light on his understanding of Neo-Platonism.

This first description of his conversion by Augustine is brief to the point of obscurity. It describes three separate stages in that conversion: the reading of Neo-Platonist books, the comparing of their teaching with that of the Scriptures and especially of St. Paul, and finally his consultation of St. Paul in obedience to the command *tolle lege*. These three stages are described in the *Confessions* also — but separately and successively. The description of the first stage is, in the passage just quoted, completed with the words: "Swiftly did I begin to return to myself." But the other two stages are telescoped in what remains; and it is the final stage, being the most memorable — which dominates — as far as most of the expressions go. In content the text does not describe the *tolle lege*, but rather his careful reading through *all* of St. Paul and comparing it with Neo-Platonism. But the expressions that he was later to use in the *tolle lege* scene do dominate even to the extent of obscuring the sense.

The true explanation for the excitement of the passage and for the words which have always seemed unintelligible: "Therefore, stumbling, hastening, yet with hesitation I seized the Apostle Paul," is that Augustine allowed his memory of the *tolle lege* scene to intervene and come to the forefront of his mind so as to over-shadow his memory of the first consultation of St. Paul. So vivid, in fact, was his recollection of that excited reaching out for the volume of the Apostle at the bidding of the *tolle lege*, that in this and other places, to be seen presently, he uses not only "therefore" (*itaque*), but also "seized" (*arripui*), and always with words denoting great expectation. These passages graphically reproduce the dramatic motions of getting up from the ground where he was lying and seizing St. Paul's text from the table — motions which are particularly if not exclusively, applicable to the garden scene.

Similarly the words: "these men would not have lived as they evidently did live" certainly refer to the followers of Antony, as do the corresponding words in the *tolle lege* scene in the *Confessions*; for, again, his memory of the story of Antony was very vivid a few months after he had heard of it when he was writing the *Against the Academics*. It is possible, but not so certain, that the passage: "religion which is implanted in us in our *childhood* (*pueris*) days and bound up in the marrow of our bones; but it indeed was *drawing* (*rapiebat*) me unknowing to itself" may echo the *child* of the *tolle lege* (as perhaps do the expressions of the "tender heart" and "drunk in with mother's milk" of the *Hortensius* description also). Other even less certain echoes can be observed by one skilled in these matters, but the point cannot be pursued here.

The memory of that excited seizing of St. Paul consequent on the child's *tolle lege* was so great that, when in a companion volume to the *Against the Academics*, namely, *On the Happy Life*, he is even more briefly referring to his recent conversion, the note of excitement creeps in again and some of the expressions are used in a strange way. He writes: "Having read a few books of Plotinus (?, that is Neo-Platonist books) and compared with them the authority of (the Scriptures), I was so aflame that I wanted to break all those anchors that held me, but was influenced by the opinion of certain men. What remained then but that as I dallied with vanities, a storm, which was considered adverse, should come to my aid. *Therefore* (*itaque*) *such* a pain in the chest *seized* (*arripuit*) me that, not being able to stand up to the burden of my profession I gave up everything" (4 f.).

This passage, addressed to the Christian philosopher Mallius Theodorus, turns the account in a way which that Platonist might be supposed to appreciate: the passage has Neo-Platonic echoes. In addition it is somewhat less intimate than the passage in the *Against the Academics* which is addressed to his friend and patron Romanianus, and so he gives Theodorus the ostensible (but also true) reason for resigning from his profession and retiring to the country — his illness — and not a more important and personal one — his conversion to Christianity. Nevertheless some of the phrases which his memory of the garden scene had dictated for his use in the *Against the Academics* strangely work their way into this more impersonal account too. It is well to notice that the passage seems to bear out the evidence of the *Confessions* that Augustine, although he had already compared the Scriptures with the Neo-Platonist books, had taken no further step immediately.

It cannot be without significance either that in his account in the *Confessions* of his comparison of the Scriptures with the Neo-Platonist books, the memory of the later seizing of St. Paul seems to have influenced him when he wrote: *"Therefore (itaque) most avidly did I seize (arripui) that venerable writing of Your Spirit; and chiefly the Apostle Paul"* (7:27).

It is suggested here that the experience of that agitated seizing of St. Paul in obedience to the *tolle lege* made such an impression upon his memory that whenever he attempted to describe the whole episode, or part of it, or some experience even remotely like it,[5] the same thoughts came and with them much the same words. This does not, of course, in itself prove that the episode is historical: for even a pure fiction can leave a strong impression; but it is an indication which cannot lightly be set aside. If Augustine, when

---

[5] For example *Confessions* 8:14 where Pontitianus *tulit, aperuit, invenit apostolum Paulum*: he observed a book, took, opened it, and contrary to his expectation, found it the Apostle Paul.

he came to describe the garden scene in the *Confessions* reverted to the phrases which he employed for the first time some fourteen years before in the *Against the Academics*, then the continuing recollection of a real event is a more likely explanation than the continuing recollection of a fiction. Moreover, while one can have reserves about the general historicity of the *Against the Academics*,[6] one can have little doubt about the historicity of most of the matter mentioned in the prefaces — and the description of his conversion is one of them. The accord between the *Against the Academics* and the *Confessions* on this matter is indeed remarkable. It is based on fact.

Augustine represents the *tolle lege* episode as *the* moment in his life. Generations of readers have felt it to be so. Teresa of Avila was one. Newman was another. Not the least indication, perhaps, in favor of the historicity of the *tolle lege* and Augustine's precipitation towards the table on which rested the text of St. Paul, is the fact that his whole subsequent career and outlook on life was, as will be indicated in the following epilogue, finally determined by that fateful consultation of St. Paul.

---

[6] See J. O'Meara, "The Historicity of the Early Dialogues of Saint Augustine," *Vigiliae Christianae*, July 1951, pp. 150-178.

EPILOGUE

ABOUT THE FIRST WEEK of August of the year 386, when he had emerged from the crisis the climax of which was marked by the scene in the garden, Augustine felt more strongly than ever his previous impulse to throw up his profession immediately and devote himself to a life of Christian philosophy. Nevertheless he was deterred from doing so by a number of considerations. The vintage vacation would begin in a few weeks and the convenience of authorities, parents, and even of the students would be better served if he were to postpone his resignation until then. As against that his rapidly deteriorating health and, indeed, almost complete exhaustion of mind and body urgently invited him to take the step immediately. Moreover a dramatic break-off would not fail to impress Christians and non-Christians alike: in this he would be another Victorinus. The gesture was expected of him, he felt, and later he was to fear that in carrying on at his worldly work he had been guilty of sin. But he was, he tells us, most anxious not to draw upon himself too much the attention of certain people — doubtless those non-Christian patrons whose influence had helped him in getting his position in the first instance, and whose interest he had up to this date never ceased to canvass most assiduously. His desire to keep on friendly terms with these may easily, by the way, account for his want of intimacy with Ambrose. In any case it would take a little time to make provision for himself, his dependents, and friends in the new life which lay before them. Accordingly he carried on until the vacation came to release him from his task. He then retired to Cassiciacum, a country place some distance from Milan, and in due course sent in his resignation. Thus, quietly, he put an end to his worldly career in which, for all his diligent cultivation of it, he can never have had his whole heart.

He had great need of rest, for his health was nearly broken under the strain of his work, but even more of his exhausting mental and moral experiences. The thought of death had come before his mind frequently of late. His lungs had been giving him much pain and anxiety. A toothache would come suddenly and as suddenly depart. The relaxation of living at his ease in the country, the strain now over, must have been great indeed.

The pleasant villa in which he was to live for some months was placed at his disposal by his friend Verecundus, who in compensation was given the services of Augustine's companion Nebridius to help him in his teaching. Verecundus himself wished to become a Christian, but only if he could also be a celibate. As he was married to a Christian wife, however, his wish could not be fulfilled immediately. Consequently he still remained without the fold, to us an interesting example of the exaggerated ideals some such men had about Christianity.

Augustine's was a less complicated case, at any rate in this particular. He now sent in to Ambrose a request that his name be put on the list of those to be baptized at the following Easter, and also for advice on reading. Ambrose acceded to his wishes and suggested that he should read Isaiah. But Augustine found that he was unable to profit by the advice.

During those leisurely days of the autumn and early winter of 386, Augustine with his mother, brother, son, some cousins, Alypius, Evodius, and two young men who were entrusted to him for instruction, spent their days attending to the chores in the house and in the fields, sitting under a tree by the meadow or, when it was wet, in the baths discussing philosophy and reading Cicero and Virgil. Augustine prayed and wrote when he was not otherwise engaged. The fruit of his labors are the three dialogues, *Against the Academics*, *On the Happy Life*, and *On Order*, and a dialogue between his soul and himself, the *Soliloquies*. Other writings were projected — for he proposed to write a series of works treating of the disciplines introductory to philosophy — and some (such as *On the True Religion*) may have been begun. It would seem that for the moment, at any rate, he proposed to devote himself to philosophy, philosophical or semi-philosophical writing, and the sweet companionship of his friends — while at the same time integrating all of this into his new life as a Christian. There is no hint of any further plan.

His first dialogues were modelled mainly on Cicero and there can be no doubt but that they were intended for publication as literary works. It was often customary in such dialogues to pretend that the discussions actually took place and consequently a number of conventions were employed to lend verisimilitude to the claim. Among these conventions was the supposed even verbal accuracy of the report of an actual discussion. Augustine conforms very closely to the conventional practices in all these matters, and the historicity of the discussions between him and his circle must inevitably be suspect. One notable point is that whereas his first dialogue, the *Against the Academics*, starts as a general discussion in which two interlocutors come to grips at close quarters, but ends in a very long set speech, delivered by Augustine himself; the further dialogues in the series are catechetical and are conducted in the form of question and answer. The former type of dialogue is loosely called Platonic —and Plato himself did not always succeed in overcoming the difficulties inherent in this dramatic type of composition, where progress in the exposition of the matter of the discussion was hindered by the exigency of trying to make the discussion sound as if it had actually happened. Augustine remarks that the reader can notice how he himself became more successful in this kind of composition according as he practiced it. What the reader will certainly notice is his complete want of success in the Platonic style and his early switch over to the other kind.

It is not unlikely, however, that Augustine attempted to hold the discussions, and either recorded them for editing afterwards, or wrote up discussions that had just taken place. For the inter-

locutors of the dialogues were in Cassiciacum and were engaged
in such exercises as are described in the *Dialogues*. Moreover, the
prefaces to the works give without any doubt many historical facts,
and there are other detailed points favoring the historicity of certain episodes.

But in the main, although there may be much solid fact enshrined in them, the *Dialogues* of Cassiciacum are works of fiction
and must be treated with appropriate reserve.

It has been sometimes contended that these *Dialogues* are
truly historical, that they represent Augustine as more interested
in Neo-Platonism than Christianity, and that they are in flagrant
contradiction with the *Confessions*, which by implication is not
historical. These charges are quite unfounded. Of the writings concerned the *Confessions* are — it is only right they should be — the
more historical; Christianity in the *Dialogues* is preferred, although
quite naturally less talked about, to Neo-Platonism; and not only
is there no contradiction between the one and the other but a remarkable harmony can be observed.

The case of the first extant work, the first of these dialogues,
the *Against the Academics*, will not only illustrate the last two points
but provide an opportunity of discussing Augustine's outlook on
life, religion, and philosophy at this interesting juncture, this
breathing-space, as he calls it, between his conversion and his baptism.

The work is a refutation of the scepticism of the New Academy and particularly of Cicero's *Academica* in which that scepticism is explained and defended. It will be remembered that a short
while before he had been troubled by scepticism. It would be out
of place here to give a summary of the book's arguments; but the
final argument amounts to this: man can assent to truth, if truth
can be found; but truth is found in Christ; therefore man can assent to truth. It will be noticed that the argument rests significantly
on the acceptance of Christ as very truth. Augustine developed
the theory not only that the Neo-Platonists had recognized the
necessity for a man-God to elevate and lead mankind to the Fa-

ther, but that the scepticism of the New Academy was feigned! In reality, he suggested, they held to the true immaterial doctrine of Plato, now so gloriously revived by Plotinus, and resorted to the stratagem of preaching the negative doctrine (that nothing could be perceived and no assent should be given to any proposition), only in order to prevent the mass of mankind, already through weakness enmeshed in the flesh, from abandoning themselves with a good conscience to the rank materialism of the Stoics. In Augustine's time, however, men had been elevated by the Incarnation, and the immaterial, the true, doctrine of the Academic followers of Plato was being preached again. The real case against the Academics was that there were no Academics: they were only pretending; for they were Platonists in disguise.

His book culminates in the following passage:

> Not long after, all obstinacy and pertinacity had died down, and Plato's doctrine, which in philosophy is the purest and most clear, the clouds of error having been removed, shone forth especially in Plotinus. Today, therefore, in that which concerns erudition, doctrine, and morals, after many generations and many conflicts there is strained out at last, I would say, one system of really true philosophy. For that philosophy (Platonic) is not of this world — such a philosophy our sacred mysteries most justly detest — but of the other, intelligible, world. To which intelligible world the most subtle reasoning would never recall souls blinded by the manifold darkness of error and stained deeply by the slime of the body, had not the most high God, because of a certain compassion for the masses, bent and submitted the authority of the divine intellect even to the human body itself. By the precepts as well as deeds of that intellect souls have been awakened, and are able, without the strife of disputation, to return to themselves and see once again their fatherland.
>
> This theory about the Academics I have sometimes, as far as I could, thought probable. If it is false, I do not mind. It is enough for me that I no longer think that truth cannot

be found by man. Here in brief is my course of procedure. Whatever be the position of human wisdom, I know that I as yet have not attained it. Though I am in my thirty-third year, I do not think that I should give up hope of reaching it some day. I have renounced everything else that men regard as good, and have proposed to dedicate myself to the search for wisdom. No one doubts but that we are helped in learning by a twofold force, that of authority and that of reason. I, therefore, am resolved in nothing whatever to depart from the authority of Christ — for I do not find a stronger. But as to that which is sought out by subtle reasoning — for I am so disposed as to be impatient in my desire to apprehend truth not only by faith but also by understanding — I feel sure at the moment that I shall find it with the Platonists, nor will it be at variance with our sacred mysteries. (3:41-43)

Augustine returns to this peculiar theory of his about the Academics more than once but never with any confidence, because he must have known that he had no satisfactory basis for it. It was, in fact, a rounding-off of the idea which he got from Porphyry of the absolute necessity for a mediator, if mankind was ever to find its way to the Father. It was also an extension to a wider field of his own personal experience that until he submitted to Christ he failed to win either truth or moral reform. It should not surprise us that Augustine should so lightly have had recourse to the idea of a secret doctrine: secret doctrines of all sorts were the order of the day. This synthesis absorbed all his attention in those days at Cassiciacum and even as late as the year 410 he gives it in full detail in the letter to Dioscorus; but it was in the early days above all that it occupied his thoughts so much as to fascinate him. In the first of his extant letters — to Hermogenianus, written at this time — he uses a phrase which has so puzzled editors that they have always suggested that the reading was corrupt. He refers to his theory that the Academics countered the materialism of the Stoics by concealing their true doctrine, as an *ars Dei*, a neat disposition of Providence. More explicitly he says in the *Confessions:* "Nor was I sated in those days with the wondrous sweetness of considering the depth of Your counsels concerning the salvation of mankind." (9:14)

It is evident from all this that Augustine not only fully accepted the Incarnation, but regarded it as central both in his own life, in which he found its acceptance so momentous in its impact and consequences, and in the lives of all mankind. In this all important point the *Dialogues* and the *Confessions* are in striking agreement and show that he put his allegiance to the organized authority of Christianity above and before his allegiance to the vaguer claims of reason and Neo-Platonism. In point of fact he rejected the Porphyrian view on the Incarnation, as also for example its view on the nature of the soul.

At the same time one must draw attention to the fact that when he was writing the *Dialogues* of Cassiciacum he thought of the claims of reason and Neo-Platonism quite differently from the way in which he thought of them when he came to write the *Confessions*. In those early days he seems to have held the view that a man could understand the content of revelation — and his remarks on this point show why. Briefly they come to this: one cannot reason without God's help; his illumination of the mind and its object make reasoning possible. Hence as he is the one source of the truths of both reason and revelation, what can be communicated by the latter can also be communicated by the former. Augustine added that reason could not operate in a kind of vacuum: it needed some authority to raise the questions — but once started it could proceed in its own way, with God's illumination, on the independent search for truth. Reason and revelation were, in fact, independent but coordinated ways to the one truth and used the one source of illumination. Hence Augustine at this stage was full of expectations from Neo-Platonism, expectations which could not be fulfilled. In this he was following to some extent the lead of Porphyry, for example, who insisted, as we are told in the *City of God*, that there was the way of reason for the few, and there should be a way of authority for the many. He differed from Porphyry however on a most significant point: he accepted the authority of Christ. In effect the way of revelation came first with him. Already at this stage his famous phrase was true: *credo ut intellegam*, I believe in order to understand. But he himself even in the beginning complained that in those days he was perhaps too enamored of what he calls his darling reason. If one can hardly demand from even a pious Christian that he should frequently refer to his religion in the course of a work on, for example, epistemology, still less should scholars ever have come to any conclusions about the insincerity of his religious conversion, because Augustine who held such optimistic views on reason and its relation to revelation, did not in those *Dialogues* constantly refer to his newly-found faith. In point of fact he does more than once refer to it, as we have seen; but his general position was something like what has been described, and the philosophical tone of the *Dialogues* and their many echoes of both Porphyry and Plotinus are fully accounted for in that way.[1]

One might have the legitimate curiosity to ask what degree of certitude did Augustine believe himself to have on the truth of Christianity? One might get the impression from the *Confessions* that all doubt and difficulties vanished for ever. It would indeed be wonderful if it were so, but it is too much to expect. His position was much the same as Newman's later: he had difficulties, but not doubts. He had an impressive convergence of probabilities, but no evident certitude. For him, as for everyone, faith was belief in things unseen. He knew neither the origin nor the nature of the soul, for example. And he had the idea, to which we have referred, that he would, with the help of Neo-Platonism, eventually understand some of the things which he was prepared to believe. But his assurance in the rational order was that of great probability: no more.

An equally fair question might be raised as to Augustine's moral reform. Did this man, who represents himself as not having

---

[1] See J. O'Meara, "St Augustine's View of Authority and Reason in A.D. 386," *The Irish Theological Quarterly*, Oct., 1951, pp. 338 ff.

been able up to his conversion to do without women, and for all his stern resolution in dismissing his former mistress had nevertheless quickly taken another in her place, quite suddenly find himself so strong in the face of temptation that he could resist it altogether? It is doubtful if we have enough information to give an entirely satisfactory answer on this point. A modern writer of confessions would supply us with full and perhaps lurid particulars; but Augustine did not feel any need to do that, although he was far from squeamish. It has been contended in this book that Augustine was not the kind of sensualist some biographers suppose him to have been. His emphasis upon these matters in the *Confessions* is partly accounted for by the inevitable polemics of a bishop entrusted with the care of souls, partly by his desire, conscious or unconscious, to make himself a more conspicuous instance of the triumph of grace over fallen nature, and partly by a certain obsession, a preoccupation with the flesh, perhaps mainly Manichean in origin. In other words, the ground to be covered by him, so to speak, in this kind of moral conversion was not as great as is commonly believed. In addition, even before his conversion there seems to have been a serious, if not successful, attempt at reform. Again the feeling of having to do without pleasures enjoyed in the past obsessed him more as he approached the crisis than great, immediate, and positive fondness for the pleasures themselves: "'Do you cast us off? And from that moment shall we no more be with you for ever?' [...] And now I much less than half heard them — they did not openly show themselves and contradict me, but muttered as it were behind my back, and privily plucked at me, as I was departing, to only look back on them. [...] But now [the powerful habit] spoke very faintly. For on that side to which I had set my face [...] there appeared to me the chaste dignity of Continence" (8:26). Continence had been beckoning to him with increasing urgency before his conversion and it is hard to believe that this had not had some effect.

In the *Soliloquies*, written in Cassiciacum, he says, in a somewhat exaggerated tone (addressing himself):

> How sordid, filthy, and horrible seemed to you a woman's embrace, when we were discussing the question of the desire for a wife. But that very night when we were lying awake, when going over again the same matter in our own mind, you saw how — contrary to what you have supposed — those imagined charms and bitter sweetness caught your interest: far indeed, far less than it used to, but also far otherwise than you had thought. I should be ashamed to look back again upon those darknesses that I have left. (1:25)

This text, while showing that with Augustine, as with St. Paul, was left the sting of the flesh, also shows that so far he was resisting. In the *On Order* (1:29) he speaks also of wounds not yet being healed as quickly as he would like: but this information is too vague, if not even irrelevant, to be of much use. All we know is that by the time he became a dispenser of the sacrament, he was more assured in this matter:

> You enjoined upon me continency from concubinage; and, as for wedlock itself, You have counselled something better than what You have permitted. And since You gave it, it was done, even before I became a dispenser of Your Sacrament. But there yet live in my memory (of which I have spoken much) the images of such things, as my evil habits there fixed; which haunt me, strengthless when I am awake; but in sleep, not only so as to give pleasure, but even to obtain assent, and what is very like reality. Yes, so far prevails the illusion of the image, in my soul and in my flesh, that, when asleep, false visions persuade me to that which when waking, true sights cannot. (*Confessions* 10:41)

Augustine was no disembodied saint. The precautions which he took in later years to keep away from all contact, however innocent, with women cannot justly be taken as evidence of neurosis. Rather should they be interpreted as practical measures taken by one who disciplined himself, and with no small measure of success.

❦

Some time before the beginning of Lent in the year 387 Augustine with his son Adeodatus and his closest friend Alypius repaired to Milan to prepare for baptism. There they underwent the usual course of instruction and preparation as described, for example, in St. Ambrose's *On the Mysteries,* and in due course were baptized with all the ceremonies attached to that impressive rite as practiced in Milan at the time. He tells us of the joy and consolation he found in the singing of the psalms in church, and that joy is an indication of his feeling of true happiness and contentment in his new state.

He remained in or around Milan for about a year, and then in company with his mother, son and brother, and some others made his way to Rome preparatory to returning to Africa and to the cradle of his early years, Thagaste.

While waiting to cross over from Ostia there occurred what, with some exaggeration, has been called "the Vision of Ostia." The incident is widely known through Scheffer's painting of the scene. Augustine's account of it is as follows:

> The day was now approaching when she [Monica] was to depart this life (which day You well knew, we knew not). It came to pass, You, as I believe, by Your secret ways so ordering it, that she and I stood alone, leaning in a certain window, which looked into the garden of the house where we now were staying, at Ostia. There, removed from the din of men, we were recovering from the fatigues of a long journey, in preparation for the voyage. We were talking then together, alone, very sweetly. Forgetting those things which are behind, and reaching forth to those things which are before, we were enquiring between ourselves in the presence of the Truth, which You are, of what sort the eternal life of the saints was to be, "which eye has not seen, nor ear heard, nor has it entered into the heart of man." [1 Cor 2:9] But yet we gasped with the mouth of our heart, after those heavenly streams of Your fountain, the fountain of life, which is with You; that being sprinkled from it according to our ca-

pacity, we might in some sort meditate upon so high a mystery.

Our discourse was brought to the point, that the very highest delight of the earthly senses, in the very purest material light, was in regard to the sweetness of that eternal life, not only unworthy of comparison, but even of mention. We then raised up ourselves with a more glowing affection towards the "Selfsame," and by degrees passed through all things bodily, even the very heaven whence sun and moon, and stars shine upon the earth. Yes, we were soaring higher yet, by inward musing, and discourse, and admiration of Your works; and we came to our own minds, and went beyond them, that we might arrive at that region of never-failing plenty, where You feed Israel for ever with the food of truth, and where life is the Wisdom by whom all these things are made. [...]

And while we were talking and panting after her, we slightly touched on her with the whole effort of our heart; and we sighed, and there we left behind the first fruits of the Spirit; and returned to vocal expressions of our mouth, where the word spoken has beginning and end. And what is like Your Word, our Lord, who endures in Himself without becoming old, and makes all things new?

We were saying then: If to anyone the tumult of the flesh were hushed, hushed the images of the earth, and water, and air, hushed also the poles of heaven, yes the very soul were hushed to herself and by not thinking on self surmount self, hushed all dreams and imaginary revelations, every tongue and every sign, and whatever exists only in transition — if anyone could hear, all these say, "We made not ourselves, but He made us that abides for ever." [Ps 100:3, 5] If then having uttered this, they too should be hushed, they would have roused only our ears to Him who made them, and He alone would speak, not by them, but by Himself. Then we may hear His Word, not through any tongue of flesh, nor angel's voice, nor sound of thunder, nor in the dark riddle of a similitude, but we might hear Him whom in these things we love, might hear His Very Self without these (as we two now strained ourselves, and in swift thought touched on that Eternal Wisdom, which abides over all) — if this could be continued on, and other lesser visions be withdrawn, and this one ravish, and absorb, and wrap up its beholder amid these inward joys, so that life might be for ever like that one moment of understanding which now we sighed after; would not this be, "Enter into your Master's joy"? [Mt 25:21] And when shall that be? When we shall all rise again, though we shall not all be changed? [cf. 1 Cor 15:51]

Such things was I speaking, and even if not in this very manner, and these same words, yet, Lord, You know, that in that day when we were speaking of these things, and this world with all its delights became, as we spoke, contemptible to us, my mother said: "Son, for my own part I have no further delight in anything in this life. What I am doing here any longer, and to what end I am here, I know not, now that my hopes in this world are accomplished. One thing there was, for which I desired to linger for a while in this life, that I might see you a Catholic Christian before I died. My God has done this for me more abundantly, that I should now see you despising earthly happiness, to become His servant. What am I doing here?" (9:23-26)

Courcelle has justly remarked that the experience at Ostia itself was, doubtless, less specifically Plotinian than is the account in the *Confessions*. Ever since the work of Henry on this subject[2] the Plotinian elements in this account have been much stressed by most scholars. Theiler, however, again with some reason, sees here the immediate influence of Porphyry rather than Plotinus. It is indeed difficult to be certain in the assignment of such influences at any time, but especially when there is question of these two Neo-Platonists. In any case too little account is taken of Augustine's own originality and the many other possible influences which could flow into this kind of experience. One should suppose the influence of either Plotinus or Porphyry, or both, only when it is clear and

---

[2] *La vision d'Ostie*, Paris, 1938.

unmistakable. For example, one should refrain from seeing in the phrase *primitiae spiritus* an attempt by Augustine to find a biblical equivalent to a Neo-Platonic formula: one should rather, as M. Pépin[3] does, give it its Pauline significance and leave it at that.

But a more important question is concerned not with the description of the experience but with the experience itself. Too many writers have disputed at length on whether or not the Vision of Ostia proves Augustine to have been a mystic, or at least to have had on this occasion a mystical experience. Their arguments unfortunately have been based mainly on the language of the *Confessions* written many years after the event. Some — Henry, Boyer, for example — have contended that on this occasion Augustine's experience was one of mystical ecstasy; others, such as Hendrikx and Cavallera, that it was solely intellectual.

It is easy to agree with Courcelle that the experience was, however different in some respects, roughly of the same order as the experiences described in connection with his reading of the Neo-Platonist books at Milan. But none of them could properly be called mystical. One must disagree, however, with Courcelle when he speaks of ecstasy; for again the word "ecstasy" cannot properly be used of any of these experiences. That Augustine and Monica, each all the more on account of the other's presence and evident emotion and thoughts, should have had an intellectual and emotional experience quite above the ordinary, one can readily allow; but technical terms such as "mystical" and "ecstasy" should not lightly be employed of an intellectual and emotional experience devoid of any of the characteristic signs of mystical states, and described much later in language apparently, at least in part, borrowed from the Neo-Platonists. If the Vision of Ostia left Augustine satisfied and without a feeling of frustration such as he experienced at Milan — and it is possible that the difference in this point between the two experiences is much exaggerated — a variety of explanations can be offered and they need not, as some scholars

---

[3] J. Pépin, "Primitiae spiritus," *Revue de l'histoire des Religions*, 140 (1951), pp. 155-202.

seem to think, be mutually exclusive. Augustine did find satisfaction in the Christian teaching on the relation of the vision of God in this life to that in the life hereafter; he did undoubtedly derive support from the presence of Monica; and he had profited by what might be called Platonic purgation and the knowledge necessary for contemplation.

This is not to say that Augustine never had mystical experiences. For the moment we are concerned solely with episodes that occurred immediately before and shortly after his conversion, and were in both cases related to Neo-Platonist books. The larger question of Augustine's ever having mystical experiences in later life is not immediately relevant here. Perhaps it might be true to say that Augustine, like many others, had many potentialities not all of which could be realized. If he had not been chosen — against his will — for the See of Hippo, a certain mystical vein in him might have made itself more manifest. For that there was a streak of mysticism in him can hardly be doubted.

It is going too far to say, as Henry says, that Augustine was a born mystic. It is more convincing to say that the intellectual side of his conversion greatly stimulated those aspirations in him which were always present, manifesting themselves in his long and ardent pursuit of wisdom, truth, happiness, and God. Henry writes finely of his natural taste and indeed nostalgia for God, and his radical love of the Divine. Augustine does indeed show in this matter both an exquisite sensibility, an enduring passion, and the greatest generosity.

A few days after the Vision at Ostia, Monica fell sick and soon it was evident that she was dying. She amazed her sons and those who surrounded her in her last hours by asking to be buried, not with her husband in Africa, which had always been her desire, but in the place where she was. For she too had progressed in her indifference to material things. On the ninth day of her sickness then, and the fifty-sixth year of her age, and the thirty-third of Augustine's, she died.

> I closed her eyes; and there flowed a mighty sorrow into my heart, which overflowed into tears; my eyes at the same time, by the violent command of my mind, dried up their fountain; and woe was me in such a strife! But when she breathed her last, the boy Adeodatus burst out into a loud lament; then, checked by us all, he held his peace. In like manner also a childish feeling in me, which, through my heart's youthful voice, found its vent in weeping, was checked and silenced. (9:29)

Augustine, a raw recruit to asceticism, steeled his heart against weeping, although his whole life was being rent asunder, for their two lives, as he says, had been as one. She had spoken softly to him before she died of how kind and dutiful he had been to her, and he could not help feeling that her life had been a slavery, however devoted, to his. Still he drove back the tears and occupied himself in discoursing with his friends on a topic which would fortify them in their sorrow. He shed no tears at her burial. Even a bath, which was claimed to have peculiar virtue in this regard, did not banish the grievous oppression that lay cold upon his heart. In the end he burst out into a flood of tears before God, made no further excuses for his human feeling, and prayed for the charity of forgiveness for his sin.

> And I gave way to the tears which I before had restrained, allowing them to overflow as much as they desired. I reposed my heart upon them; and it found rest in them, for it was in Your ears, not in those of man, who would have scornfully interpreted my weeping. (9:33)

The twentieth century will easily forgive Augustine his weakness. It should also try to realize how ruthless was the indifference expected of him by himself and others.

This part of the *Confessions* ends with a prayer for Monica — and Patricius — which cannot be omitted:

> May she rest then in peace with her husband, before and after whom she never had any; whom she obeyed, with patience bringing forth fruit to You, that she might win him also to You. And inspire, O Lord my God, inspire Your servants my brethren, Your sons my masters, whom with voice, and heart, and pen I serve, that as many as shall read these *Confessions*, may at Your altar remember Monica Your handmaid, with Patricius, her sometimes husband, by whose bodies You brought me into this life, how, I know not. May they with devout affection remember my parents in this transitory light, my brethren under You our Father in our Catholic Mother, and my fellow citizens in that eternal Jerusalem, which Your pilgrim people sigh after from their Exodus, even until their return there. That so, my mother's last request of me, may through my *Confessions*, more than through my prayers, be, through the prayers of many, more abundantly fulfilled to her. (9:37)

Since this study, following the *Confessions*, must end with the death of Monica, and some writers have seen in that physical death the death also in Augustine of one part, even the better part, of his own soul, one must attempt to assess the extent of her influence[4] over him and in doing so give some verdict on his character.

Augustine himself speaks, as we have seen, of his life by her death "torn asunder as it were, which, of hers and mine together, had been made but one" (9:30). This is an admission that his life was greatly influenced by her. The *Confessions* portray her as playing a dominant part in his life and in this they doubtless only represent the truth. Henry speaks of her part in Augustine's conversion in representing for him Christian living in its most intense, most delicate, most austere and most seductive form: he was

---

[4] See L. Daly, "Psychohistory and St. Augustine's Conversion Process," *Augustiniana* 3-4, 23-54, 231 ff. (1978). See also my *Understanding Augustine*, Dublin, 1997, pp. 34 f.

brought to Christianity by conviction, but also by "contagion." One might add that her influence was much more positive as well. It would not be an exaggeration to say that so far as lay in her power she tried almost to compel him by every force at her disposal to become a Christian.

Nevertheless her efforts were not the decisive factor in his conversion and in his life. One can rule out of account any notion that Augustine was completely dominated by his mother. In point of fact he had defied her in his whole manner of life and more than once in important issues. Naturally, however, she had considerable influence on his actions.

The most interesting and important question is concerned with the characteristics which Monica transferred to him at birth and developed in him in childhood. Through them she could influence him greatly. Certain writers have placed much emphasis here. It has been stated that from his relationship with his mother springs his inability to find happiness in the love of women; from this, his desperate pursuit in philosophy, in friendship, at last in religion, of an elusive substitute for that happiness. This is a serious charge — if meant seriously. It seems to suppose that for Augustine, philosophy, friendship and religion were never anything more than a *pis aller* for happiness in the love of women which, because of Monica's absorption of that love in herself, could never be satisfied.

Without going into the question of what is meant by "happiness in the love of women," but giving that happiness its lowest or noblest meanings (by any standards), one might ask if Augustine in the context of his times and circumstances did not fare as well in this matter as most of his contemporaries? He had a variety of experiences and had one long *liaison*, which he broke up voluntarily although reluctantly: he had not lost all happiness in it. When he gave up happiness in the love of women he gave it up, we suggest, because he hungered, not for more of such happiness, but a happiness elsewhere. Not everyone will agree that a man must find happiness in the love of women or suffer the penalty of what is called maladjustment. Such a view on life is far too simple.

On the further point that Augustine's relations with Monica explain why Augustine did not find happiness in the love of women, one must admit that their relationship was closer, perhaps, than that which may be said to exist on the average between mother and son, and one cannot deny that Augustine may have been so affected. But, as against that, one can point out that no such result can be proved to be inevitable; that Augustine did, in fact, live in relative happiness with a mistress for many years; that for the important first sixteen years of his life he cannot have escaped altogether from the influence of his father; and that for much, if not most, of the rest of his life he was not only far removed from the influence of Monica but living independently in an atmosphere that might be supposed to counteract it greatly.

Those who would see in the Monica episodes of the *Confessions* a life of Monica are doubtless right in doing so. It is only natural then that in that life of Monica would be stressed her great services to and preoccupation with her son. It is only natural too that that son, now a bishop, thinking back on her happy death following on his conversion on which she had set her heart, and to honor her memory, should describe their relationship more from what had been her viewpoint perhaps, than from his own. It is indeed possible that the *Confessions* might convey a misleading impression on this point.

In short, too much has been made in this matter of questionable psychological theories; too little care has been taken in their application, and not enough attention has been paid to the evidence. It is only fair to add that Augustine himself is partly to blame for all this, and that what was left undone by him was overdone by the overpious who parade him either as a prodigal son returning to, or a pious priest honoring, a devoted and loving mother.

A psychology which is now somewhat outdated went further: it spoke of the tragic destiny of Augustine to combine in a small and sickly body the warring souls of both his parents, and a fastidious intellect which served each in turn. It simplified the matter even further by saying that until he became a bishop Augustine's character was dominated by a chaste and tender mother, but that afterwards there asserted itself in him his passionate bully of a father: Augustine's supposedly bullying attitude towards the Donatists, for example, whom he would compel to become Catholics, is alleged to reveal this. Whatever little truth there may be in all this does not justify the tidy conclusions which have been drawn, and again too little account has been taken of the evidence. Augustine's father may have been a physical bully — although he never once indulged in the then fashionable practice of striking his wife — but the moral force in the house was without any doubt Monica: and if Augustine ever was a bully, he was a moral one. Part of this notion of a conflict in Augustine's soul is based on the idea that Augustine witnessed conflict between his mother and father and that he took the side of his mother and never had a good word to say for his father. Again the facts are wrong. Augustine explicitly states that their house was unusually harmonious: "there had never been any domestic difference between them." And he does commend his father for the sacrifices that he had made in order that Augustine himself should be educated. He says that he was choleric and had been unfaithful to his mother — that in the circumstances is rather faint blame. He also says that he was fervid in his affections, and it is too much to suppose that this fervor was reserved solely for those outside of his family. In the end he became a Christian and succeeded in being faithful to Monica. With her finally Patricius is found in Augustine's prayer: "May she rest then in peace with her husband. [...] Inspire, O Lord my God, Your servants that as many as shall read these *Confessions*, may at Your altar remember Monica Your handmaid, with Patricius, her sometimes husband, by whose bodies You brought me into this life, how, I know not. May they with devout affection remember my parents" (9:37).

On the other hand it would be nonsense to suppose that from his parents and his contact with them Augustine derived little or nothing that was marked in his character. One may choose to discover in him the religious spirit of his mother, her perseverance, singleness of purpose, discretion and refinement of sensibility. From his father he inherited ardor, passion, and generosity. From them both he derived ambition and courage, ease in making friends and fundamental goodness. But one should not insist too much on such handy classification. Augustine was different from his parents and greater than them. They may have been potentially intellectual; he was intellectual, even if he was not primarily interested in philosophy. His constant absorption in the beginning was neither religion nor women, but truth: he was always interested in ideas, and captivated by them. Whatever qualities he inherited from his parents, these in him were developed to a greater intensity, met a greater challenge, and came to greater issues. Later he was an ascetic and at the same time a humanist, a man who tried hard to control his senses but who freely confessed that in spite of his efforts the senses still succeeded in giving him pleasure. He sometimes eats too much, although drunkenness is far from him; he delights in music, so much so that he wonders if after all the psalms recited might not for him be safer than the psalms when sung; and he remains curious: "I do not go now to the circus to see a dog chasing a hare; but in the field, if I am passing by, that chasing perhaps will distract me even from some weighty thought, and draw me after it" (10:57). He was a vital human person to the end.

The two great facets of his conversion, the intellectual and the moral, symbolize his outstanding characteristics — his love of ideas and his love of life. The two are not very often combined and he was great in having combined them. Both loves remained with him to the end. Hence his long series of writings and his long and active career as the administrator of a see. His mother's (and doubtless father's) influence, the influence of the Manichees, the influence of the Neo-Platonists, and the influence of asceticism as represented by St. Antony — all of these play their parts in his conversion. With all these forces and with his own nature, intelligence and will he wrestled for the mastery, and the victory gained was a victory remembered throughout his life. He never ceased to be Monica's child, nor (in a certain sense) a Manichee, nor a Neo-Platonist, nor a follower of Antony. But the Augustine that emerged from the conversion was one who wrote books such as the *Confessions*, *On the Trinity*, and the *City of God* which, whatever their inspiration in events or writings, repeat over and over again two great ideas that came to him in his great experience: the grace of Christ that saves men and his illumination that enlightens the mind. The truth of these ideas, he felt, he had experienced in his conversion, and his whole life was devoted to their propagation.